O-BON IN CHIMUNESU

O-BON
IN
CHIMUNESU
A COMMUNITY REMEMBERED

~

CATHERINE LANG

ARSENAL PULP PRESS
VANCOUVER

O-BON IN CHIMUNESU
Copyright © 1996 by Catherine Lang

ARSENAL PULP PRESS
103-1014 Homer Street
Vancouver, B.C.
Canada V6B 2W9

The publisher gratefully acknowledges the support of the Canada Council and the Cultural Services Branch, B.C. Ministry of Tourism, Small Business and Culture.

Photographs reprinted with permission by Bill Isoki, Tosh Kamino,
    Bruce Martin, and Mutt Otsu
Front cover photo used with permission from the Kawahara family
Back cover photo by Bruce Martin
Back cover translation by Deirdre and Yusuke Tanaka
Song lyrics from "Chemainus Harbour, April 21, 1942" used with
    permission from Allen Desnoyers
Typeset by the Vancouver Desktop Publishing Centre
Printed and bound in Canada by Printcrafters

CANADIAN CATALOGUING IN PUBLICATION DATA:
Lang, Catherine, 1953-
  O-bon in Chimunesu

  Includes index.
  ISBN 1-55152-036-2

  1. Japanese Canadians—British Columbia—Chemainus—Biography.*
2. Chemainus (B.C.)—Biography. 3. British Columbia—History—
1918-1945.* I. Title.
FC3849.C54527 1996   971.1'203'0922   C96-910483-98
F1089.5.C47L36 1996

CONTENTS

ACKNOWLEDGMENTS

I WOULD LIKE TO ACKNOWLEDGE the Japanese Canadian Redress Foundation and the department of Canadian Heritage (former department of Secretary of State for Multiculturalism) for their financial assistance with the writing of this book. In particular, I wish to thank Dick Nakamura for his vital support of my application to the Redress Foundation. This book would not have been possible without it.

I am grateful also to Ann Sunahara. The meticulous research in her book *The Politics of Racism* provided me with important background material. I understand that the National Association of Japanese Canadians gained a great deal of the legal ammunition that they needed to win compensation because her research proved that racism—not national security issues—motivated the government in its treatment of Japanese Canadian citizens.

I am indebted as well to a host of friends who have encouraged me in countless ways. Among those I wish to thank are Frank and Betty Moritsugu, Kyoshi Shimizu, Midge Ayukawa, Reverend Harry Costerton, Ruth Loomis, Kim Goldberg, Rachel DeCaria, Norene Price, Nancy Sine, Roma Sedgman, Linda Bateman, Miki Hansen, and Daphne Armstrong. Last, but by no means least, I am grateful for the loving support of my husband, Bruce Martin, and my parents, Art and Kay Lang.

To the memory of Jerome.

FOREWORD

BY TOYO TAKATA

WHEN JAPAN STRUCK PEARL HARBOR in December 1941, 3,400 men, women, and children of Japanese descent lived on Vancouver Island and the Gulf Islands. *Nikkei* settlements ranged from colonies that sprouted up around sawmills to lonely pockets of fishing families.

The earliest Japanese stepping ashore on Vancouver Island were visitors, not immigrants. In June 1880, a naval training vessel sailed into Esquimalt Harbour, the first Japanese ship to dock in Canada. Its three weeks in port were thoroughly covered by the *Victoria Colonist*. Settlers from Japan followed shortly.

As the provincial capital and a military base, Victoria was Canada's Pacific port of entry, and the logical choice for many early arrivals to begin their new life in a strange land. A substantial upper class, living in opulent residences and accustomed to an aristocratic lifestyle, required servants. The incoming young Japanese, eager to learn English and western customs, willingly became cooks, houseboys, and handymen.

The Victoria Japanese Methodist Church (later the Japanese United Church) opened in 1894 with a resident minister, a clear indication that its congregation was firmly established. It remained until 1942, serving as a place for meeting and worship, and as a Japanese language school. The record of the city's Ross Bay Cemetery reveals that twenty-three Japanese were buried there before the turn of the century, the first death occurring in 1886. The list includes two females, one likely an infant.

As in most Pacific Coast towns and cities, both Canadian and American, the inflow from Japan gave birth to a Japanese sector in Victoria. This eased language and cultural difficulties for their people. Within these enclaves, merchants and businessmen emerged who, generally better educated and more articulate and aggressive than the labouring types, became the leaders and spokesmen. But the real entrepreneurs ventured beyond their ethnic domain to engage in more rewarding enterprises in their quest for wealth and prestige.

One notable case was a future *taikun* or tycoon who began his career in Canada in 1888 at Victoria's "Japanese Bazaar" owned by Charles Gabriel. This was a shop selling silk, bamboo, lacquerware, Oriental porcelain, and curios from the Far East. Earning the owner's trust and confidence, Shinkichi Tamura was quickly promoted from clerk to buyer where he arranged purchases from Japan and learned about international trade and commerce. He left for Vancouver to pursue a very successful endeavour in the import-export field, establishing several firms, including a trust and savings company called "Tamura Bank" in *nikkei* circles. He was the key negotiator in the first major Canadian wheat sale to Japan. Tamura's achievements were instrumental in his election to the Upper House of Japan's parliament.

Around 1892, Charles Gabriel undertook an unrelated venture. He recruited a team of coal miners from Kyushu in southern Japan to dig for coal on one of the Gulf Islands. It proved to be a disaster. Two white men were killed in an explosion that collapsed the digging, and the operation was abandoned.

When the Wellington Collieries of Nanaimo expanded its Cumberland pits around 1890, they imported more Kyushu miners with better results, at least for the managers. For the Japanese, it was far from ideal. They joined the Occidentals and the Chinese in extracting coal under intolerable and treacherous conditions. When union miners struck in Nanaimo, the Japanese were dispatched as strikebreakers. They suffered fatalities in two major underground explosions, as well as in lesser accidents: in 1901, nine were among sixty-four killed, and five more perished in 1922. In spite of these tragedies, exploitation by management and the hostility of the union, its coal pits made the Cumberland *nikkei* community the largest on Vancouver Island. With the arrival of wives and picture brides, and the births that followed, the population reached well over 500.

Unlike mining, no clear sign pinpointed where or when Japanese began farming on Vancouver Island. Most young Japanese arriving in Canada 100 years ago were sons of farming families all too aware of long dreary hours and meagre rewards in tilling the soil. The only experience that was worse, they claimed, was being conscripted into the Imperial army to suffer harsh military training. In order to escape the draft as well as the drudgery of farm life, they left Japan before reaching age twenty.

During the First World War when demand and prices of produce were steady, owning a modest spread became more attractive and profitable. Japanese bought or leased acreage on the Gulf Islands, at Cordova Bay on the Saanich Peninsula, in Crofton north of Duncan, and near Courtenay in the Comox

Valley. They kept poultry and grew a range of fruit, vegetables, and grains, and some special Oriental produce for their people. With abundant sun, Saltspring Island strawberries were large and luscious. Being short and agile, Japanese growers were more adept at cultivating and picking the earth-hugging fruit than their taller, heavier Occidental counterparts. On nearby Mayne Island, *nikkei* were among the first to produce the best hot-house tomatoes. The sweet corn from Cordova Bay tasted even sweeter if boiled in the local brine. Japan had little grazing land and dairy products were not a staple in the Japanese diet. But novice dairymen herded bovine in the lush pastures of Comox Valley. However, they were shut out from the Courtenay creamery because white competitors protested.

When fishermen from the seaside villages of Wakayama, south of Osaka, heard of the great salmon run, they rushed to the Fraser River during the final decade of the last century. Indeed, so many Wakayama folks disembarked that they dominated the *nikkei* fishery in Canada. From Steveston on the Fraser they spread to other fishing areas: north to Rivers Inlet, to the Skeena and Nass Rivers, and across the Strait of Georgia to Vancouver Island.

Due west of Steveston, the fishing settlement at Nanaimo became the largest on the east coast of the island. Smaller groups, mainly cod fishermen, chose protected coves in the Gulf Islands, Victoria, Sidney, and Chemainus, or farther north on Quadra Island. In Alert Bay on Cormorant Island, one family engaged in building fish boats. A feature of the tides around Nanaimo were the massive herring runs. In 1900, the first herring saltery was built there to preserve and market the huge catches. Other plants located later on Newcastle and Galiano Islands, where ocean freighters docked alongside to load herring and chum salmon destined for the Far East.

Overcrowding on the Fraser, the government slashing the number of *nikkei* fishing licences, and the introduction of gas-

powered motor boats for salmon trolling on the open sea contributed to the trek to the outer coast of Vancouver Island in
the 1920s. Fishermen and their families settled in the remote
villages of Tofino and Ucluelet, which were then accessible
only by sea. Though only forty-two kilometres apart, most
inhabitants of either hamlet never visited the other. A few
anchored at Bamfield across Barkley Sound from Ucluelet.
Also at Barkley Sound, the B.C. Packer cannery employed
nikkei men and women, and a Japanese-owned saltery was
built at Kildonan.

After Steveston, the main group bought shoreline properties of multiple lots in Ucluelet. They helped one another build
less-than-modest shelters of shiplap, shingles, and rough floor-
ing, without electricity or indoor plumbing. A co-operative
was formed to oversee fishery-related issues and problems, and
to buy a packer to collect and transport the catch to the cannery
or saltery. Like any proud *nikkei* enclave, the co-operative
erected a multi-purpose hall to serve as a Japanese school and
church, and for solemn functions such as funerals or joyous
occasions like wedding receptions. Most eagerly awaited were
Japanese movies sent from Vancouver—samurai sagas for the
men and tear-jerkers for the ladies. To operate the projector,
the packing boat engine generated the power.

The isolated villages had many concerns. The womenfolk
worried when men set out in perilous seas without radio communication. In case of a serious injury or illness, the nearest
hospital was in Port Alberni, an eight-hour trip in calm
weather from Tofino. Young people hoping to graduate from
high school either took correspondence courses or moved to
the city to attend classes. The villages offered no employment
for young women. They were often sent to a sewing school in
Vancouver to learn a skill considered a requisite to marriage.
The family could not move to benefit the children since the
father's licence limited him to trolling on the west coast, and

he was barred from securing any new licence. White and Native Indian permits, obtained by application and a fee, were unrestricted.

Japanese immigrants came ashore in British Columbia as miners, farmers, or fishermen, but never as forestry workers. Except for bamboo, which is a type of grass and not a tree, Japan did not possess vast stands which could be cut down for wood and wood products. Still, the logging and lumbering industries became the largest employers of the *nikkei* work force on Vancouver Island.

With what seemed like an endless source of timber matched by an insatiable demand, logging camps and sawmills abounded everywhere. The Japanese, who proved willing and reliable, were hired almost as quickly as they landed. But the real impetus was the outbreak of war in Europe in 1914. Not only did it create an urgent military need for forestry products but it also led to a shortage of workers as young men enlisted in the armed forces.

When war erupted, Japan, committed to a military alliance with Britain, which included Canada, declared war against Germany. Its navy patrolled the Pacific waters off Canada's shore and its warships steamed in and out of the naval docks of Esquimalt. The *nikkei* of Canada greeted Japan's action with total approval, ever hopeful that it would lead to their acceptance as full Canadian citizens. In a demonstration of allegiance, over 200 volunteered to fight for Canada. Of those, fifty-four were killed and ninety-seven were wounded.

On Vancouver Island, the logging camps and sawmills were pleading for men to restore and augment their army-drained labour force. *Nikkei* heeded the call and were readily accepted. Of special note were two bustling mill towns: Port Alberni and Chemainus. Port Alberni, built at the head of the Alberni Inlet—where the first Japanese were hired for the grim task of chopping up huge mammals at a whaling station—was set among one of the best stands of centuries-old Douglas fir. Several sawmills opened in the region, requiring a large influx of loggers and mill workers. In 1911, Port Alberni was linked by rail to Nanaimo, where flatcars loaded with lumber were rolled on to barges. Destined for the mainland, they could then travel east without unloading their cargo.

Chemainus, where growth was not as dramatic, had only a single mill, but it was a modern, highly productive operation with a steady supply of logs from the booms. Those who came were attracted by the year-round employment, a developing *nikkei* community, and the amenities of a town, rather than a remote, cash-poor, and timber-short venture that many had already experienced. Most of all, they sought a proper environment to raise and educate their young families.

South of Chemainus, Duncan was the hub of woodland activity in the Cowichan Valley. Some ran retail businesses as grocers, tailors or shoe repairmen, or drove log-hauling trucks. Most Duncan men worked in the woods, returning home on weekends or when weather or danger of fire closed the forest. Sawmills were located at nearby Hillcrest and Paldi, which employed *nikkei* workers. Among them were logging contractors who supplied these mills with timber.

Nikkei-owned as well as Japan-financed forestry operations were active north of Nanaimo. The first and most extensive was Royston Lumber Company, which was purchased by a syndicate of three *nikkei* families in 1916. It owned timberland with considerable reserves and a sawmill complete with planer to produce finished lumber, which were linked together by ten miles of rail. Many of its hundred employees were recruited from nearby Cumberland where coal mining was winding down. The lumber was sold locally and in adjacent districts from Campbell River to Nanaimo.

Japan was the chief buyer from Deep Bay Logging Company established in 1923, sometimes called "Kagetsu Camp" in reference to its owner. Japanese freighters called in at Fanny Bay, south of Royston, to load logs bound for Japan. Japanese capital initiated a logging venture in Coombs. A more ambitious logging undertaking was launched at very remote Port McNeill, with a million-dollar investment from a Japanese corporation a few years prior to the Second World War.

Apart from the above firms, other sawmills of various capacities north of Nanaimo used *nikkei* work crews. These locations included Nanoose Bay, Bowser and Bloedel, and across from Alert Bay, the works at Englewood had a good-sized output. Not to be overlooked is Port Alice, once the locale of the only pulp mill on Vancouver Island. In order to be profitable, the mill ran twenty-four hours a day, seven days a week, shutting down only three days each year. Employees toiled in twelve-hour shifts, switching from day to night and back in two-week intervals. If workers wished to retain their jobs, they were required to put in a two-year stretch before they could board the Union Steamship boat for a brief respite. It was a monotonous grind with little relief or diversion.

During the span in which forestry was making noteworthy impact on the island, significant change was also affecting *nikkei* life in Canada. As noted before, young men left impoverished homes in an austere land in the hope of quick gains and a triumphant return. These were shattered dreams. Instead of heading home to grim reality, most chose to remain, in search of a stable family existence in their adopted country.

After an anti-Asiatic disturbance in Vancouver in 1907, Japan agreed to limit its annual emigration to Canada. But no restrictions were placed against women entering as wives and prospective brides of men already here. As a result, from 1910, Japanese women proceeding to Canada each year constantly outnumbered incoming males. This peaked during the 1914-18 war years when the Dominion was booming and the awaiting men were prospering. However, this policy was changed in 1928 and their entry was slowed to a trickle.

The aspirations of these pioneering men and women, called the *issei*—meaning first generation—was to provide a secure home in a domestic environment for their Canadian offspring, the *nisei* or second generation, whose numbers were increasing rapidly. Coming from a homeland that stressed a strong family bond and respect for tradition, the *issei* hoped to instill these values in the *nisei*. This was the goal of the community language schools.

They varied in enrollment (as few as ten students to a hundred in two schools combined in Cumberland), quality of teaching (housewives to qualified educators from Japan) and frequency of classes (one night a week to Monday to Friday after regular school). Except for the few *nisei* who learned to read and write passably, the worth of these schools is debatable. Moreover, it deprived youngsters of after-school romps that others enjoyed and added fuel to fiery rhetoric of some politicians that Japanese schools were hives of subversive activity.

Academic achievement, whether in English or Japanese, or commercial or technical training, did not open doors to suitable employment. The *nisei* were barred from fields such as law and pharmacy, and trades such as morticians and locomotive engineers. Denied the right to vote federally and provincially in B.C., they lacked the political power to protest or combat these injustices. For the men, leaving school meant going off to a logging camp, sawmill, or to some menial job. More fortunate were those with a family-owned business. The plight of women was similar. A university graduate found that the only position open to her in Victoria was as a domestic. Though it was the provincial capital, she could not join the civil service. No *nisei* women on Vancouver Island were nurses, teachers, stenographers—not even a clerk in a candy store, unless it was owned by a *nikkei*.

All problems and issues became academic when the bombs fell. It was a shock beyond words. From Port Alice south to Victoria, the unexpected stunned the *nikkei* community.

That night, tomato growers on Mayne Island, shopkeepers in Duncan, mill workers in Port Alberni and a community leader in Chemainus—eleven men, all Japanese nationals—were arrested and interned but never charged. Within twenty-four hours, language schools were shut, Japan-owned logging assets seized, and *nikkei* workers at Victoria's Empress Hotel fired without notice. In a week, fishermen were ordered to steer their craft under escort to New Westminster.

Shortly, all Japanese nationals (those not naturalized or born in Canada) were ordered to report monthly to the RCMP, a dusk-to-dawn curfew was imposed, and cameras, radios, and motor vehicles were confiscated. Finally, the inevitable came: exile of everyone of Japanese descent from the Pacific coast. The Vancouver Island exodus began in mid-March, with Japanese national males first, followed by the families and others. By the end of April 1942, all 3,400 were cleared off the island. Their half-century presence was obliterated.

Seven years later, in April 1949, all restrictions against the exiles were lifted, including political, social, and economic injustices. They could now move freely, vote, take any employment, and recall to Canada family members stranded in Japan.

Five years after full citizens' rights were granted or restored, barely fifty of the original 3,400 were back in their former towns or villages. They include two families in logging in the Cowichan, some fishermen who returned to Nanaimo and Ucluelet, and a widow who moved to Victoria with her new husband. But not a soul reappeared in the former *nikkei* centres of Chemainus or Cumberland. Only the dated grave markers with Japanese names attest to the existence of these and other communities on Vancouver Island that vanished more than fifty years ago.

INTRODUCTION

> The spring wind blows
> Sharpened
> on the edge of the Rockies
> —*Haruyoshi Tanouye, written about
> the Japanese-Canadian evacuation*

O N A FINE DAY IN JUNE 1990, I drove south from Ladysmith on Vancouver Island along the scenic old island highway, where the sapphire depths of Stuart Channel augment the comfortable residential landscape stretching along the route. It was the beginning of a journey that led to the writing of this book.

As a reporter for the local paper, I drove this windy road almost daily. I covered all manner of stories in the year I worked in the region, including an interview with a man who had just celebrated his 100th birthday. Scandinavian by birth, he had come to the west coast as a young man, abandoning his homeland to carve out a future in the rugged frontier. He worked as a longshoreman at the Chemainus docks in the days when sailing schooners from around the world carried cargo harvested from immense old-growth forests that once covered the bottoms of the Chemainus and Cowichan valleys. Much like old-growth stands today, his memory had faded into quiet oblivion. Nonetheless, he was part of the local history, a part which had remained where it set down roots.

On another occasion, I drove this road to catch the ferry to Kuper Island, home of the Penelakut Indian Band. As the ship approached the dock, the former residential school loomed in the middle of a large clearing of land, a bleak symbol of the injustice perpetrated against generations of Natives up and down the coast. Like First Nations people across the country, the Penelakut fell victim to a century of cultural genocide. Still, they maintain an undeniable presence in the local landscape, and are reviving their culture and pride on home turf.

Driving to Chemainus that day in June 1990, I was about to encounter another chapter of local history, one which was all but gone from view. I had vague memories of learning something in school about the Japanese Canadian war experience, and I was aware that they were offered compensation in 1988. I studied Joy Kogawa's *Obasan* in a Canadian literature course at the University of Victoria, and was deeply moved by her lyrical prose and the poignant testimonies of the novel's characters. But for reasons I still can't explain, it was the plight of aboriginal people that engaged me on an ongoing basis. In one sense, my outrage regarding their treatment was homeless—until I met a Haida man in the 1970s. His name was Jerome Parnell, and his legacy was like that of so many: a childhood torn apart by death, illness, alcoholism, and poverty, leading to apprehension by provincial authorities and a life in foster homes, leading in turn to a life on the streets. When we met, I was naïve enough to think I could help him heal and restore some inner pride. It was an ill-fated goal: my good intentions and feelings for him were no match for the depth of commitment and sheer hard work involved. Less than a year after the relationship failed, I gave birth to our daughter, Ellen Sarah. Five days after she was born, I gave her to close friends to adopt.

Ellen was ten when I met Shunichi and Hanaye Isoki in the Chemainus Festival of Murals office in June 1990. Because the adoption arrangement was open, she was then, and is now, a big part of my life. But the year and a half I had lived with her father was well in my past. Hearing the Isokis' story touched all those chords again, except here were people who, somehow, had triumphed. I rushed headlong into a history lesson of a different colour, with a tangible and memorable face.

Accompanied by Kyoshi Shimizu, a Vancouver-born woman spearheading a mural project, the Isokis were in town to help with reunion plans to commemorate the Japanese community. It had been as much of a pioneering influence as that of any other immigrant group in the valley, yet all that remained of the Japanese presence in Chemainus a generation after they were scratched from the picture was locked inside memories: of school children who cried when classmates suddenly disappeared; of baseball chums and churchgoers, friendly and hostile alike; of labourers who gained jobs and shop owners who lost patrons when the community evacuated.

To be honest, I felt lukewarm about the Chemainus murals. It was not that I didn't appreciate the local history that the paintings offered so much as the trivializing of it that accompanies such tourist-oriented ventures. Nonetheless, the town's economy depended in large part on the internationally renowned murals, and they did offer graphic insights into the region's past.

When I heard the Isokis' story, I set aside my biases about the murals. Perhaps I couldn't resist such a meaningful encounter with living history; maybe it was because the story had a "happy ending." Whatever drew me to it was forceful, and I quickly became absorbed in learning about the community that had virtually been struck from the local history fare.

A year passed. I left my job at the newspaper and began freelance writing in Victoria, where Kyoshi Shimizu lived. Over a series of interviews, I learned that her involvement in the Chemainus project grew out of an association with Shige

Yoshida when she was a social worker in Tashme. Near Hope, British Columbia, it was one of the largest Japanese Canadian internment camps. Mr. Yoshida was a scoutmaster whose boy scout troops were formed as a result of racism, and thrived in spite of it. As an adolescent in Chemainus, he had been rejected by the local scout troop on spurious grounds. So he took a correspondence course and formed his own troop in 1930, which had the distinction of being comprised exclusively of Japanese Canadian boys. In Tashme, he organized a troop that numbered over 200 by the end of the war, the largest boy scout troop in the British Commonwealth.

More importantly for Mrs. Shimizu and many others, Mr. Yoshida's efforts offered the boys a bridge to the white man's world, a way of instilling pride in themselves and a means of demonstrating loyalty to king and country. A retired social worker and ardent community spokesperson, Mrs. Shimizu felt that the history depicted in the Chemainus' murals was woefully incomplete without the story of the intrepid scoutmaster. With characteristic determination, she set about to change that.

As one of Shige Yoshida's assistant scoutmasters, Shunichi Isoki returned to his birthplace for the first time in forty-eight years to help plan for the mural. But he had another motive as well, one much closer to his heart. His baby brother was buried in the Chemainus cemetery, and his grave was among those whose markers had been bulldozed after the community was uprooted. In the 1960s, replacement headstones were erected along a fence because the whereabouts of the original graves were unknown. Those markers also disappeared. Mr. Isoki believed passionately that the memorial monument planned for the cemetery would help restore dignity to the deceased and their families.

It had been a long time coming. A Shinto-Buddhist organization based in Vancouver had been trying in vain to establish the whereabouts of those interred in Chemainus as part of a project to restore Japanese sections of cemeteries on Vancouver Island. Until Reverend Harry Costerton became pastor of the Anglican church in 1988, the committee was told there was no record of Japanese graves in Chemainus. Costerton determined otherwise. During a cemetery clean-up after his arrival, five stone markers were discovered under a pile of debris just outside the cemetery fence. A sixth was found in 1991.

The reunion was planned to coincide with the *O-bon* festival, an annual Buddhist tradition which had not taken place in the Chemainus cemetery since August 1941. In *A Child in Prison Camp*, Shizuye Takashima explains: "In August is O-bon, the festival for the dead, to wish joy for their souls and to remember them." Burning candles to light the way for their ancestors, family members welcome home the spirits of their beloved in a simple, dignified ritual.

So it seemed that the reunion in 1991 would be a homecoming on a grand scale, a rare opportunity to heal the wounds so many had stubbornly tucked away for better or worse. They would return to the place their parents called Chimunesu, for the immigrants were unable to wrap their tongues around Chemainus. As with pioneers from other lands, the Japanese had forsaken a great deal to forge a better future for their offspring on the wild west coast. But Chimunesu evolved into an enclave of shacks and boarding houses destined to be torn from their grasp, a place which nonetheless harboured memories of all moods for those who once called it home.

The reunion homecoming on August 10, 1991 was as charged with emotion as one would expect. Old baseball friends mingled in the heart of what had been Kawahara camp as if nothing had changed in fifty years—except everyone knew that virtually everything had changed. For those who participated, the celebration was all-consuming.

Predictably, not everyone who lived in Chemainus during the war years came out for the reunion. There are some in the community who still call the town's exiled residents "Japs" and who mistrust their motives, those who still harbour deep hatred against them because of atrocities perpetrated in Japanese prison camps. Some still have curios they stole or picked up at auctions, just as there are residents with Japanese gravestones on their properties—in chimneys and fireplaces, in a retaining wall, in the corner post of a house. But there are also those who came forward with headstones and discreetly turned them over to the pastor. And there are many, perhaps the majority, who deeply regret what happened and yet maintain that the evacuation and internment were justified. It is what happens in a climate of racial hostility and war: extremists wreak havoc with normal sensibilities, moulding a hysteria based on ill-founded fears and hatreds. Against the advice of senior military officers and the commissioner of the RCMP, the government went ahead with the evacuation to further its political agenda.

From the outset, the opportunity to record the reunion seemed all mine. What started as a simple article for a community newspaper evolved into a magazine article and then this book. I was overwhelmed by the generosity of spirit, humour and pride of those who returned to Chemainus in August 1991. It struck me as important to offer a window into those early years of Chimunesu as they remembered it, a portrait of a community that perhaps would disappear with their passing. I wanted to find out how they got on with their lives and succeeded in spite of all that had happened. And I wanted to celebrate the goodwill of those in Chemainus whose efforts helped to exonerate the wrongs of the past, even though an undercurrent of resentment about the "The Lone Scout" mural tainted the occasion. Many felt the focus on Shige Yoshida was inappropriate, given the contributions of others that would go unnoticed.

With the emotionally charged experience of the reunion behind me, I travelled to Ontario to interview former Chemainus residents in the winter of 1992. I needed a more in-depth picture of their lives, as well as a sense of the places where they had set down roots—the places they now call home. Many struggled to gain acceptance in the industrial heart of Ontario after the war. They succeeded, but not without further incidents of racism in their efforts to find housing and work.

A few years ago, I cruised through Chemainus on a blustery October night. It was my first time back since the reunion, and I parked the car a block from the mural of *The Lone Scout*, directly behind the mill compound where Tomoki Kawabe's crew had once sweated to stack lumber up higher than the roofs of nearby homes. I glanced at the modest piles of milled lumber, processed and stacked mostly by machinery, on the other side of the MacMillan Bloedel fence. Everything was still, except for a strong gusty wind blowing up from the harbour. I crossed Oak Street and found myself peering into the faces packed around the community hall in the mural. Whispering their names, I ran my fingers across their tiny faces. Behind me the street was black, deserted. Yet I knew I was not alone: the spirits of those who lived there were watching. I was not alarmed by their presence; I was reassured by it.

No Japanese Canadians have lived in Chemainus since the war. Restricted from returning to the coast until 1949, they were forced to start over elsewhere when the war ended in 1945. But if you walk along Croft Street and ponder the faces in *The Lone Scout*, you may feel a wind bearing spirits that will lift you back to the heart of a community that laughed and cried in its time.

A few miles south in a small cemetery, the Japanese community is no longer censored from the town's history. The desecration of the graves of babies, children, women, and men in their prime, and the elderly is vindicated by a memorial monument. Old headstones engraved with calligraphy are stark, eloquent reminders of the past; modern marble plaques complement them, the names of the deceased etched in bold black letters: *Yoneji Isoki, Miki Okada, Takeshi Okada, Towa Izumi, Nobuyuki Izumi, Shigeru Yoshida....*

Ironically, there is also a stone marker bearing the name "Lang" in the Chemainus cemetery. Although that family is no relation of mine, no doubt we share a similar racial background. It makes me an unlikely candidate for this material, except that the hope in this story is irresistible to anyone concerned with justice. Writing and learning about this black episode in our history has been a catharsis of sorts, putting my anger, sadness and frustration in perspective. More importantly, it has also taught me about the resiliency of the human spirit, as well as what life offers and what it takes away from all of us, regardless of race or class.

Some may consider it inappropriate for me to tackle this subject matter. I understand that point of view. Indeed, I may have misconstrued some cultural subtleties. However, I believe that we do not necessarily need to suffer racism personally in order to bring life experience, compassion, and insight to any subject that moves us.

To the people from Chemainus now scattered across the nation, I offer these final comments. For the benefit of consistency, I adopted the order of given name first and surname second, even though your *issei* parents used their surnames first.

In writing your stories, I have taken great liberties by creating dialogue and fleshing out scenes with details which may or may not have been true to the moment. If I have misrepresented anyone in any way, I apologize in advance for my lack of understanding. While I adopted fiction techniques to develop this book, the stories themselves are based on the true events of your lives.

Not everyone's story is included, but I will remember the trust, generosity, kindness, and strength of all those I interviewed. Meeting you has touched me in ways that won't leave me ever.

Regrettably, I did not finish this book in time for some. During the spring of 1996, four former Chemainus residents died. To the surviving members of their families and the former community, these deaths were among many since the war years to which I made little reference: for example, Satoshi and Mitsuo Izumi, Norboru Yoshida, Mitsuhara Otsu, Satoru Okada, and, naturally, most of the *issei*. Although the book includes references to deaths affecting many families over time, I did not anticipate that some of those I interviewed would be gone before the book was in print, and it draws my attention to the ailing health of a number of the aging *nisei* from Chemainus.

I note their passing with sadness, for each in his or her own way offered something to ponder or to cherish: Aiko Nakahara (nee: Higashi), a rebel in her youth with the guts to elope with the man she loved; Shizuka Okada (nee: Taniwa), an artisitic woman who believed in the goodness in people; Mitsuyuki Sakata, a once proud judo expert who fought Parkinson's disease with courage; and Yuki Yoshida, a proud and gentle woman who set herself apart as an award-winning producer for the National Film Board.

O N E

YOSHIKO KAWAHARA

Y OSHIKO PUTS THE LETTER ON THE TABLE and leans her head against the wall. Sunlight floods her kitchen through the window above the sink. Along the window ledge, African violets sparkle like a cluster of rough amethyst. She feels the sun's warmth find her face as she closes her eyes and sighs.

The quiet in her kitchen is surreal, having once been the stomping grounds for ten children. Not quite twenty-one when her first child was born in 1940, she was forty-three when her last one came into the world in 1962. Oh, the meals she had prepared in this kitchen while the kids ran amuck until their father came home from work. Today, her children have families of their own.

Even Takayoshi isn't home. It's his afternoon to play mahjong with the boys, giving her solitude to digest the letter from her brother, Shunichi.

He is back home from his trip to Vancouver Island, where he went to make arrangements for next year's reunion in Chemainus. Yoshiko has been expecting news from him, but

28

somehow isn't prepared for it now that it's here. Oddly, his letter reminds her of the day when her mother told her she would marry Takayoshi Kawahara. She was eighteen and asked that they wait a year, but when 1938 turned over she still felt everything conspiring to make her insides lumpy. Little knots of excitement and dread, happiness and fear rolled round and round like the conveyor belt in the clam cannery where she worked. In those days she had her youth to sustain her; now, at seventy-one, strength cultivated from survival supports her. But she resists the idea of returning to Chemainus, knowing it will drag her through all the memories that have brought her here.

Her brother is suggesting they drive across together: she and Takayoshi, and he and his wife, Hana. Yoshiko has only travelled across Canada by train, never by car. No one had a car back then. The train took them pretty much wherever the government ordered them to go; it brought them here to Fort William in 1947. She hasn't cared to travel much since.

Passenger trains don't come through here any more, but Yoshiko hears the distant rattle of a freight train chugging along the shore of Lake Superior. The whirr of steel on steel grinds to a halt, echoing across the water and prompting old memories to life. Closing her eyes, she finds herself en route to Lemon Creek in 1942, holding baby Shirley in her arms.

Yoshiko listens to her baby breathe, watching her little body rise and fall. It has been too hot to keep the window closed from the onslaught of gritty coal smoke that spews inside the old rail car. She sets the flannel diaper down that shielded Shirley from the smoke. It is black with soot. Now that dusk is upon them, Yoshiko shoves the window shut. It hits the bottom of the frame with a crack. As dusk deepens into night, the steam engine propels them inland.

She rocks the baby and smoothes her hair off her forehead.

Shirley's face is porcelain white in the dark. On the facing bench, Yoshiko's sister-in-law lies under a scratchy, grey army blanket: it is Hana's turn to sleep on these cursed wooden benches. With nowhere safe to lay the baby, they take turns holding her through the night. The boys are already asleep on the benches across the aisle.

Her bones are aching. She shifts her weight and stares at the dark sliding past her reflection. "What will Lemon Creek be like, and how long will we stay, and when will we be allowed to go home?" She whispers each question to the rhythm of wheels grinding them inland. Wilderness sped past and loomed before her all day—nothing but trees, mountainsides of deep impenetrable green. It is September, but this forest has not changed colour; this forest will stay green until it snows.

Yoshiko is afraid. Nonetheless, she feels that what lies ahead cannot be worse than Hastings Park, cannot possibly be worse than leaving Chemainus to live in horse stalls. Within days of arriving in that wretched place, the pains started and they whisked her off to Vancouver General to give birth to Shirley.

Yoshiko leans her head against the train window, recalling the afternoon her husband came to see them.

"Hello, Yoshiko," Takayoshi says, shuffling over to her bedside.

Yoshiko suffers a thin smile and peers into her husband's face. "What's wrong, Tak?" she asks.

"It's a long story. I can't stay, because I'm going to road camp soon," he replies, his eyes downcast.

"Road camp? Where?"

"Somewhere in northern Ontario. Everything's in a turmoil, Yoshiko. Some other Chemainus boys are going too."

She turns away and says nothing. She doesn't have the strength to be outraged. "How are the boys?" she asks, twisting a corner of the bedsheet around her finger.

"Mom says they are fine," he replies. "They are like all the kids, having fun with all their new friends."

"Oh," she says. Takayoshi is standing over the bassinette, staring blankly at the baby. "Go on, pick her up. She'll be fine."

Takayoshi puts his hand under her wee head and lifts her into his arms. Yoshiko can see that he is not connecting, however. His eyes are clouded, fragmented by the chaos and not with this world.

"Well, I'd better go. I'll write when I get to road camp," Takayoshi says, looking briefly into his wife's eyes.

"Okay. Bye." Yoshiko takes Shirley back, cradling her against her breast. She listens to her husband shuffle out the room the same way he shuffled in, but she does not watch him go. When she returns to Hastings Park with her new baby a few weeks later, Takayoshi is long gone.

Then she gets the fever, and a nurse puts her in the Hastings Park hospital, a converted chicken house. Perhaps she is the only young mother who doesn't cross the cement floor to feed her baby at night. Once a day they let her out to visit her infant, while her husband's mother and her two sisters-in-law look after Shirley and the boys.

The fever will not come down; she starts dreaming. In her dreams, Yoshiko escapes to the Chemainus she knew when she was little herself.

On April 15, 1919, Yoshiko Isoki is born at home on the edge of what the *hakujins*, or white people, call "Japtown." Located on the north side of Chemainus, it is an enclave of boardwalks, shacks, bunkhouses, garages, and gardens where bachelors and families live. Most men work in the sawmill across the street; others, like Yoshiko's father, fish and find odd labouring jobs.

Yoshiko only has one brother and an older sister in their

home on Oak Street when she is a baby. Two more children
are born before her mother, Shyobu, reaches the end of her
childbearing years in her early forties. She was in her teens
when her firstborn arrived in the mountainous seaside village
of Taiji, Wakayama.

Yoshiko's father, Jiroichi, came to Canada around 1910, followed by his wife in 1914. They left three daughters and the
memory of their only son, Ichio, who died as a child. Hard
times necessitated this wrenching of roots, which they intended to be temporary. Jiroichi only earned a meagre living as
a whaler, in part because hundreds of foreign boats whaling
off the coast of Japan in the mid-1800s contributed to declining
stocks. To make matters worse, fire-powered harpoons and
modern boats were beginning to replace hand-held harpoons
and Japanese-style rowboats. He could no longer compete.
The way whaling had been done in Taiji for 700 years was
dying, and with it, his livelihood. Just as some whale species
faced the threat of extinction, Jiroichi weighed his options and
chose to seek his fortune in the abundant fishing grounds off
Canada's coast. He was thirty-five when he booked his passage
across the Pacific, hoping to make his fortune quickly and
return. Four years later, less impoverished but by no means
wealthy, he sent for his wife.

In time, Yoshiko will lose all of her sisters to Japan or to the
gods, those sisters she knows and those she doesn't. Separated
by 4,000 miles of ocean and unbridgable circumstances, she
never meets her sisters born in Japan. But she imagines that the
ghost of Isoyo, her oldest sister, sometimes drifts down the
street outside her bedroom window.

Occasionally, she wakes when the screen door slips from
her mother's hand and slams shut. Shyobu is roaming the
streets while Chemainus sleeps. Yoshiko imagines her wandering down Oak and along Esplanade to the bluff behind the

hospital, where the sea stretches to blackened islands nearby; or perhaps she slips down to the wharf to listen to water lap against the shore. Leaning against the wooden railings and facing the stars, she implores Isoyo to brush a breeze across her temples. Her beloved firstborn died in childbirth, but Shyobu did not light candles for her daughter's safe journey to the afterworld. She did not know Isoyo's fate until it was too late. Her grief is all tangled up with her estrangement from home, like seaweed pushed by the tide against the pier's pilings.

Back in the cluttered room that Yoshiko shares with her two Canadian-born sisters, the young girl closes her eyes and tries to picture Isoyo's face. Did her sister have her broad nose and flattened cheeks? Had she grown from being tall and gangly into the graceful woman Yoshiko dreamed of becoming? Had she wondered about the land that enticed her parents away as Yoshiko wondered about the land that they pried themselves from? Midway through her imaginings and long before her mother slips back inside, Yoshiko falls asleep again. When she wakes in the morning, eager to play, she has forgotten it all.

It is Saturday, which means that before Yoshiko can play with her friends, she and her sisters have to scrub the wooden floor. Like the other houses that people rent from Mr. Kawahara, the Isokis' home is small and neat. There is nothing fancy about its rooms and roughly-hewn furniture, but it cradles the family nonetheless. Yoshiko's father and brother are out fishing today, and the girls waste no time hauling water to heat on the stove.

Soon Yoshiko is on her hands and knees, scrubbing circles on the floor. No one speaks, for they wish the job done as quickly as possible. When it is, Yoshiko runs around the corner past Mr. Kawahara's garden and garage to Miyoko Nishimura's house. Miyoko is waiting for her, and they race each other down the alley, past the dirt playground behind the community bathhouse, all the way to the table by the apple tree to join the other girls playing jacks.

Taller than most of the girls, and with big hands that spread out wide, Yoshiko has an advantage at jacks. They play for hours if it is warm, but summer is over and the air has a fall bite. They decide to play hide-and-seek instead and soon the neighbourhood boys join them. At the heart of Kawahara camp, the children establish home base on the trunk of the apple tree and spread like roots taking hold in new-found crevices, squirming their way into corners behind stacks of firewood or backing into nooks around the bathhouse that only children can find.

Yoshiko is the first to be "it." Although her mother doesn't speak English, she recognizes her daughter's voice yell "ready or not, here I come," followed later by several bursts of "home free." Laughter and the scurry of running, jumping feet echo down the alley and along the boardwalk all afternoon.

When Yoshiko comes home for dinner, she is pooped and hungry but happy. Her father and brother are home from fishing; she can smell the ling cod cooking the moment she runs inside. Shunichi is in his room reading, but Jiroichi is sitting in the kitchen, smoking a cigarette and watching his wife cook. He is a kind man who isn't a drinker like many of the men. Nonetheless, Yoshiko knows her place and doesn't need to be reminded of her inferior status to boys.

Before she goes to bed that night, Yoshiko asks her father to tell her the story about the baby whale again. She loves his lilting voice; somehow, his Japanese sounds softer when she is cradled in the nook of his arm.

"Papa, how did those babies learn to swim?"

Jiroichi smiles. Yoshiko never seems to tire hearing about his whaling days in Taiji.

"Well, I didn't see the baby whale being born, but I saw the mama whale swimming alongside it very closely. The water was whooshing around my boat in great waves as they went by, and the mama whale looked me right in the eye."

"Did she, really? Weren't you afraid?" asks Yoshiko.

"No, I wasn't. We never killed a mother whale, so I just watched her glide through the water with the baby suckling as they swam."

"They swam together?"

"Yes, like petals drifting in circles, they danced through the water."

Yoshiko closes her eyes, trying to imagine the great mama whale and her baby dancing in the sparkling blue water. She looks into her father's eyes. Perhaps she, too, could swim off to another space, somewhere deep and gentle where the warmth is like a wave washing over.

Jiroichi is out fishing when she gets up the next morning, and Shyobu is packing a lunch of rice and fish cakes. After breakfast Yoshiko and her older sister Misako set out with their mother in search of *matsu take*, a wild mushroom that is a delicacy. Yoshiko likes going into the forest on these outings, where towering Douglas firs shelter all sorts of critters and moss squishes softly underfoot.

Mr. Nakaki was an old man when he showed them the way to the *matsu take* patch, which he said no one else knew about. Because there was no path, he nailed markers into trees. But that morning they miss one, and now the forest looks the same in all directions.

Yoshiko wonders if they missed the marker when they stooped to pick mushrooms along the way. Perhaps they were too busy watching for the flat, brown caps peeking out from the forest floor and forgot to watch for the next turn in the woods. Although she has long legs for a ten-year-old, Yoshiko finds it difficult to keep up with Misako and her mother.

Before long, she is soaking from the heavy dew and dirty from walking through dense brush. They stop to eat their lunch and take a rest.

"Just calm down," Shyobu tells her daughters. "We'll get out. Nothing to worry about." Yoshiko doesn't like the pinch in Shyobu's voice, though, and notices the colour has drained from her mother's face.

After lunch, they trudge through more bush in single file. Yoshiko hears a loud crack to her left and everything goes still. She imagines that it is a bear, then a cougar, perhaps a wolf. Near tears, she forces herself to focus on the back of her mother's head. Cold, damp sweat streams down the nape of her neck. Maybe they will join her baby brother, Yoneji, in the Chemainus cemetery—although she doesn't know how anyone will find their bodies. Yoneji has been dead for about five years; pneumonia killed him when he was nine months old. Shyobu always said that if the vaporizer she ordered had come sooner, he might not have died. Yoshiko doesn't remember him well, but every August the family lights candles and burns incense at his grave, welcoming his spirit home. She wonders whether they will be remembered in the cemetery too.

Suddenly, Shyobu spins about to face her daughters. "We must go where we can see sky more than trees," she says. She had been sure that by going ahead they would come to the mushroom patch and could follow the markers back. But hours later, there is still no sign of the patch. Yoshiko wonders if they have been walking in circles, for lengthening shadows are closing in on them.

Shyobu pivots around and sets their course. Yoshiko glances at her sister, but Misako says nothing. They seem to be walking into forever, losing hope as the afternoon light fades. Before dusk sets in, however, Yoshiko catches a glimpse of sky beyond her mother. Excitement overcomes her fatigue, and she hurries to catch up. Her mother's jaw is set as she plods ahead, but Yoshiko sees relief flood her eyes as they step into the clearing above the highway. Misako chatters like a squirrel as Yoshiko rushes forward down the hill, her long hair streaming on the wind.

Watching her mother knit by the kerosene lantern that night, Yoshiko studies shadows flickering across Shyobu's face. Her mother has donned her mask again. Their brush with disaster will linger with other ghosts from the past, away from public view.

They go mushroom picking again in the autumn months that follow. Yoshiko tries in vain to find the marker they missed, but the forest remains elusive. Now she takes extra care picking the succulent stems, patting the mossy earth afterwards with firm, gentle pressure to coax a new crop to unfold.

Yoshiko's school days are over when she finishes grade eight at the Chemainus public school. Fluent in English and studious, she passes all her grades. But times are harder in the thirties than they have been before. Earning money to help the family is what she has expected all along. High school is just not part of the picture.

Also, her parents are saving every penny to send her sister Chizuru to school in Japan next spring. Misako will accompany her and rejoin her husband in Fukuoka. He was deported months after their marriage because he could not get immigrant status, but Misako stayed behind until their son was born. Now she is taking little Shigeru to Japan to make a new home.

Their brother Shunichi goes fishing for days and sometimes weeks at a time. Yoshiko misses his gentle sense of humour when he is gone. When her sisters and baby nephew go, she will miss him even more. She remembers when Genichi Nakahara used to show up on their doorstep, eager to share his steaming bowl of food. An only child, Genichi liked the foofaraw in the Isokis' kitchen and often ate with them. Now it seems that Yoshiko is about to be the only child in her kitchen.

But she is a loner at times, given to moody bouts of resentment toward Misako and Chizuru, whom her mother favours. Now they are going to Japan and she isn't. For once, she is glad she isn't the chosen one. Leaving home seems a high price to pay for favouritism. But Chizuru is excited about travelling to a strange country and meeting her sisters there. Adventurous and naïve, she has no fear.

Misako is caught in altogether different circumstances and could not feel more torn. She knows it is her duty to join her husband, but she is leaving without illusions. This goodbye will not be temporary. The week before they leave in March 1933, Misako watches her mother with new respect, recognizing the twist of fate that is about to plant her in the country Shyobu was forced to abandon. Women go where their husbands bid, without argument or negotiation.

Misako and Yoshiko return the Robinsons' laundry the last time together. A weekly chore for some years, it takes on the status of a ritual this Friday. Walking across to their neighbours, the sisters cling to all that is familiar.

"Look, Misako, the snowdrops and crocuses are peeping through the snow," Yoshiko says, pointing down at the path.

Misako nods, glancing at the delicate clusters of flowers poking through shiny patches of snow. "I wonder if spring has arrived in Fukuoka yet. I guess they won't have these kinds of flowers there."

"I bet they do, and they'll remind you of home when you see them," Yoshiko offers.

"I don't want to be reminded of home, not for a while anyway," Misako says, glancing sideways at her sister while they wait on the porch for Mrs. Robinson.

"Let's put this basket down. It's getting too heavy," Yoshiko says, rubbing her hands. She wishes she could think of something to make her sister feel better.

Misako closes her eyes, inhaling the sweet fresh smell of sheets that Shyobu boiled on the stove with washing soda. They sparkle in the sunshine. She might never see her mother starch and iron laundry again, or share the task of folding it with Yoshiko.

Her thoughts are interrupted when the door opens.

"Ah, you've brought my laundry, girls," Mrs. Robinson says, reaching into her pocket for the money. "Thanks, kindly."

The sisters smile at their matronly neighbour and turn to go. Misako grips the seventy-five cents Mrs. Robinson drops in her palm as they walk out the yard. "Yoshiko," she asks, "did you notice Mama's hands when she finished the laundry this morning?"

"Not really. Why?"

"They are red and sore from scrubbing. Maybe we should buy her some hand cream from Kawahara's."

Yoshiko pauses before replying. "You know that Mama would just make you take it back."

"You're right. It's a silly idea," Misako says as they turn into their yard. On her last spring morning in Canada she can think of nothing more important than to rub some cream into her mother's cracked hands. However, Misako knows they have more urgent needs. It will take years for her parents to recover the cost of sending Chizuru to Japan.

Without a word to Yoshiko, she bounds abruptly up their stairs. Shyobu is counting the coins when Yoshiko comes through the door. Misako is at the front window with her baby, whispering in his ear and waving his little arm at someone on the street.

Yoshiko says goodbye to Misako and Chizuru at the train station beside the *hakujin*'s community hall the next day. They do not hug or cry but wait awkwardly on the platform, not knowing what to say. Yoshiko glances at Chizuru's profile and notices the scar on her cheek is less pronounced. Chizuru is twelve now, seven years after the accident.

Yoshiko recalls the day it happened. She was seven then, playing jacks by the apple tree. She looked up to watch a boy running by, pulling Chizuru in a box behind him. One minute her young sister's head was flung back in total abandonment and glee, her long black hair flying; a split-second later, Yoshiko heard her scream as a wire sticking out from the trunk of the tree gashed across Chizuru's face. They ran home together, blood spurting along the boardwalk, pain raging through the air. Shyobu laid her iron on the woodstove when she heard the screams. Taking control, she fetched water from the stove to wash away the blood. The cut revealed her daughter's cheekbone, but Shyobu didn't think to go to the hospital. She couldn't speak English, and it was a strange world to her where they did. Besides, she hadn't the money to pay, so she laid the child on her bed and cleaned the deep gash with peroxide while Yoshiko stood by.

Chizuru is leaving Chemainus with a happier memory. Shifting her weight impatiently, she wonders whether there are Easter bunnies in Japan. She will miss the Easter egg hunt this year by a few weeks, one of few events where *hakujin* and Oriental children scramble over each other in their indiscriminate pursuit of brightly coloured eggs on the sawmill manager's estate. One year Chizuru found a chocolate bunny, killing her suspicion that fat Mr. Humbird told the *hakujin* children where to find the best treats. She plopped herself on a nearby knoll and began nibbling at the ears, munching blissfully through its thick chocolate belly.

With those sweet moments on her mind, the train pulls into the station, hissing steam. Chizuru hops happily up the stairs and skirts down the aisle to pick a seat. Her fate in Japan will not be so happy. After finishing high school, Chizuru will marry. Like the other women of her generation, she too will go where her husband bids—to Manchuria, where he is drafted during the war. The hardship will contribute to heart problems and her death at the age of thirty-six.

Misako will not fare so poorly, but she drags her feet as she climbs aboard. She cuddles Shigeru and smiles wanly, waving his wee hand through the train window. Mr. and Mrs. Nakahara, neighbours accompanying them on the long trek to Japan, board the train next. Sedate but inwardly pleased, they are going home.

What is left of the Isoki family in Canada waves goodbye. The train blows its whistle and chugs out of sight in a cloud of black smoke. In time, everyone but Yoshiko will see them again.

With her sisters gone, Yoshiko goes home to sort through her belongings. They are moving to Sidney soon, where her brother hopes to make more money fishing. Everything in her world is shifting. Like the little tremors she sometimes feels beneath her feet, the subtlety is disquieting.

As promised, Misako writes often. The three-week journey across the Pacific was marked by terrible seasickness. Her husband and their Japanese sisters greeted them warmly, although it was difficult to get used to the customs and lifestyle. When Misako found that people scorned her because her Japanese wasn't good enough, she diligently improved it.

Yoshiko tries to imagine how her sister is managing. Life in Sidney is predictable, if uneventful. Every day she walks along a dirt road to her job at the Sidney cannery and to the *hakujin* houses that she cleans. Shunichi works hard too, fishing and selling everything from herring and dogfish to fish heads at a fox farm nearby. Due to increasing restrictions against Japanese fishermen, their father hasn't fished for years. Jiroichi finds odd jobs where he can, but Shunichi is the primary breadwinner. Yoshiko knows that her parents are waiting for her to marry so they can go home to Japan, but at eighteen she is in no hurry.

One afternoon, she is reading in the light of the window at the foot of her bed. A bank of fog rolls along the shore where Saltspring Island rises above calm grey seas. She looks up to see Shyobu standing in her doorway.

"Yes, mother?" she asks, thinking she has an errand.

"Yoshi-san, our go-between has found you a husband."

"What?"

"It is as I say. Takayoshi Kawahara will be your husband."

"Who?" Yoshiko stammers.

"Takayoshi, Gihei Kawahara's son."

"But Mama, I am only eighteen. I do not want to marry yet."

"When will you want to marry, Yoshiko?" Shyobu snaps back.

Yoshiko knows better than to argue with her mother and softens her voice. "Please, Mama. Let me wait another year."

Shyobu hesitates and walks over to Yoshiko's window. She sees the letter from Misako on the bed and sighs. "I will ask your father. Perhaps we can wait one year," she says and turns to leave.

Yoshiko holds her breath and counts to ten. She fumbles Misako's letter back into the envelope and puts on a sweater. Going out the back door quietly, she heads for the rocky beach at the end of the lane to think things over.

Yoshiko knows she can refuse altogether, but to do so doesn't make sense. Takayoshi is her brother's friend, so she knows him better than most young men her age. There is no dazzling chemistry between them, but she understands that marriage is not about romance. It is about securing a provider. Takayoshi will inherit the business dealings of his father, one of few with money and land in Chemainus.

Back in her room, she writes Misako of the news.

Jiroichi drives Yoshiko to Victoria to buy her wedding dress. They motor into the heart of downtown in the truck her brother uses to haul fish. The lady in the store is very English, with an accent as pointed as a hat pin. Yoshiko has never had a fancy dress in her life, let alone one that is brand new. Drawing a gown over her head, she holds her breath tight, fearful that the fabric will tear or a button pop. The saleslady is in the change room with her, supposedly helping but really making matters worse. Yoshiko decides on the second dress, squirming uncomfortably when Jiroichi hands over twenty-five dollars in payment.

They step outside into pouring rain on Government Street. Holding the bag under her umbrella as if the dress is made of eggshells, Yoshiko is flighty and more than once almost trips on the slick city streets. Glancing at her wavy reflection in the store windows, she envisions white lace falling to her feet in soft swirls. Unbelievably, the dress in her arms is not imaginary; it is hers for keeps.

When the Isokis move back to Chemainus later that year, Yoshiko sits in her brother's truck with the wedding gown in a nest of tissue on her lap. She watches for groves of Arbutus trees alongside the dangerous narrow road that twists over the Malahat mountains before it emerges at Mill Bay. As dusk descends, the deep auburn bark on their smooth, sinewy trunks glows. The scenery calms her nerves and takes her mind off the multitude of unanswered questions she has about the future.

In the few months before the wedding, Yoshiko and her family settle back into Chemainus and its familiar rhythms. They move upstairs from Noboru Kawahara's laundry room on Oak Street for the winter months. On the western edge of Kawahara camp, it is around the corner from Dwyer's Confectionary, where Yoshiko once bought penny candies during school lunch hours.

Because of the Depression, the streets are quieter than she remembered them. But several landmarks look the same: the community hall where they went to Japanese language school, Kawahara's store, Taniwa's pool hall and Ning Chang's store. Perhaps the cedar siding is a bit more silver, like strands of Jiroichi's hair.

The *hakujin* community to the south and west of the mill did not notice their departure a few years earlier any more than their return, but families like the Robinsons who live among them know they are back. One afternoon Yoshiko walks along Esplanade to her former home. The apple tree from Mr. Robinson's back yard still branches over the fence. She remembers the delicate sweet jelly her mother made from those apples. It was not for that reason alone that the bungalow had been her favourite home. More spacious and comfortable than the row houses along Oak Street, it was where they first had electricity. Among other conveniences, it put an end to her least favourite chore: cleaning the glass globes of kerosene lanterns.

She notices Mr. Robinson leaning over his flower garden in the late afternoon sun, cutting the last of his huge dahlias. He looks up and calls her over.

"How did you like Sidney, Yoshiko?" he asks, snipping at the base of the flowers.

"It was fine, Mr. Robinson," Yoshiko replies. "But I'm glad to be home. I missed Chemainus."

"Well, welcome back," he says, thrusting a bouquet of crimson, canary yellow, and lavender dahlias into her hands.

The next day, she cuts across her yard to help a neighbour make tofu. The innocence of childhood is behind her, obscured in the shadow that darts over the ground she covers.

Standing for a moment in her neighbour's doorway, Yoshiko watches Fude Nakatsu grinding soybeans in the crushing wheel. The pasty yellow mush gushing out the side of the stone wheel reminds her that even beans as hard as rocks can be made malleable.

Fude is not the only woman in the area who makes tofu, but hers is among the best and in demand. It is a mystery how she managed on the pennies she earned when she was first widowed. Her son Kanichi is a fisherman himself now, but when her husband drowned twenty-three years ago, the boy was too young to work.

The night it happened, a frantic Fude ran to Yoshiko's father. It was dark and her husband hadn't come home for dinner. Jiroichi organized a group of fishermen to drag for the body around Bare Point at dawn. They found his boat all right, running circles in the chop. Many speculated that his foot got caught in the net as he let it out, but they dragged up the net without his body. With no explanation or remains to bury, Fude mourned her loss and somehow carried on.

Yoshiko helps Fude finish forming the tofu cakes and pack them in a wooden bucket. Carrying it between them, they march along the Oak Street boardwalk and onto the sawmill grounds, where Mr. Kawabe's crew strain like slaves, piling lumber as high as the rooftops of the row houses they face. The women skirt past the grunts and sweat of the labourers, while the grinding lurch of gears hauling huge timbers from the booming grounds into the saws eclipses all other sound. They step onto the shore where the Okadas established their camp years before and knock on the doors of the shacks strung across the beach. They have lightened their load by the time they move up the hill into Chinatown. Yoshiko hears pigs squealing where the shacks meet the forest. Some Japanese families live among the Chinese and Japanese bachelors here.

Some say they are the poorest of the poor and condescendingly refer to the neighbourhood as "Nanking town."

Fude is selling her last slab of tofu and talking to Mrs. Shiozaki. Yoshiko turns toward Horseshoe Bay. Beyond the squalor of the settlement, the sawmill stack and booming grounds, the rugged ridge of land they call Bare Point stretches like a fortress between them and open water.

On February 25, 1939, two months before Yoshiko's twentieth birthday, she marries Takayoshi Kawahara. Reverend Rensin Tatibana performs the Shinto-Buddhist wedding ceremony in the Kawaharas' living room above the store, where the newlyweds sip sake to consecrate their vows. Then the photographer stations them on the stairwell and frames the moment in his viewfinder, capturing smiles more of adolescents than adults.

Caught between the solemnity of the occasion and the awkward excitement they feel, Yoshiko and Takayoshi trundle with their escorts to the community hall for the reception. The weather has co-operated generously. For February, the breeze is exceptionally warm and the only clouds in the sky are high flying wisps.

Once seated at the head table, the newlyweds watch their party unwind at the edges. Women in kimonos perform funny skits as plates of chicken yakitori and sushi are endlessly replenished. Although not a drinker, Takayoshi is expected to drink excessively on his wedding day. But the sake makes him sick, so they leave before the singing finally stops spilling onto the street. By the time Chemainus goes quiet, the bride and groom are asleep at the World Hotel in Vancouver.

The stars shine more brightly above Chemainus than over the Powell Street hotel, for Vancouver is a city and Chemainus a tiny town. But as wedding guests wind their way home, they notice that the bride's radiance has shifted skyward. Life is evolving in Canada. Although many *issei*, or first-generation

Japanese immigrants, still cling to Japan the homeland, the future now has roots in the same fertile soil that also covers their dead.

When Yoshiko and Takayoshi return from their honeymoon in Seattle two weeks later, they join Takayoshi's parents and sister for dinner. Yoshiko sits through the awkward silence and nibbles at her food, recalling the constant chatter during mealtimes at home. She will not miss her fierce arguments with her mother, but she recognizes that adjusting to married life will take time.

The living quarters above the store are luxurious compared to the homes Yoshiko knew. The rooms are big and airy, furnished with upholstered sofas and chairs from the Eaton's catalogue. In addition to linoleum floors, they even have an indoor bathtub, unheard of in other homes. Of course they have electricity, although no indoor plumbing for toilets. But her mother-in-law, Shigeri, has an electric wringer washer, whereas most women scrub and wring their laundry by hand.

Yoshiko catches whatever private moments she can in the bedroom. She sits in the burgundy stuffed chair by the window and peers out to sea over the rooftop of Ning Chang's store. She recalls running down the wharf below when she was little, scanning the bay for her father's boat. She loved the smooth cut of the hull plying the water without effort or regrets.

Within a month of the wedding, Jiroichi and Shyobu board a steamer for the last time. Yoshiko knows she will not see them again. Now in their sixties, they hope to salvage part of their past with another wedding, that of the youngest daughter they left behind twenty-five years before. Once in Taiji, they will stay and live out their days.

Yoshiko tucks her sorrow away and buries her loneliness with work. She spends her days helping her mother-in-law prepare food for the few remaining boarders and, as is expected, accepts a good deal of the household chores. Her mother-in-law is an attractive but stout woman, efficient and businesslike in all her endeavours. For her part, Shigeri has little patience with her daughter-in-law's daydreaming spells, but she recognizes Yoshiko as a determined young woman who does not shirk hard work.

Takayoshi is always out in his truck, hauling everything under the sun from what Yoshiko can see. His father, Gihei, has been pressured to turn the store over to a manager from his Vancouver supplier in order to pay off his debts. When the sawmill slowed production in the 1930s, most of their boarders left, some with outstanding debts that Gihei absorbed. He relies on his son more than ever now to help maintain their standard of living, combined with the rents they collect and the money Gihei makes on his taxi business. The thirties are hitting others harder, but times are still not what he would call good.

Yoshiko understands why Takayoshi is never around. If there is one constant in her life it is that men go out to work and women work at home. Although they add to the workload, children bring a purpose to women's lives that would otherwise be marked by drudgery alone.

In March 1940, Yoshiko gives birth to a healthy boy in the Chemainus hospital. Tom is not quite seven pounds, a robust urchin with a mischievous smile. Cradling him, she feels the safe, warm glow of times when her father told her tales of mama whales. Nearing her twenty-first birthday, she is beginning to fulfill her destiny and submits peacefully to motherhood.

The second son comes a week before her second wedding anniversary in February 1941. Yoshiko marvels at how loudly her newborn protests his arrival while she rocks his perfect tiny body. They name him Brian, but like his brother before him and siblings to follow, he has a Japanese name as well. Giving their children names from both cultures is a carry-over from their own generation, and it signals the ongoing transition into Canadian culture. Among the *hakujin* community, her husband Takayoshi is known as Tommy. The difference is that the second generation, or *nisei*, give their children English names at birth, and they are their names of choice through life. Many *nisei*, on the other hand, adopt English names that suit them in an effort to assimilate with the mainstream.

One morning later that spring, Gihei strolls into the kitchen where Yoshiko is working. Brian is sleeping in a box by the table, and Tom is playing happily with pots and pans on the floor.

Gihei is short and stout like his wife, with fine polished features. Tom pushes himself up and staggers forward with a grin. Gihei lifts him into his arms and whispers his Japanese name, Takaaki, in his ear. Yoshiko smiles after her one-year-old as he waddles out the door, holding his grandfather's hand. He has only just learned to walk and is so proud of himself. They are going to inspect the big strawberry patch that Gihei just planted across the alley. Tom helps him tend the patch with his way of it all that summer. He comes home totally muddy and wet from the watering, but Yoshiko does not care. Next year when the plants bear fruit, Gihei will pluck a ripe strawberry for his grandson and watch his eyes widen, smacking his lips together and pawing the plants for more.

One Sunday morning in December Yoshiko passes her neighbour Yoshi Higashi on the stairs. He is out of breath, which strikes her as odd. She is on her way to the kitchen, but he stops her short.

"Japan bombed Pearl Harbor this morning," he blurts. Wiping his brow with his shirt sleeve, he waits for Yoshiko to respond before continuing upstairs to find Gihei.

"Japan did what?" Yoshiko shouts.

"I heard it on the radio. Japan bombed the American navy base in Hawaii and casualties are heavy."

Yoshiko leans against the wall to let Yoshi pass. She isn't sure where Hawaii is exactly, but it doesn't matter. If Japan attacked America, it might attack Canada—and Vancouver Island would be first. Instinctively, she clutches her growing belly, rubbing it in smooth wide circles with the palm of her hand. Her gut is queasy. A prickle speeds down her spine, leaving her cold. She continues down the stairs, steadying herself on the banister. Tom isn't two yet, and Brian just ten months. Now six months pregnant, Yoshiko has never felt so vulnerable in her life.

All community activity shuts down, perhaps in anticipation of the seven p.m. curfew police will impose in a few months. Everyone in Chemainus blackens their windows at night so invading Japanese cannot see the town lights. Takayoshi starts looking for a buyer for his truck right away, and Gihei stores his taxi at McBride's Garage. The Mounties seize their radio and cameras. None of it makes sense to Yoshiko, but it soon becomes clear that the *hakujins* lump her in with the enemy.

The uncertainty nearly drives her wild. She has heard rumours that the government may ship them away, but she doesn't know where or when, or why for that matter. When she falls into bed at night, memories of schoolmates hollering racist slurs revive old hurts. She steels herself against these visions and eventually falls into a fitful sleep. Within a few hours she is up again, tiptoeing down the hall to check on the boys.

Yoshiko stands at the kitchen counter mashing hard-boiled eggs for sandwiches. Looking out the window at the apple tree that was home base long ago, she realizes with a start that her boys may never play hide-and-seek here. It may be years before they are back. Her sadness turns to anger when she remembers the strawberries across the alley. She wonders if some *hakujin* boys will enjoy them, or whether they'll be a sweet feast for the slugs.

Takayoshi's cousin, Kiyoko, is helping prepare lunch. Yoshiko glares past her and pounds the egg mush.

"May I have the bowl, please?" Kiyoko asks quietly, ready to add mayonnaise, salt, and pepper. Yoshiko slides it over without comment and butters six white slabs of bread.

Kiyoko passes the bowl back. "Yoshiko, I've never seen you like this," she says.

"No, I shouldn't think so," Yoshiko replies, flinging the egg mixture onto the bread. She hears the back door slam as her mother-in-law arrives for the sandwiches. The women pack them in a bag, and Shigeri slumps down the alley toward the community hall where the Mounties wait for their lunch.

It is fingerprinting day in Chemainus.

"Kiyoko, do you know what I thought when that Mountie pressed my finger onto that card?" Yoshiko asks, watching Shigeri disappear down the lane. "I imagined thrusting my belly right into his face, just to embarrass him."

"You didn't!" Kiyoko is shocked. Her cousin is one of the most modest people she knows.

"I wish I had. I've never been so humiliated in my life."

"Me too," Kiyoko mumbles.

Yoshiko's head is screaming. "You know, Kiyoko, when I was mashing those eggs, I was really mashing that Mountie."

The young women are still laughing when Shigeri comes back from the hall.

"What are you two so happy about?" Shigeri asks.

"Oh nothing, Mother," Yoshiko replies. "Nothing at all."

Yoshiko and Takayoshi are not going on the evacuation ship with everyone else. With the baby due the same week Chemainus is scheduled to be evacuated, Yoshiko fears she won't be fit to travel. So they prepare to leave in February with Gihei, who will be going through Vancouver and on to road camp. Because they need someone to look after the boys when Yoshiko has the baby, Takayoshi's sister, Chiyoko, reluctantly tags along too.

Yoshiko exhausts herself sorting and packing what to take and what to leave behind. The boys' festival dolls—exquisitely crafted samurai warrior and emperor dolls—and her wedding dress are among the treasures she can't possibly add to their load. She packs them carefully in a wooden chest, hoping moths won't ruin them before they return.

Everything is finally in order. Looking out her bedroom window, Yoshiko scans the street below. Black, sinewy branches will blossom in a profusion of pastel pink next month. She recalls the day late last April when a petal snow-storm danced around her. Gusts of wind tossed the blossoms haphazardly through the air, settling in a spontaneous mosaic at her feet. She felt momentarily blessed, swept by beauty.

Turning to the task at hand, Yoshiko dresses Tom and Brian for the trip to Vancouver. She pulls a new red sweater over Tom's head and pushes his arms into the sleeves. Before she can smooth it over his little belly, he is wriggling out of her arms and running to the door.

"Wait!" Yoshiko calls out, running after him as she hauls Brian into her arms. Tom is at the top of the stairs. "You must wait for Mommy," she says, taking his hand and turning back to the bedroom.

"I want Daddy," he says, pushing out his lower lip.

"Daddy is busy," Yoshiko snaps. Her patience is thinning, but she must divert him somehow if she wants to avoid a temper tantrum. He turned two last week, and Brian had his first birthday a month ago.

"Come over to the window, Tom," she says, setting Brian on the floor and pulling Tom into the chair. "Look at the pigeons on Ning Chang's roof."

Quickly, Yoshiko turns her attention to Brian. Tom will

T W O

TAKAYOSHI KAWAHARA

Y OSHIKO HEARS A DOG BARKING and comes to with a start. She looks at the clock. It is five past five. Takayoshi will be home soon, expecting his dinner. Daydreaming for well over an hour, she gets up from the table to put on the rice.

She pours water into her rice cooker, listening to it tinkle. Her life is uneventful now, but the past still haunts her. After the war, they joined thousands of families searching for somewhere to put down permanent roots. Their family had grown during their years in Lemon Creek, where two more children were born. Yoshiko was pregnant with her sixth child when they left the internment camp in 1946. Life would have been so much simpler had they been allowed to return to Chemainus, but the ban prohibiting them from the coast was not lifted until 1949, the same year they finally won the right to vote.

There was nothing for them in Chemainus at any rate. Whatever possessions left behind had long since been sold for pennies. Yoshiko sometimes wonders if her lace wedding dress graced the body of another bride. It would have looked lovely on either of her two daughters, but that was not to be. She prefers to think some young woman wore it, rather than it be rendered useless by mildew or moths.

In 1947 Takayoshi finally found work in Fort William, a grain port and twin city with Port Arthur on the northwestern shore of Lake Superior. Over the years they became accustomed to the mind-numbing temperatures in winter and black flies in summer—but not the merger of Fort William and Port Arthur, of all things. They'll never get used to calling it Thunder Bay.

When they arrived, Yoshiko believed the worst was behind them. In many ways it was. But political machinations aside, life did not spare her further tragedy. In 1983, one of her sons took his own life. Born during the family's trek to the east, Dick was brilliant and schizophrenic. He spent many years in and out of psychiatric institutes, at times refusing medication to control his illness. Nothing in life prepared Yoshiko for his suicide. She always had a special fondness for him, praying that he would improve one day. She wonders if the disorder was a result of so much upheaval when he was in her womb. Perhaps it was her fault: she worried so while she carried him. Eight years after his death, it still cuts deep. She has come to accept that it always will.

Life carries on. Her grandchildren take their place in mainstream Canadian society for granted, a fact that comforts her. As for personal pleasure, summer sojourns fly-fishing in a tributary of the Upsala River offer hours free from the ache of memories. Perhaps it is the icy draft that reaches her nostrils when she wades into the rushing, frigid waters of the Seine; for Yoshiko, there is no smell quite so clean and fresh and alive.

Supper is almost ready when Takayoshi walks through the door at 5:30. Throwing his cap on the table, he slides into one of the chairs, ravenous. Takayoshi loves food, although he is

not a big man. His children easily identify him in old Chemainus pictures by his cherubic smile. Now he wears thick-
rimmed black glasses, a sedate choice that doesn't obscure the
mischievous sparkle in his eyes.

He leans back in his chair, describing in some detail the
mah-jong game with the boys. Yoshiko stands at the stove and
breaks an egg into the ramen noodles. She is setting his bowl
on the table when he sees the letter.

After reading it, Takayoshi looks at his wife. "Well, what
do you think?" he asks.

Yoshiko smiles, hesitating for a moment. "I think it would
be nice to go back now," she says.

"So do I," Takayoshi says. He has longed to go back for
years but didn't have the nerve to suggest it. "Won't it be fun
to see all our old friends?"

"I suppose so," Yoshiko replies. "I can't even think who
would still be around. But those murals they are going to paint
and that cemetery monument they'll be building. . . . I don't
know what to think of that."

"Oh, it's not going to be an ordinary reunion," he says. "But
I don't think much about the town's change of heart. Times
change, and war is war. It's as simple as that."

While Yoshiko does up the dishes, Takayoshi retreats to his
cellar. The idea of going back prompts him to rummage
through the boxes of memorabilia they have somehow managed to keep. His wool wedding suit is down here somewhere,
along with his King Scout trophy, his parents' passports and
old family pictures.

So much has come and gone in their lives since a Vancouver
photographer arranged a family portrait in front of the old
store. Takayoshi runs his finger across his father's name above
the entrance. Painted on the window in white capital letters,
G. KAWAHARA faced the street on an angle to catch passersby
where Oak and Esplanade converged. Takayoshi counts the

windows on the second floor, trying to locate his bedroom. It
faced Esplanade, right above his dad's glass gas pumps on the
street.

The picture puts a nice façade on life inside the building,
where his childhood tumbled through good and bad times. On
the far left, his father appears proud and gentle, the soft light
on his face emphasizing his easy, relaxed smile and plump
cheeks. Gihei lined up his accomplishments for the portrait:
his business is the backdrop for his brand new 1925 Chrysler
Royal, in front of which his family stretches. Takayoshi sits on
the car's running board, his Cocker Spaniel panting at his feet.
His parents are on his left and his uncle, aunt, sister and the
cook huddle together at the rear of the car.

Takayoshi remembers the suit and bow tie he had to wear
for the occasion, although not the picture-taking itself. The
suit was unspeakably awful; unless he sucked in his tummy,
the fabric wouldn't lie flat. Whenever his mother made him
wear it, he was the object of ridicule in the neighbourhood.

It was the Tanouye boy who most often riled Takayoshi.
He can still hear the taunts as they leave school.

"Fat pig, fat pig," Haruyoshi yells.

Flying into a defensive rage, Takayoshi lashes out at
Haruyoshi with a vengeance. But who wins the fist fight is
immaterial. Gihei takes his son aside that afternoon.

"The Tanouyes are our tenants. You will not fight their son.
You have disobeyed me before, and I will not stand for it,"
Gihei shouts.

"But Papa, he was. . . ."

"I don't care what he was doing. You must behave," Gihei
clamours. He marches Takayoshi outside, where he ties him to
a telephone pole in the back alley, the community's main thoroughfare. His mother, Shigeri, rescues him before long, but
not without a reprimand.

"When will you learn, Takayoshi?"

"But it's not fair, Mama," he says, pushing out his lower lip and rubbing his arms where the rope cut into him.

"Do as you're told," Shigeri snaps.

Takayoshi bursts into tears and darts inside, bounding up the stairs two at a time to his bedroom.

Despite such incidents, many consider him a spoiled child. An only son, Takayoshi knows he has privileges and freedoms that few children have. He runs into the store and helps himself to candy bars whenever he wants, sometimes sharing them with friends. But both his parents are so busy running various aspects of the business that he eats his meals alone and often falls asleep with his head on the parlour table, too afraid to go upstairs in the dark to his room.

His mother works in the kitchen, where the men from the bunkhouse eat, always with an ear for the bell in the store. Gihei drives taxi and runs the pool hall in back of the store. Some days the business associated with the bachelors in his bunkhouse and families in his motley collection of houses is a full-time job in itself. Gihei is in his mid-thirties in the 1920s when business in Chemainus peaks. He has come a long way for this.

When he was sixteen, Gihei left his father's farm in Fukuoka prefecture and boarded a steamer bound for Hawaii. He went as an emigrant labourer in 1906, the twenty-ninth year of the Meiji era. It was a period of historic transition in Japan, for the emperor encouraged emigration to North America when he ushered in the Age of Enlightenment. After he came to power in 1868, Emperor Meiji moved to diminish the crippling effect brought on by the isolationist policies of his predecessors. Japan was desperately short of land and resources, and the emperor promoted emigration as a way of easing pressures at home. For the first time since 1637, Japanese citizens could leave their island nation legally. Most who did sought adventure, wealth, and prestige, intending to return home with elevated status.

But some left Japan without looking back. Takayoshi can't be sure, but he feels his father is one. Gihei worked hard and risked much to establish himself. He never speaks of the two years he laboured in Hawaiian sugar cane fields or how he managed to get to Vancouver in 1908. It is not unusual for *issei* to keep those stories to themselves, along with the history of the families and conditions they left behind.

His mother, Shigeri, may have been a "picture bride," for they were common among her contemporaries. Marriages were arranged through parents of eligible offspring and pictures were exchanged across the Pacific. A Shinto-Buddhist marriage ceremony often took place in Japan with a picture of the groom substituting for the groom himself. Once in Canada, they registered the marriage by marrying again. This practice served two purposes: it perpetuated the ancient custom of arranged matrimony and enabled Japanese bachelors to marry within their race, some 4,000 miles away.

A Methodist reverend married Shigeri Takahara to Gihei Kawahara on October 3, 1913 in Victoria, about five weeks after she emigrated from Fukuoka. The twenty-two-year-old merchant's daughter may not have been happy about marrying a total stranger in a foreign land. Although women had the right to refuse, many were pressured to accept their fate.

Gihei took his bride to the farm where he was working on the outskirts of Duncan. Pioneers from Europe, other parts of Canada and the United States had settled in the region for over fifty years, but huge chunks of wilderness remained untouched. The sight of towering Douglas fir forests and calamitous gullies torpedoed what was left of Shigeri's composure as the Esquimalt and Nanaimo Railway jostled its way up island. She concentrated on the centre aisle rather than look outside. It was best to keep her eyes lowered in any case. Japan bred a surface stoicism into its women and men, often for the purpose of saving face. Gihei had no concept of the depth of his wife's anxiety. He was too preoccupied with maintaining his own composure to consider hers.

When Takayoshi is born in October 1915, Gihei is working in the bush for the Hillcrest Lumber Company, and Shigeri is a maid for Mr. and Mrs. Fall on their Cowichan Valley farm. The Kawaharas live in one of the lumber company shacks beside the sawmill, but Takayoshi's earliest memories are from the inside of a wooden box on the Falls' kitchen floor. As a toddler, Takayoshi plays with the Falls' daughter, learning the hard way his place in life. Shigeri spanks him in the woodshed every time the children squabble. Who is at fault is not the issue. The Kawaharas are the peasants, and her son must learn to show respect for his superiors.

When he turns six, Takayoshi walks about five miles to school in Hillcrest. The isolation forces him to find ways to amuse himself. His best games are the ones he develops from his outings to the bush with his father. Takayoshi is in awe of the men and machines at work, mesmerized by the smell of sweat and the wood-fired steam engine, the elegant strength of re-volving cables, the high-pitched whistle that sails through the air to give the all-clear, the scraping of logs across the forest floor.

Gihei is the "whistle-punk," the one who signals the steam donkey operator to pull the logs into the spar tree. He never lets his son pull the whistle though, because a split-second error in timing could cost the chokerman's life. Takayoshi is a content observer, however, enthralled with mechanics. At home, he simulates the operation and makes himself a model steam donkey. Takayoshi creates an engine out of an old clock, attaching a handle onto a motor he makes from the spring.

Then he rigs a miniature spar tree with line and gathers branches to substitute for logs, cranking them into the spar tree with the handle.

When he isn't playing with his donkey-clock engine, Takayoshi dons the caulk boots he fashioned by tying spikes onto the soles. He scrambles into the bush, pouncing on fallen logs and chasing squirrels madly. Hours go by in this soggy domain before hunger sets in and he trundles home, soaked but invigorated by the clean forest air.

Takayoshi is eight when his sister Chiyoko is born and the family moves to Chemainus, putting an abrupt end to the isolation. While Chemainus is a small town of less than 1,000, the Japanese population of 300 constitutes a significant minority. In addition, Gihei establishes himself as a community leader in Chemainus. Sugar cane fields, farms, and the woods are now lodged in his past. Gihei becomes a businessman and his own boss when he buys a store and surrounding property from Giichi Nakashima early in 1924. With $1,300 down and a mortgage of $3,700 on the six lots he purchases, Gihei invests his life savings with confidence. It is only months after the sawmill burned to the ground and shattered the town's economic base. But when the company announces plans to build what will be the most modern sawmill in the world, Gihei swells with pride. He could not be better situated.

Takayoshi feels odd about this step up in life. Everything is so strange, like the way women wear their hair. He has never seen his mother hold her long black hair in her hands and roll it onto the top of her head so that it bulges out on the sides. Shigeri wears her hair up, but it curves smoothly against the side of her head into a soft twist at the back.

Before long, Takayoshi doesn't give it any thought. He's too busy playing with friends in his new neighbourhood. Compared to Hillcrest, there's a lot to do, playing cowboys and Indians among the trees and rock bluffs, fishing for "shiners" off the wharf with a safety pin and string, running to Ning Chang's for a steaming bowl of noodles topped with slices of hard-boiled egg.

When it's too wet or cold to play outside, Takayoshi often slides into his father's pool hall in the L-shaped room behind the store. He watches men playing pool, sitting among them on the thick wooden benches that straddle either side of a huge drum woodstove. Takayoshi dangles his feet and rocks back and forth on the bench, surrounded by the steamy warmth of rain evaporating off men's wool work shirts. A cacophony of Japanese spits through air laced with thick cigarette smoke; those not playing pool are reading Japanese newspapers, talking politics and sipping small cups of hot green tea.

Masa Nishimura's barber shop is partitioned off in a corner, where most of the Japanese men and native Indian stevedores come for a haircut. The stevedores find her barber shop convenient while they wait for the next ship to dock at the wharf down the street. Unbeknownst to them, Masa charges her Japanese customers a penny less.

Next to the pool hall on the other side, Takayoshi's mother works in the kitchen, preparing meals for the bachelors living in his father's two-storey bunkhouse. The bunkhouse is across the alley that cuts through the heart of Kawahara camp. Set on the northern edge of Gihei's property, it rises above the collection of homes that line the north side of the alley. It towers over the upstairs floor of the Hashimotos' home, where students take Japanese lessons until the community hall is built in 1927. A few doors down from there, boys gather to practice judo in the *Dojo Bah*. Without mats to break their falls, they lay canvas over a sawdust-covered wooden floor and leave bruised and sore, sometimes injured in this tough process of becoming a man.

Gihei's garage is at the far end of the alley near a vegetable garden and a small orchard in the haphazard complex. And somewhere in the middle of it all, somewhere secret because it is illegal, cases of Japanese sake are stashed behind a large wood shed.

On the south side of the alley across from the *Dojo Bah*, the community bathhouse, or *ofuro*, attracts daily traffic from early evening on. Gallons of scalding water splash into a large wooden tub just before the day shift ends at the mill. The tub is soon full of aching bodies steeped in steam. After the men are done, it is the women and children's turn, slipping out of their kimonos into the deep, still calm of hot water.

A few families have the resources and space to build their own baths, but most come to the communal tub and think nothing of the nudity. Occasionally a peeping tom from the *hakujin* community skulks his way along the alley to feast his eyes on flesh, but few are nervy enough. For the Japanese, the everyday routine is one of few pleasures in lives marked by long hours of hard work.

Like other Japanese Canadian children in Chemainus, Takayoshi joins his friends for an hour of Japanese school after the public school day is over. He doesn't like either school much and has little incentive to excel, knowing he will inherit his father's business.

He may not like school, but Takayoshi wastes no time in joining the 2nd Chemainus Troop that Shige Yoshida forms in June 1930. The troop often competes against the all-white 1st Chemainus Troop, which spurns any Canadians of Japanese ancestry. For boys like Takayoshi, scouting is enormous fun. Mingling with *hakujin* troops at jamborees in Victoria and Washington State, Takayoshi rides on a wonderful sense of belonging to a world normally out of bounds.

Over the next three years, he earns twelve badges and becomes a King's Scout. No other boy of Japanese ancestry in

Canada has attained this rank, prompting the mill manager, Mr. Humbird, to award him the Humbird Cup for his efforts. In the summer of 1933, patrol leader Takayoshi Kawahara puffs up like popcorn as he climbs the stage to accept the trophy. He surveys the crowd below and grins at the 1st Chemainus Troop.

But Takayoshi has to earn different points among his own. The year before becoming a King's Scout, Gihei celebrates his forty-second birthday with a sumo wrestling tournament. In the days leading up to the May 30 celebration, many in the community lend a hand. Shigeri's nephew builds a wooden platform in front of Gihei's garage at the west end of the alley. Baseball coach Bari Kasahara crouches on Yoshiko's kitchen floor painting oriental landscapes onto one *kesho-mawashi* after another. Tomorrow the men will wear the floor-length aprons in the ring-entering ceremony. Others drape colourful banners and flags above the garage, while the women prepare delicacies. And someone, perhaps Gihei himself, digs out a sake stash for the all-night party.

Takayoshi takes the day off from his trucking business on Gihei's birthday, sprinting here and there to help with last-minute chores. He is a chunky seventeen-year-old, proud of his father's ability to celebrate with such fanfare, and equally proud to take his place in the ring-entering ceremony.

One by one the young men mount the platform, as Gihei announces the names of the east and west divisions: Satoshi, Iwao, Kaname, Norimichi, Hitoshi, and Mitsuyuki; Takayoshi, Yoshitero, Harunobu, Shunichi, Kanichi, and Noboru. They face the community in a circle, displaying the elaborate aprons, and then turn inward to face each other. After clapping, they lift their arms skyward and hitch up their aprons to show they carry no weapons—each movement a ritual dating back to the sport's ancient links with Shinto worship. Thus a generation of future community leaders announces their purity to the gods, and the tournament begins.

When his turn comes to wrestle, Takayoshi throws his weight against his opponent with particular relish. He wins some fights that way, but others he loses to more skillful peers. The street echoes with the sound of stamping feet and shouting all afternoon. Mothers rock babies in their arms at the back, while older children slice through the crowd for a better view.

The community rallies around the same location on other memorable occasions. Just down from the hall that they built to celebrate Canada's Diamond Jubilee in 1927, the area is the pulse of the community. On a sultry night in 1939, they congregate here again.

Now married, Takayoshi and Yoshiko join friends and neighbours in the lot beside the garage. Tomorrow's July 1 parade will mark the fiftieth anniversary of the sawmill, which so many depend on for their livelihood. Tonight they will finish the wooden-frame float that carpenters hammered onto Takayoshi's flatbed truck.

Kaname Izumi is rushing about when the couple arrives. "Hello, Yoshiko, Tak. Sure glad you're here. Need all the hands we can get."

They set to work, listening to Kaname ramble on about one of his escapades. Earlier, he and his brothers sped out to Westholme to dig some moss-covered earth.

"Well, it wasn't me who tripped over the old grump, but I got us out of there with the moss," Kaname boasts. "That old Indian, he just bolted up out of nowhere, hollering, 'What the Sam hell are you guys doing, stealing my earth?'

"I walked up to him and said, 'Oh, we didn't mean any harm, sir. We just want some moss for our float in the parade.'

"He grumbled something under his breath and waved us on. 'Well, okay,' he says. 'Just don't leave any mess behind.'

"We dug that moss like there was no tomorrow. Never seen my brothers move so fast. Back on the road, we laughed so hard we had tears in our eyes," Kaname says, winking at Yoshiko.

She smiles. "Kaname, you really are a character." Looking over the frame, she adds: "But you did the job well. There isn't a bit of wood showing. It looks like a perfect little moss-covered hill."

"Heck, that was easy," Kaname replies. "Sticking those branches in the moss so they'd stay, that was the tricky part. Well, getting them to look like real trees wasn't easy either. But now comes the fine artwork, and I think you women better take over." They laugh and nod, deft fingers already skittering over the branches.

Yoshiko has been folding delicate Japanese paper into cherry blossoms for the last two weeks. Piles of soft flowers were accumulating in corners, drifting across the floor. Now she works alongside the others, fastening them onto branches and chattering in the twilight. As the float transforms, a warm evening breeze rustles the paper flowers with the same chirring sound of a zephyr combing life into a stand of bamboo.

The next morning feather-tipped clouds skirt through blue sky. By ten o'clock, it is pleasantly warm. Inside several homes, *issei* women knowledgable in the art of kimono dressing fuss over the young girls who will wave as their float drifts along the dirt streets.

Takayoshi is busy buffing up the shine on his truck. His German Shepherd, Rex, loiters close by. Inside, Yoshiko is pressing his favourite royal blue shirt and navy slacks. She is almost done when Takayoshi walks in.

"Is my suit ready?" he asks. "I've only got half an hour to wash and dress."

"I'll be done in a minute. What's it like out?"

"Gorgeous. It's going to be a great parade," Takayoshi says, heading to the washroom.

He is securing his red bow-tie when the kimono-clad misses arrive for their escort, giggling with excitement.

"Oh, don't you girls look beautiful!" Yoshiko exclaims. "Let me see you twirl your umbrellas," she says, turning them around one by one. Takayoshi steps into the room. "Don't they look adorable?" Yoshiko asks.

"Sweet as sugar," he replies, winking. "Let's go."

Outside, Rex lingers alongside the truck. Takayoshi never goes anywhere without him, but today he'll have to sit in the cab. The girls climb the wooden steps onto the spongy moss and they are off. Yoshiko strolls around the corner onto Oak Street, where friends are milling about.

Other townsfolk stream out from every corner of the community, lining the boardwalks along the parade route. Unlike other parts of the country, Chemainus has escaped the worst of the Depression. Although the sawmill is curtailing production and has cut wages, at least it hasn't shut down. This occasion celebrates their good fortune and calls for nothing less than their Sunday best.

The mill whistle blows at noon, signalling the military band to begin its brassy version of "God Save the King." The crowd sings along as the band marches past. Mill manager John Humbird rides behind in his sleek black limousine, his plump wife at his dark, bulky side, smiling like a Cheshire cat. Then the procession of floats begins its descent along Oak Street, turning up Esplanade to swing by the hospital for the patients' enjoyment.

Takayoshi gears down as he heads towards his community at the bottom of Oak Street. He searches for Yoshiko and his parents as he rounds the corner onto Esplanade, waving proudly when he catches Gihei's eye. Absolutely everyone is there when the float shimmers like a mirage down the hot, dusty street.

Driving past the hospital and up towards the train station in the centre of town, Takayoshi sees some *hakujins* pointing at them. Women whisper in their children's ears, lifting their little hands to wave. Others stiffen and turn away when they see Takayoshi at the wheel. He shrugs, pushing his feelings out past the hood of his truck where nothing can bother him today.

He brakes at the train station and leans out the window. People are hanging over the platform above him to see what's coming. To their disappointment, the parade is over. Humbird is talking to parade officials near the podium, getting ready to announce the winner.

Takayoshi and Rex jump out and wander back to visit the girls, who are still giggling and twirling their umbrellas. Yoshiko and several friends arrive, thronging to fuss over their flowery kimonos some more.

Humbird climbs onto the podium and surveys the townsfolk. He is thinking that they aren't a bad lot, obedient and law abiding for the most part. Humbird's namesake, his late grandfather, created the Victoria Lumber and Manufacturing Company when he bought the old sawmill off coal baron Robert Dunsmuir in 1889. Although there have been fatal accidents, the mill has none of the violent history associated with striking coal miners in nearby Ladysmith. Even though he pays the Orientals twenty percent less than the white workers, they have still put together the prettiest float.

The crowd is restless, so he begins.

"I want to say how proud grandfather would have been today," Humbird says. "Everyone knows that these are hard

times, yet you have outdone yourselves with so many ingen-
ious and beautiful floats. You all deserve a big pat on the back.

"My wife and I want to thank you for your ongoing loyalty
during these difficult years. You're one heck of a town, Chemainus!"

The crowd breaks into applause. Humbird raises his hand.

"And now, folks, what you've been waiting for. The winner
is . . . the cherry-blossom float."

Takayoshi beams. He is so excited he doesn't even hear who
the runners-up are. The girls are jumping up and down, ex-
claiming, "Yoshi-san, we won, we won. Can you believe it?
We really won!" Yoshiko and her friends are dabbing their
eyes with handkerchiefs. Rex leaps onto the float, wagging his
tail so that his whole behind moves wildly, and everyone
laughs.

Takayoshi works hard during these years. As a community
service, he hauls batches of cast-off Douglas fir from the mill
and builds fires to heat the forty-five-gallon tank of water for
the *ofuro*. If Gihei isn't taxiing someone in his 1937 Chrysler
Royal, he helps his son get the communal bath ready.

This daily chore is time-consuming, but Takayoshi still has
to earn a living. He hauls booming chains up to Parksville for
the sawmill and returns with 100-pound sacks of coal that he
sells for a small profit. He hauls hay for local farmers, all kinds
of lumber and furniture for families moving away. He hauls
bricks off barges for fireplaces and chimneys. He drives his
uncle to Duncan to sell fish.

Takayoshi feels free driving his five-ton GM truck with
Rex. He can't explain it, but something stirs every time he
starts the engine. When Takayoshi got his first truck and
started his hauling business in 1932, Rex used to jump right on
top of the hood and ride up there, his nose to the wind. Someone put a stop to it, claiming it was dangerous. From then on,

Rex rode in the back when it was empty and, when it was full, in the cab with Takayoshi.

While he was still a bachelor, Takayoshi shared that freedom with his chums too. They are the best years of his youth—the truck bursting with friends as he races along dirt roads, the radio blaring, spinning the wheels into nowhere. They bump along as far as Maple Bay or Cowichan Bay and even go to Koksilah if he has enough gas. They hatch plans most Saturday nights to see a movie—Takayoshi likes westerns—or put lotteries on men playing Fan-Tan in a Chinatown backroom in Duncan.

One afternoon Hitoshi and Noboru climb into the cab and Kaname and Satoshi hop in the back. They pick up some Cumberland girls working in Duncan and drive out of town. Suddenly, Takayoshi stops the truck. "Sorry, girls," he says, "looks like I've run out of gas. You'll have to hike it home."

They walk about a quarter of a mile before Takayoshi starts the truck again and drives up alongside. "Just kidding," he says, laughing. "Hop in."

The girls eye one another. It's a long way back to town, so they jump in the back. Takayoshi is whistling, oblivious to the silent daggers the girls are throwing his way. Kaname and Satoshi are chuckling and teasing them about the trick, but they aren't humoured. "Stupid boys," they yell when they get out in Duncan. Heads held high and hands linked together, they march down the street leaving the boys rocking back and forth in laughter.

Takayoshi and his friends head toward Konkui House, a cheap Chinese restaurant that serves the most divine smoked pork tenderloin. They savour the rich morsels of meat, watching Chinese cooks in food-smeared aprons stir sizzling concoctions in huge woks. Steam from the cooking mixes with thick clouds of cigarette smoke while the boys jabber about the latest baseball scores.

Takayoshi has seven years of such fun before marriage crimps that lifestyle. He has other responsibilities now, so weekends on the road with the boys become part of his past. Still, every morning he climbs into his truck and goes off to work. On the road with his faithful friend, he is free again.

Three years after marrying, Takayoshi is the father of two beautiful boys and Yoshiko is expecting again. Fatherhood has not been a terribly difficult adjustment, given the fact that his wife does most of the work. But it has changed him in some ways, settling him down to more serious thought about providing for his children in an increasingly uncertain world.

One morning he is in the pool room listening to the *issei* men, many of whom believe Japan is winning the war in Asia. He fears their views will bring trouble. Otoji Okinobu, a divorcee who works as a tally clerk at the sawmill, is holding the floor.

"Emperor Hirohito's power descends from the gods. Japan will rule the world," he crows. "The west is weak and inferior. Soon they will surrender."

Murmurs ripple around the room, but Takayoshi cannot stand it. "You are wrong, Okinobu-san," he says, stiffening his shoulders. "Japan is losing. Your newspapers are spreading lies."

"And yours underestimate Japan's might," Otoji snaps back. "Just wait and see."

"Why don't you go back then? Canada isn't good enough for you, is it?" Takayoshi retorts.

Fuming, Gihei interjects. "Okinobu-san does much for our community. Now, apologize!"

"Yes, father," he mumbles, retreating like a defensive child. "I am sorry, Okinobu-san."

Otoji nods abruptly and buries his head in a newspaper. Takayoshi sips his tea, hoping to ease the slight nausea in his gut. Relations with the *hakujin* community are more strained than ever. There's a new edge in people's voices when they call him "Jap." Long after they spit it out, Takayoshi feels the sting.

Suddenly Gihei turns the radio up, hearing the broadcaster announce a special news bulletin.

"We have confirmed reports that Japan bombed Pearl Harbor early this morning, sinking or crippling nineteen naval vessels. Casualties are estimated at over 3,000, including some civilians."

Takayoshi meets his father's eyes across the room.

The jabbering that follows the broadcast forces him into the cool December fog outside. Rex lumbers up alongside. He lays a hand on the dog's head and stumbles toward the highway. It is Sunday, the one day when the mill shuts down, and the street is quiet. He tries to sort out his thoughts, but they just go around in circles. He thinks out loud, talking under his breath: "Japan has bombed the American navy. That is so stupid, I can't believe it. But if they can do that, they sure as heck could invade here. The *hakujins* may call me a 'Jap,' but I am Canadian and will fight for my country. I will defend my home and wife and children. Oh God, what will happen to us now?"

Takayoshi's heart is pounding at the prospect of going to war and the tensions that that will create among his people and the wider community. He reaches the highway and turns to look down the street. The lumber yard is disappearing between folds of grey mist. He must go home and talk to his wife. Watching Rex sniff his way back down the street, Takayoshi wishes his world were so simple.

The next day the United States declares war on Japan and begins arranging to intern its citizens of Japanese ancestry in prisoner-of-war camps. A white supremacist group and right-wing politicians from British Columbia use the American precedent to force an issue they have clammered about for years: to rid the province of all Japanese, once and for all. Using the powers of the War Measures Act, Prime Minister MacKenzie King and his parliament begin passing orders-in-council. Individuals and communities up and down the west coast stagger from the shock of each successive order. At the same time, they adopt an attitude of *shikataga-nai*, meaning it can't be helped.

Takayoshi feels an epidemic of sorts is on the rampage. He wonders how this world ever felt secure, whether it was an illusion now torn apart like a body dragged up from the sea bottom, half eaten by crabs. Yoshiko worries constantly. He is hot-tempered and easily riled, unable to concentrate.

Meanwhile, rumours are rampant.

"Did you hear what they're going to do now?" Kaname asks Takayoshi one day.

"I've heard so many things. I don't know who or what to believe," Takayoshi replies.

"Well, I heard that police are going to confiscate our cars and then they're going to ship us out."

"Where?"

"God only knows. Papa says we should prepare for the worst. He keeps whispering *shikataga-nai* over and over again. He is almost as depressed as when Mama died."

One by one, the rumours are confirmed. They learn police are going to confiscate not only their cars but also their radios, guns and cameras. Gihei decides to store his taxi at McBride's service station before the RCMP come for it.

Takayoshi follows his father's Chrysler to McBride's in the pouring rain. The windshield wipers in his truck can't keep up with the torrents sloshing over the glass. He can barely see the rear bumper through the rain as the Chrysler passes the Horseshoe Bay Inn. Gihei is handing over the keys when Takayoshi arrives.

"That's it, then, Mr. McBride," Gihei says, giving him the storage money. "You'll take good care, won't you?"

"You bet," McBride replies. "I'll turn the engine over regular, make sure she keeps purrin' along. Don't you worry."

"Goodbye," Gihei says, turning to go.

"See ya."

Gihei jumps in the truck, soaking. Rain streams down his face and neck. Takayoshi points toward home and checks his rear-view mirror. McBride is driving the Chrysler into his garage.

"There she goes, Papa. I wonder if you'll see her again."

Gihei is looking straight ahead, mopping his face with a handkerchief. "We'll be back. The war can't last forever."

Takayoshi decides to find a private buyer for his truck. He works throughout December, although his *hakujin* clientele falls off dramatically. In January, he sells his five-ton truck to the sawmill sales manager for about $1,200, unhappily absorbing a $2,000 loss.

Next he finds a home for Rex. Takayoshi gives him to a Mountie one day in February, when spring makes a fleeting, unexpected appearance. He wishes it hadn't. Somehow the sunshine focuses unforgettable detail on the parting. Sliding his calloused hands over Rex one last time, he says goodbye as the officer leads him to his car. Takayoshi feels like someone has thrown a brick at his stomach. Rex is the kind of dog who will go with anyone. Of all people, it has to be a Mountie.

The nightmares start that night. He sees Rex through a small window in a shiny steel door. A bulky man with no hair is tying the dog to a long, steel table. Then he sticks needles into Rex's rump and brands him with a hot iron. No matter how hard he pushes, Takayoshi can't budge the steel door.

Orders come and go from January to March. They hear that Japanese nationals are going to be shipped to road camps in the

province's interior. Sure enough, a Mountie knocks on their
door one night to serve Gihei his notice. Takayoshi translates.
His wife and him are accompanying Gihei to Vancouver tomorrow, and he will go to road camp from there. They finish
packing last-minute things and are ready in the morning.

Takayoshi hates goodbyes. He is almost panicky about
pushing off. Trying to rush past the pain, he manages a farewell wave of sorts to his mother. Within a few weeks, he
wishes he hadn't been in such a hurry. They stay with Gihei's
friends in Vancouver at first, where Gihei draws up a will
before leaving. Everything is so chaotic when Gihei boards the
train the next morning that Takayoshi can't hear his father's
parting words of advice. It's all a blur after that, but Hastings
Park jolts him out of his daze soon enough. The stench alone
makes him thoroughly regretful that they left home early.

A few days later, Takayoshi overhears some men in nearby
bunks whispering about not going to road camps in Ontario.
Their plan is to hide out in the *Tairiku Nippo* offices, a Japanese
newspaper in Vancouver, and he gets swept up in the scheme.

It is a windy day in March when Takayoshi and his com-
rades get passes to leave the compound. About seventy young
men leave separately and meet at a prearranged spot outside.
The walk to the newspaper building on Cordova Street gives
him plenty of time to regret his decision. When they reach the
building several hours later, Takayoshi is hungry and tired.
After spending a long night on a cold hard floor, he knows in
his bones the plan won't work. The RCMP raid their hideout
that day, making a mockery of their futile escape.

The Mounties escort them to the immigration building and
then the police barracks where they undergo physicals. Arrangements are progressing to send them to work on a stretch
of the Trans-Canada north of Lake Superior.

Meanwhile, Takayoshi learns that Yoshiko has had the
baby. A Mountie accompanies him to the hospital, waiting

outside the ward while he visits his wife and newborn. A week later, he is gone.

It is late March when he arrives in Schreiber. The temperature will not warm for another two months. Takayoshi jumps down from the cattle truck that brought him from the train station and decides right away to work in the cookhouse. No way is he going to build roads in this cold.

The air freezes his nostrils as he surveys the landscape. Nothing but scrub trees stick out of miles and miles of snow. Takayoshi pulls his wool cap further down. He finds his bunk, throws his bags on top and slips over to the cookhouse. The next morning he is peeling potatoes for the lunch meal.

Life settles into a routine, and the men become friends. The food is better than the slop they ate at Hastings Park, which isn't saying much. But for the first time since leaving home, Takayoshi can cook himself bacon and eggs for breakfast.

Spring finally arrives in May. Takayoshi is accustomed to the flat, barren land now, but familiarity switches to more discomfort when blackflies descend. In June the river starts to run. He leaves the cookhouse in Schreiber to work on the log drive for pulp mills in the area, landing a job in a Sudbury mill. Summer is followed by a spectacular autumn. The ground has frozen over again when an envelope with censored contents arrives. Dated several months before, the letter informs him that Yoshiko is sick. Now he understands why she hasn't replied to any of his letters. It wasn't because she was angry with him for getting into trouble after all.

Unable to leave the area without permission, Takayoshi runs to the mill superintendent's house and knocks on the door.

"Who is it?" a gruff voice shouts.

"It's me, boss," Takayoshi replies.

The door opens and he finds himself staring down the barrel of a shotgun.

"Sorry to bother you, sir," he sputters, waving his letter in the air. "Just found out my wife is sick."

"So?"

"Well, can I go tomorrow?"

His boss stares at him for a long minute and finally lowers the gun. "Yeah," he says.

Takayoshi shuffles his feet.

"Well, go on. What are you waiting for?"

"My pay, sir."

"We'll mail it," he says, slamming the door.

Walking back to the bunkhouse, Takayoshi kicks rocks out of his path. He'd like to pitch a boulder right into his boss' living room. He packs his belongings in a fury and tries in vain to sleep. Every time he closes his eyes the ugly grin above the shotgun leers larger than life. Takayoshi creeps out of bed at dawn. He can't get out of Sudbury soon enough.

But he can't go west immediately either. First he has to report back to Schreiber and get an RCMP permit. Once there, he finds that a special constable substituting for the regular Mountie can only issue him an unofficial permit. Takayoshi boards the next train heading west, panicking at every whistle stop where Mounties might check his papers. He can't overcome the fear that they'll haul him off to jail.

Feeling like a fugitive, Takayoshi can't relax between stops either. A group of air force men harass him for two days, threatening to string him up. Among them is a Métis man who intervenes, moderating the threats somewhat. Cowering in his wooden seat as the train chugs across the frozen prairie, Takayoshi is a nervous wreck when the men finally get off in Moose Jaw. Two days later, he disembarks among a throng of RCMP in Nelson, where the threat of them checking his permit is greatest. When he finally hops on a bus to Lemon Creek, he stops shaking inside and goes momentarily numb. It is late November, not as frigid as Schreiber, but damp and penetrating nonetheless.

Yoshiko has been healthy for months when Takayoshi arrives. Hearing footsteps crunch through the snow, she looks out the window and grabs Shirley off the floor. She opens the door and smiles. His daughter is eight months old and acts strange, but Tom and Brian jump up and down, clamouring for a hug. Finally they are together as a family again, including Gihei, who is back from road camps along the Yellowhead-Blue River highway. With his brother-in-law, sister-in-law, his parents, and his own family, Takayoshi adds one more body to an already cramped hut. But they concentrate on making the best out of the situation, still hopeful that one day they will call Chemainus home again.

Those hopes are shattered two years later when Gihei gets a cheque for the sale of his Chemainus property. The news does not come as a complete shock, but the will to wrestle on dies. When he was still in the road camp the summer of 1942, Gihei received a letter from the government offering to relieve him of his assets. Unable to collect rents, he had defaulted on his mortgage payments and property taxes.

Rather than give in, he provided government authorities with names of people who owed him money. Aware that the likelihood of collecting those pre-war debts was remote, Gihei's strategy was to keep government agents busy until the war was over and he could go home. But the war dragged on, and he lost the battle with time.

Some months after Frank and Mary Anne Crucil bought his property for $5,000 in August 1944, Gihei receives a cheque for $1,900—the mortgage company and the municipality sharing the difference. Now in his early fifties, his life unravels before him: the sugar cane fields and the farming, the logging and the business he built up for his son, all gone.

Takayoshi is getting cold in the cellar. He stretches his legs and checks his watch. It is almost time for the evening news, so he leaves his pictures and papers to tidy in the morning.

The next day he returns to the cellar and surveys the fragments from his past strewn about the floor. A photo of his truck triggers his dream from the night before. For the first time in decades, he dreamt of Rex, the wind coursing through his pelt as they cruised down a dirt road back home.

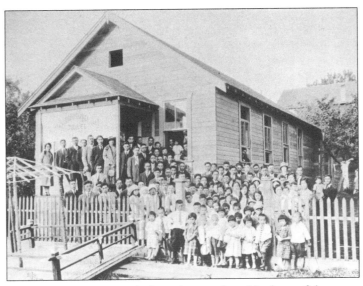

The *nikkei* community of Chemainus, gathered in front of the Japanese community hall, 1927.

The first meeting of the 2nd Chemainus Boy Scout Troop in front of the Japanese language school, 1930.

Kaname Izumi
rowing with three
young women in
Stuart Channel,
c. 1930.

Children having fun in front of the ships at Chemainus Harbour,
c. 1930.

83

The 2nd Chemainus
Boy Scout Troop
marching in
Victoria at the
World Scout
Jamboree,
early 1930s.

Noboru Yoshida
refereeing a *sumo*
match at Bare Point
in Chemainus,
c. 1935.

Michio Inouye and
Mutt Otsu logging in
the woods, 1936.

Jiroichi Isoki (Shunichi and Yoshiko's father) and Gentaro Nakaki
unloading herring to be kippered in Victoria, 1938.

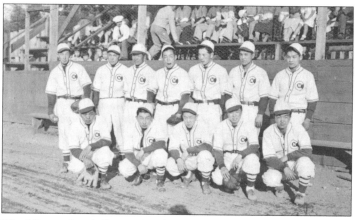

The Nippon baseball team in Chemainus, c. 1938.

Young girls on the steps of the Kawakara camp's bunkhouse, 1938.

Three dashing young men—Noboru Yoshida, Kaname Izumi, and Toki Yoshida, in 1939.

Girls enjoying a day at the beach, including Tosh Kamino (nee
Yoshida), second from right, 1938.

Bill Isoki and Genichi Nakahara on the boat *Joker* in Sidney, 1941.

Men relaxing in an *ofuro* at a road camp in Jackfish, Ontario, c. 1942.

Bill Isoki (centre) and friends, including Minoru Nagasawa (second from right) and Kanichi Nakatsu (right), enjoying lunch on the Hornby Island wharf, 1941.

Genichi Nakahara
displaying dogfish on
Kanichi Nakatsu's boat
off Hornby Island, 1941.

Sunao Makokoro
(nee Izumi) at the
beach, 1938.

THREE

SHIZUKA and HITOSHI OKADA

A CROSS TOWN, SHIZUKA OKADA is getting ready for her Japanese dance class at the seniors' centre. The cotton kimono jacket feels cool against her skin and brings momentary relief from the hot, muggy air wafting through the bedroom window.

Shizuka perches herself before the dressing table and lifts her brush. Her hair is completely silver now and much shorter than it used to be, but it has kept its soft lustre and is still one of her greatest assets. Brushing it slowly, she eases into the comfort of the bristles massaging her scalp. After all these years, the calm reassurance she gets from this simple solitary act is much the same as it was in her youth. In front of the mirror, Shizuka communicates with herself. Her beauty makes her feel secure, insulated from troubles.

She ponders her large, almond-shaped eyes. They are set wide apart above her high cheek bones, black and shining like her hair used to be and a marvellous contrast to her flawless white skin. The memory that springs forward is of her first

Christmas concert in Chemainus. She imagines the little girl seen through the eyes of an audience.

Shizuka is alone on the school stage. Except for the light shining on her and the rustling of paper, the room is pitch black and silent. Earlier, Miss Dyke lowered the burlap costume she had made over Shizuka's head. Then she grasped Shizuka's long, thick black tresses, dividing them evenly into three bunches and braiding them with exquisite deftness. To finish, she poked a raven feather behind the thin red band that creased the young girl's forehead.

Miss Dyke did not have any Coast Salish girls to dress as the Indian princess because they were in the residential school on Kuper Island. When Shizuka came into her class that September, Miss Dyke thought that she would make a fine substitute. The fact that she did not speak English added authenticity to the scene, for Shizuka would naturally emanate the wonder and star-struck innocence necessary for the part.

So Shizuka stands alone on stage, motionless under the beaming light, watching darkness. Soft lyrical voices sing "Silent Night" behind her somewhere. She can neither see her classmates nor understand a word they are singing.

Shizuka finishes brushing her hair and goes into the living room. Her husband, Hitoshi, has already gone to the car, so she locks the front door and walks down the steps. She opens the car door, deep in thought. A year from now, they'll be locking up for their trip to Chemainus. They had gone back once in 1972, and she had headed straight for the beach. Like a salmon returning up river to spawn, Shizuka waded into the frigid salt waters of her birthplace. Perhaps she would do so again.

Hitoshi is waiting for his wife outside her *odori* class. The summer heat is stifling. He checks his rear view mirror and sees Shizuka coming out of the seniors' complex. At seventy-six, she is still an attractive woman. He chuckles, remembering how jealous other men were when they married. She was a real beauty in those days. He recalls the sense of power he felt when they first got engaged, as if he could wrench mountains from the earth. As it turned out, life did that to him instead. It has eased off since, of course. All that is behind them, thank goodness.

Now they are going back again. He has mixed feelings about their visit in 1972, but he hopes this time will be different. Old baseball friends he hasn't seen in a long time—chums like George Ridgway—may be there. In '72, hardly anyone knew them and nothing was left of Okada camp. His former stomping grounds were within the mill compound: fenced and inaccessible. Memories of his childhood sifted through the sand along the now-forbidden shore. He did not feel he had gone home at all; that home didn't exist anymore.

What's more, he could find neither the graves of his mother nor his young brother, so they left some flowers in the area, hoping it was close to the burial sites. Standing in the cemetery in 1972, Hitoshi recalled the times when he helped clean up the grounds, with his way of it. He was just a child, but no one was excluded from the communal task; it was an annual ritual in August in preparation for the *O-bon*. The whole community showed up, carrying rakes and wearing gloves, prepared to do some serious weeding.

But Hitoshi learned that soon after the April 1942 evacuation, some yahoos drinking at the Horseshoe Bay Inn got riled up about the "Japs" buried in their cemetery. Swinging into action with plenty of beer in their bellies, they fired up a front-end loader and levelled the Japanese section at the rear of the cemetery. The jumble of headstones and simple wooden markers that they dropped from the front-end loader into a grove of trees over the fence would lie under dirt and debris for some forty-seven years—with the exception of headstones that people stole for chimneys or for use in their yards and homes. In 1989, long-time resident Pat Allester took it upon himself to try and clean up the town's cemetery. When he noticed headstones with calligraphy protruding from a pile of dirt outside the cemetery fence, the whole sickening incident came to light. No one dared mention names, but some knew who had done the deed. Almost fifty years later, no one bragged about the nasty event as they once had; now they cursed the fact that it hadn't been kept quiet. When Hitoshi heard about it, an odd mix of rage and grief rekindled the bitterness he had tried so hard to exorcise. Thinking about it made him nauseous, for some things never changed.

Shizuka opens the car door, interrupting his thoughts. She slides onto the seat beside him, and he points their Oldsmobile towards their Begin Street home in Thunder Bay.

"I guess we'd better write to Shunichi soon and let him know we'll be coming to the reunion," Shizuka says, watching the flat concrete landscape scroll past.

"Yes, he'll be wanting to know."

"I wonder who else will be there," she says, turning to study her husband's strong profile.

"Hard to say. I hope some of my old baseball buddies are around this time," Hitoshi replies as he pulls into their driveway. "But it's hard to say."

Shizuka Taniwa and Hitoshi Okada grew up quite apart from each other as children, but both had their share of happiness and heartache. Although born in Chemainus on January 31, 1915, Shizuka spent most of her first seven years in Steveston, where her father worked as a fish buyer. When Risaburo

Taniwa brought his family back to Chemainus in 1922, they moved into a house on the corner of Oak and Croft streets right in the heart of Kawahara camp. Hitoshi, on the other hand, lived in the heart of the camp named after his father, along the shore facing the booming grounds. They called it Okada camp.

Both of their fathers were prominent men among their peers. It was to Shizuka's father's credit that Chemainus had a Japanese language school, for Risaburo Taniwa spearheaded the drive to build the community hall and hire teachers. Hitoshi's father, Bukichi Okada, was one of the more well-off Japanese residents. It took some years to get established, but when he negotiated the boom contract with the mill, Bukichi achieved what most immigrants only dreamed of when they left Japan in search of wealth. He had elevated his status and standard of living well beyond what would have been possible in Kawauchimura, the village on the island of Shikoku which he left one fine spring day in 1906.

After a stopover in Hawaii, Bukichi sailed on to San Francisco, working his way up the coast into Canada. By 1907, he had found work in a logging camp near Chemainus and sent for his wife, Rakuju, and three teenaged sons, who reluctantly left their home for the wild unknown. It was a commonplace experience then, where men scouted out the territory and the wives and offspring followed. But Bukichi was a man who set himself apart in other ways. His parents had arranged his marriage to Rakuju to curb his habit of drinking in bars, but it did not work. Neither marriage nor parenthood had curtailed his drinking and carousing; what did, eventually, was love.

When Bukichi first settled his family in Chemainus, he spent most of his days in the logging camp in the bush south of town and left Rakuju, Ryoichi, Haruyuki, and Osamu to fend for themselves in the frontier. He only had one day a week respite from the back-breaking labour, doing his part to clear the land of giant Douglas fir stands. But it was not his wife and sons that he came home to on Sundays, his day of leisure. Instead, he spent his time visiting Miki Mizuta in her parent's store on the corner of Esplanade and Oak.

Bukichi fell for Miki shortly after arriving in Chemainus. He had gone into her parent's store for some inconsequential drygood and stumbled out the door without his usual keen sense of direction. The next thing he knew, he was back inside, rummaging through his brain to think of something—anything—that might enable him to linger a little longer.

"You've forgotten something, Mr. Okada?" Miki inquires, seeing him step back inside.

"Oh, yes. I believe I need some, uh, tea. Yes, tea would do."

"You already bought some tea, Mr. Okada. You would like more?"

"I need some extra," he says firmly, trying not to feel like a fool. He would have enough tea to last three years now.

Miki turned to the shelf behind her, stretching for the boxes of green tea stashed just within reach.

"Will that be all, then?" she asks.

"All? Well, no. I know there must be something else," Bukichi replies, bracing himself. "I wonder if we could. . . ."

Unsure of himself for the first time in his life, he stops. What if she says no? he wonders.

"Mr. Okada?" Miki says, a bit perplexed. She is no longer sure of herself, either. This older man is so intense; he is studying her face at the same time that he doesn't seem quite here. "Are you all right?"

"Yes, fine. Of course. I was just thinking that maybe we could have tea together sometime."

Miki smiles. "That would be very nice, Mr. Okada."

Bukichi flashes back. He feels his heart race, as if waiting for the crash of a colossal timber he has just felled. "You are very pretty."

Miki is stunned and avoids his gaze. She cannot believe what is happening. It is all so improper, for a go-between should make the first approach, with her parents' approval of course. She has, momentarily, forgotten the larger impropriety that looms—his marital status. But she is flushed with an excitement that she cannot ignore. Tentatively, she raises her eyes to meet his, and the chemistry of love begins brewing.

Bukichi continues to court Miki on his days off. The precedent he set during that first encounter becomes a tradition. He is always searching his brain for one more item, one endearment left unsaid, one kiss yet to cherish as he approaches the door to go. But he cannot leave. Like wrenching huge tree roots from the ground, dynamite works best.

Over the next two years, Bukichi works his way into town, first as a labourer on the boom, and then negotiating the contract. Meanwhile, Rakuju returns to Japan, leaving her sons to work the boom with their father while they, too, prepare themselves financially for wives and families. From the outset, she knew not to expect love in marriage; now she equates it with abandonment and retires to her homeland like a stone hurled back in time. Within months of her departure, the Baptist minister in Chemainus, Reverend Cook, marries Bukichi and Miki.

One year later, in 1910, Miki gives birth to Takeshi, followed by Hitoshi in March 1912. She brings two more boys, Satoru and Tamotsu, into the world before death reaches into their happy home and crumples hope in its hands. Tamotsu is just an infant in 1918 when Miki, now in her early thirties, falls victim to the influenza epidemic following the First World War. Bukichi spares no cost to try and save his young wife, delivering her into the hands of the best doctors in Vancouver. But his effort is in vain. It isn't him who buries her ashes or gives his three-month-old son to an Oriental orphanage in Victoria; it is his own ghost.

Hitoshi watches his father going through the motions, but he is not sure where to turn. He is six years old, standing with his feet wide apart and his hands crossed behind his suit jacket. His eyes follow the musky wisps of incense drifting over Bukichi as he places the urn in the ground. A breeze is stirring the branches of fir trees nearby as Hitoshi stares into his own wee void, thinking of the hot lunches his mother once brought to Takeshi and him halfway between school and home. He can see her spreading out a picnic in the little shed they found on the mill grounds. She is piling hot, steaming noodles, rice balls, white radish pickles, and seaweed into bowls. Hitoshi knows this will be followed by her scrumptious sweet bean cakes and pulls the food from her, smelling the sweet-sour mixture and diving into the exotic mix. He examines her face while he eats, studying the translucent glow of her skin and her dark penetrating eyes. She returns his gaze nonchalantly, dreamily.

They finish eating and grin at her, rubbing their bellies like little Buddhas. Giggling at their silliness, she deftly packs up and goes home. The two boys run all the way back to school with the comforting swell of a full belly fuelling their antics.

Hitoshi's daydream is brought to an abrupt halt when his father rests a hand on his shoulder, indicating it is time to go. Bukichi, Takeshi, Hitoshi, and Satoru leave the cemetery together, numb and aching for solace that cannot be found.

Hitoshi and Takeshi don't return to school for a year and the days roll into one another without incident. Their playground in Okada camp stretches right around the bay. There is a hard patch of dirt behind their house, where they play marbles and ball with the neighbourhood boys. Sometimes they play hide-and-seek with the Indians who live in houses on posts below the government wharf. A smaller group of Indian families live on the other side of the bay too, below Bare Point. Hitoshi likes to watch them come into shore in their canoes, which can be tricky business in strong seas. But they are expert canoeists and manoeuvre about as if nothing short of a gale-force wind presents a challenge.

Something is always happening on the harbour. Hitoshi often sits on the seashore, watching the men work the boom, or the Indian stevedores loading up scows with timber that they row out to schooners anchored in the bay. It's common for five or six great tall ships to be bobbing about at once, the sun beating down on their decks while the sea sparkles around their huge hulls. Hitoshi thinks watching a sou'easter working the harbour into a sweat is the best, though. Mounting swells rock and roll huge timbers like some god is piling them up for kindling. After such storms, Hitoshi often sees the Izumi kids out there with makeshift fishing gear in their hands, running along the logs like cats. They skitter across the bay on the logs to the base of the train trestle, which they climb with acrobatic fearlessness. Hitoshi never once sees them slip or fall.

One afternoon some years later, Hitoshi is playing marbles with his brother Takeshi and the other neighbourhood kids behind the house. It is one of those cold, crisp days in early January when the sun coats everything in primary colours. A westerly is gusting out on Stuart Channel. Hitoshi sees Gordon Cathey and Harvey McGinnis walking down the hill towards them. He looks up from the game as Gordon and Harvey walk straight up to Takeshi.

"Want to go duck hunting?"

"Where?" Takeshi asks.

"We've got a little punt out at Bare Point," Gordon says. "C'mon, let's go." He whispers something in Takeshi's ear. He smiles and nods.

Hitoshi returns to the immediate challenge: knocking his friends' marbles out of the circle. He is collecting quite a pile and doesn't pay any mind to his brother's shenanigans. The afternoon passes and he goes inside, rubbing his hands together over the stove to get warm. Takeshi still isn't home when Hitoshi hears his father's caulk boots on the wooden floor. Daylight is fading fast.

"Where's Takeshi?" Bukichi asks his son, yanking off his boots and looking around.

"I don't know," Hitoshi replies. "He went with Gordon and Harvey early this afternoon. Something about going duck hunting on a punt out at Bare Point."

Without saying a word, Bukichi stands and stares out his front window. Then he checks out back, squinting at the path leading to Bare Point, praying for his son to walk into the clearing. No one does. The landscape is hushed.

It is an engineer from a foreign boat docked in Chemainus who hears the boys. Walking along the point to take a picture of his boat, he hears their screams fighting the wind. Rushing back to his ship, he puts out a call for help. But by the time anyone reaches the point, it is too late. All they find is the wreckage of the punt floating in the chop.

For a week, fishermen from as far away as Steveston crisscross the channel, dragging for bodies. The night they find Takeshi's crab-eaten remains, Hitoshi stumbles into the living room and stops. His father's silhouette hunches against the dying light, his head in his hands.

Miki and Bukichi's firstborn son drowned at the age of thirteen. Hitoshi and his father bury Takeshi in the cemetery close to his mother's ashes. It is 1923, five years after the influenza epidemic swept Miki's spirit away, two months before Hitoshi's eleventh birthday.

Bukichi sends for his first wife, Rakuju. His younger sons need a mother, and the household needs a woman to do the cooking, cleaning and laundry. Since Miki died, the wives of

Bukichi's adult sons have done the women's work in the house. But they have children of their own now; it is time to welcome Rakuju back into the fold. Hitoshi does not love her like his mother, but he is happy to have her nonetheless. He feels a little less vulnerable with her around, although he can't say why. And now that she is back, Bukichi decides to bring Tamotsu home from the orphanage. Hitoshi's five-year-old brother is a stranger about to discover a new meaning of home and family, but it is a family that needs time to knit itself into something whole again.

Hitoshi likes his little brother, but he desperately misses his walks to and from school with Takeshi. He misses playing baseball with him too. He can't quite digest the fact that Takeshi isn't going to come busting into the house ever again. Often he turns to tell him some joke or to throw him a punch, remembering the tumbles they had—some of them so hard and fast that they hurt and made him mad. Sometimes Hitoshi reaches for Takeshi and feels the empty space surge.

Spring and summer come and go. Hitoshi goes back to school in September, as another wet winter approaches. One Saturday in November, he is with his friend George Ridgway in the ball park when they hear the fire whistle blow at the mill. Curious, they stop playing and sit on a knoll overlooking the mill grounds. Billowing clouds of smoke, like elephants roaming the sky, pour out of the east side of the mill building.

Suddenly George nudges Hitoshi. "Look, the whole roof is on fire!"

Hitoshi has already seen the burst of flame erupting out of the smoke and dancing across the mill roof. Fascinated, they sit and watch the flames consume it over the next forty-five minutes. Then they hear it crash with one tremendous crack as hordes of men work like ants to keep the fire from spreading. Hitoshi can't make out if his father or half-brothers are in there with the other men, but he figures they are. The mill, directly or indirectly, puts food on just about everyone's table in Chemainus. And now it is levelled.

A month of uncertainty follows before the mill owners announce they will build a new mill. In January 1924, one year after Takeshi's death, work begins on what will become the most modern and expansive mill of its day. Hitoshi's father gets a job cleaning up the old mill site. His half-brothers get work sawing and bucking logs from the boom to fuel the locomotive bringing the rebuilding equipment onto the mill site. Times hold the promise of prosperity again.

In 1927, when Hitoshi is fifteen, street lights appear in Chemainus and homes are wired for electricity. Conveniences they haven't dared dream about become commonplace; everything from electric lights to radios and gramophones begin to appear in the homes of those who can afford such luxuries. The Okadas are among those who can.

As it turns out, it is a short-lived prosperity. When Hitoshi starts school in the fall of 1929, he is seventeen. Whatever hopes he has of graduating from high school are thwarted when the New York stock market crashes in December, affecting the lumber market in demand and price. Operations in Chemainus are cut back, including his father's boom contract. Bukichi cannot comfortably keep all his men employed, so he fires six men. Soon after, Hitoshi leaves school to work for his father. What begins as a temporary arrangement soon becomes permanent.

Hitoshi grows into manhood on the boom. He enjoys strong-arming his way around the bay, where the pungent smell of wet Douglas fir mingles with salt air and the fishy odour of carousing harbour seals and sea lions. The work is heavy, but satisfying. Occasionally, his footing slips and he falls into the chuck. No one wears life jackets. Some years before Hitoshi started working, a young worker was crushed to death between two logs near the log dump. It isn't uncommon for the train to dump so many logs at once that it creates a log jam, and breaking it up is dangerous. Hitoshi soon learns to pinpoint a log to jump to in an emergency, never allowing his concentration to lapse. He earns less than twenty cents an hour, seven hours a day, six days a week, to take such risks.

Shizuka Taniwa is just eight years old in 1923 when news of the drowning seared the community. She barely knew the boys to see them, having been back from Steveston for less than a year. But she learns that her neighbour, Mr. Isoki, found one of the *hakujin* bodies after dragging through the waters in his fish boat, *Joker*. The day of the funerals, the whole town is shut down. Shizuka wishes she could play tag with her friends along the alley in Kawahara camp, but her mother, Naka, forbids it because it would be disrespectful.

She goes to her room, which looks onto Oak Street, and feels a bit homesick for Steveston. She has made new friends since returning to Chemainus, but she misses her classmates from the Japanese language school. Her English is improving now that she is in the local public school, but she will still think in Japanese for some time yet. This is to her parents' liking. In fact, her father is very busy these days, among other activities, organizing the other Japanese men in the *jijikai* to raise the necessary funds to start a Japanese language school in Chemainus.

Like his peers, Risaburo Taniwa thinks it more important that his children be educated in Japanese than in English. To that end, he and his wife took their firstborn, a son named Norimichi, to Japan for his first years of schooling. But they could not straddle two continents forever. With a growing family in Canada, they had little choice but to return. There was neither enough money to bring the family to Japan, nor the means to establish themselves comfortably there. In that respect, Risaburo's original intentions, like those of countless peers, were thwarted.

In 1905, when he left his small village home in Wakayama, Risaburo left his young bride behind while he got established in Canada. He had finished his apprenticeship with his father-in-law and wanted to break free from the grinding poverty of life in Wadamura. One year later, feeling raw and vulnerable, Naka Taniwa swallowed tears as she said goodbye to her family and boarded the steamship in Yokohama. She was not quite twenty-one when Norimichi was born at home in Chemainus a year later. If it hadn't been for the other Japanese women living close by, Naka believed she would perish. But she grew accustomed to the changes and, as the years rolled by, she thought back to how frightened she had been and laughed.

Her pioneering life included many unexpected hardships and some rare light-hearted moments. Helping Kume Yoshida in childbirth was, in retrospect, one of the funnier experiences. Shigetoki Yoshida arrived at the door one morning, pleading with her and her friend Miki Mizuta to attend the birth of his child until the doctor arrived. Shigetoki was clearly desperate, not knowing what had happened to Dr. Watson, so the young women went with him in his rickety Ford pickup to the Yoshida's home. They lived on Matthew Howe's property on the outskirts of Chemainus in those days, isolated from the various Japanese camps in town.

Naka is recounting the story to her daughter one afternoon, and Shizuka sits at her feet, embroidering a brilliant butterfly. "When we stepped into Kume's bedroom, I became frightened. But I walked over to her bed and took her hand. I didn't know what to do then," Naka says, looking out the window.

"Miki and I felt very queasy watching Kume grip the side of her bed with the pain. Shigetoki was pacing back and forth, muttering 'Dr. Watson,' over and over again.

"Miki had not had children of her own; in fact, she was not

even married yet. Even though I had Norey, I knew nothing about how to deliver someone else's baby. We were all in a dither, except Kume, who was oblivious to everything. Miki and I were taking turns running to the door for signs of the doctor.

"When the baby's head began to appear, we swallowed hard and set to work. Within half an hour, a baby girl was born. When it was over, Kume smiled weakly. 'Having you here is a comfort,' she said, drawing her infant to her breast. The baby stopped screaming then, and for just a little while we were in a different world. Something happens when a baby is born. . . . It's hard to explain."

Naka laughs, remembering how silly she felt at the time. Quietly, she watches Shizuka pull the bright yellow thread through the fabric, wondering if her daughter can grasp that bygone era. Her generation speaks English and goes to hospitals to have babies, whereas in 1915, Echi Tanouye coached Shizuka out of her womb with only the most rudimentary tools. A midwife who had brought babies into the world on both sides of the Pacific Ocean, she had often witnessed life giving birth and birth extinguishing life as well.

Risaburo works as a millwright in the sawmill to feed his family of five. Like all Orientals, he is paid ten percent less than his Caucasian counterparts. Their status worsens in the Depression.

Early in 1930, the mill manager calls everyone together. Risaburo thinks John Humbird a slob of a man, although he never speaks such opinions out loud. He is not alone. Most of the *hakujins* feel that way about their boss too, but workers are completely at the mercy of their employers.

A light drizzle falls as everyone gathers near the planing shed, stiff and anxiously shuffling their feet. A total shutdown has been rumoured since the stock market crash. The men wonder if they will be the next "Prairie chickens" to ride the rails in rags, thin and haggard as medieval peasants. Everyone has seen them coming through Chemainus, begging for work.

Risaburo eyes Harunobu Higashi at the edge of the crowd. He looks sober, but Risaburo can't be sure and decides to elbow his way across to stand by him. Risaburo's distrust of Humbird is equalled by his fear that Harunobu might erupt into one of his violent rages, if the news is bad enough, and jeopardize the entire Japanese working force.

Humbird coughs into the megaphone and begins:

"I have surveyed all sections of the mill, from the booming grounds to the dry kiln and planing shed. If you men are prepared to take a cut in wages, the mill need not close."

A unanimous affirmative chorus bounces back at Humbird before he draws another breath. Risaburo watches a slow smile creep across Humbird's face, but his pudgy cheeks straighten almost at once and his brow forms burrows again beneath his curly brown hair.

"Given your approval, I hereby announce that the wages of all Caucasians will drop ten percent," Humbird shouts. "And all Oriental wages will drop twenty percent."

Neither Risaburo nor Harunobu speak much English, but they understand enough to get the message. The men slump together, simultaneously angry and resigned to their fate. Humbird surveys the crowd just before he sways off the podium. For a split second, Risaburo makes eye contact with his boss. It is as penetrating as Humbird's unapologetic racism, but it doesn't phase him in the least. No matter how unwillingly, the Orientals will accept the terms without comment or be gone. It is as simple as that, and everyone knows it.

At the end of the year, the company proudly announces they have cut the equivalent of 4,800 boxcars of lumber—enough to stretch a train from Victoria to Duncan, which would require the strength of sixty locomotives interspersed among the boxcars to move it. Added to the other years the mill has been in production since 1925, it is enough to build a 347-foot wide roadway of one-inch boards right around the equator.

Before the Depression is over, the Japanese are earning seventeen cents an hour on average to do their part in keeping those boxcars full. When Humbird announces a second cut in wages in the mid-thirties, Orientals lose another twenty percent and the white workers another ten percent.

Hearing this news, Risaburo bursts out laughing. The gullible sensibility of his youth seems incredible to him now. Stories of streets paved with gold mock the tight spaces of his life.

Risaburo returns to Japan in the mid-1930s. Life in Canada has humiliated him. He must return, knowing his place in Japanese society cannot be put on hold forever. But his family is established; regrettably, his family is Canadian. Crossing the Pacific, he lets go of them as best he can, sifting through his memories and wrestling with past choices that have provoked so much pain.

Now in her late teens, Shizuka misses him terribly and writes often. Whatever his shortcomings, he is her father and the bond is strong. She checks the post office regularly for his letters. It is a bit of a hike up past Okada camp, but she enjoys the salt air and the wind blowing through her hair. She is often rewarded for her effort, for Risaburo is good about writing. Shizuka never opens the envelope until she is home in her room. No ritual could be more important than to sit at the table he made for her years before. They had sanded and polished the yellow cedar together until it glowed; like everything her father put his hand to, it was a work of art.

Today she smooths the letter open with the palm of her hand pressed hard against the tabletop and begins reading. Risaburo writes in his fine, bold calligraphy about the landscape of the passing days—the mist that hangs in the valley, the cranes nesting on a nearby slough, the opaque velvet blue of the mountains.

Shizuka tucks the letter away when she is finished and lifts her *koto* onto the table. Recalling the hours Risaburo put into its making, she runs the tips of her fingers along its exquisite curves, caressing it with the same sweet affection a parent reserves for a child. Through her sheer curtains, sunlight warms her room.

She begins to strum, seeking out keys to give expression to her melancholy. She plays a sharp, complex piece called "Disarray," which suits her mood. It echoes across the room. Outside her window, the shadow of a high-flying cloud skitters across Oak Street. She remembers the afternoon she looked up from her *koto*, startled by the silhouette of a man studying her through the glass. An officer on a visiting Japanese ship, he was walking by on the street when he heard her playing. Stunned, he stopped to float on the music. Having been at sea for months, he let the music lift him home. Later, Risaburo invited him and the ship's captain for tea, but Shizuka did not entertain them. She did not think her playing good enough.

In fact, like her father and her brother Norey, she excels at all artistic endeavours. At school she wins an award for the still life drawing she enters in the Duncan fair. The mother of the little boy she babysits across the street gives her free piano lessons, for Mrs. Jarrett recognizes the young girl's talent. She is a favoured student at the Japanese language school; her calligraphy is exceptional and her Japanese very good. She comes home from her needlework lessons with vivid magenta peonies and tiny yellow finches flawlessly embroidered on both sides of fine linen.

Although she enjoys sewing, Shizuka hates walking through the mill to Chinatown for her lesson. The men whistle as she passes by, and she can feel their eyes bore into her until she arrives at the base of the hill to Chinatown. It isn't that she doesn't feel safe, but she blushes with embarrassment and her body feels awkward. Walking along the train tracks in front of Okada camp, however, she knows nothing of other eyes watching her. Bukichi Okada has already determined she will be his favourite son's wife, for she is a picture: petite, with shiny black hair and a silky white complexion, her large dark eyes flash above her high cheekbones and classic nose and mouth.

Shizuka knows Hitoshi well because he plays baseball with her brother Norey. The two young men have been the best of friends for years. Hitoshi does all kinds of things for Norey that he maybe doesn't deserve. Shizuka loves Norey, but he makes her mad sometimes too. He often rides on the backs of others and is always up to something. As well as being the firstborn son, Norey is good-looking, very smart, and charming. No one tells him what to do.

Norey and Hitoshi have been playing baseball together since their adolescence, long before Shizuka took much notice of her brother's friend. It was Risaburo, before he returned to Japan, who took her to her first baseball games. She wasn't much interested in boys then. But now she goes with her friends, and together they cheer on the team of their choice, chatting among themselves about the strong, handsome young men on the ball field. It's always a big deal when the *Asahi* team from Vancouver comes to play against the all-star team. Everybody crowds the stands to watch those games. Once, Shizuka and her friend Chizuru Yoshida ran home like gazelles as soon as the game was over, some *hakujin* kids hot in pursuit. The girls, along with many others, were routing for the *Asahis*, and the *hakujins* didn't like it—not because they were a Japanese team but because they were from out of town.

Norey plays on two of the three teams that Hitoshi plays on: the *Nippon* team and the Chemainus all-star team. Occasionally, Hitoshi plays with the Cowichan Indian team, too. Only his friends know he isn't Indian. Shizuka learns from Norey that Hitoshi can even speak some Chinook. One of the Indian stevedores taught him when they were playing pool downstairs in their store.

Chemainus has four teams, and they play three games a week all summer long. On top of that, the *Nippon* team plays two annual series against the Cumberland Japanese team. On July 1, the *Nippons* rent a bus and go up island; on Labour Day, the Cumberland guys come down island. In the summer, baseball is a way of life.

One day Hitoshi is having a soda at Taniwa's store when the Furuya salesman comes in. While he and Norey are taking care of the order, they talk baseball. Mr. Ryujin knows all the baseball teams on the island because he supplies stores in Japanese communities from Duncan to Port Alberni.

"No use you fellows going to play the Port Alberni team," he tells Norey. "They got an all-star team there that's pretty good, so you watch out if you go up there."

"You don't know who you're talking to," Norey replies, laughing. "I bet you five bucks we can slaughter them."

Norey wins the bet.

They play at the ball field in Port Alberni, halfway between the east and west coast of the island. The day is a scorcher, up in the nineties, without so much as a breeze. As usual, Norey is pitching, and Hitoshi is on second base. Norey works his fast ball on them for five innings and they keep striking out. The *Nippon*'s manager, Torizo Yamashita, finally decides they should ease up a bit.

"Let them hit a little bit," he tells Norey.

Norey nods. In the sixth and seventh innings they start hitting, but Hitoshi usually catches the ball before they get to second base. In the eighth inning, Torizo tells Hitoshi to pitch.

"Shall I let them hit?" he asks.

"No, it's too hot. I want to get it over with," Torizo says.

Hitoshi throws nothing but curve balls. He faces six batters and the game is over with a score of 23-0.

The *Nippons* go home cocky as hell.

But there are also teams they can't touch. In the summers from 1935 to 1938, the Chemainus all-star team plays against barnstorming teams from the United States. Most of them are black men—barred from American professional leagues by virtue of their race—who come to Canada on buses and roam the countryside for competition.

Everyone from Duncan to Ladysmith comes out for these games. One time a team called the Zulu Giants plays in grass skirts, their Olympian legs running like thunder and stirring the dirt into clouds around their skirts. Then there is the House of David team, all six-foot-plus giants with long beards and muscles the size of small boulders. One time the Kansas City Monarchs beat out the *Nippons* neatly. Two of their players went on to the majors: Satchel Paige and Jackie Robinson. Satchel didn't play in Chemainus that day, but Jackie did. Hitoshi pumps adrenalin for the next two weeks.

Of course, most of the time it is simply the hometown boys on the all-star team, the cream from each of the four teams: Bob and Dick McBride, Joe Horton, George Robinson, Jack McKinnon, Babe Work, Cy Shillito, Gus Crucil, Jack Naylor, Haley Jackson, Norey Taniwa, and Kaname Izumi. One big happy-go-lucky bunch who play hard together like tight brothers and love every hot, dusty minute of it.

Every now and then Hitoshi wonders how a certain ball game might have ended up if Takeshi had been part of the team. He'd be standing on second base and, without warning, his brother would appear in front of him, smiling his big, gangly grin. Just as quickly, he was gone.

If Hitoshi isn't coming around to pick up Norey for baseball, he is playing pool with him in the family's store on the corner of Oak and Croft Streets. Although the Kawaharas' store and pool hall is just down the street, it is Taniwa's place that becomes popular in short order. It is more of a confectionary store than the Kawaharas', and friends often gather for soda after the baseball games.

One day Hitoshi has lunch with a friend who lives in Chinatown. Impressed with the delicious fruit pies made by the Chinese cooks in the bunkhouse, Hitoshi wonders if Norey could make a profit by selling single pieces. He finds out that they can order as many as ten pies at a time for thirty-five cents each. As soon as he tells Norey, Hitoshi has himself a volunteer job, transporting pies stacked across the back seat of his Buick. Norey sells each piece for twenty-five cents. Hitoshi doesn't even think about his time or gas money any more than Norey thinks about sharing his profit. They are the best of friends, and money is never an issue.

Naturally, Shizuka notices how strong and handsome her brother's friend is. But even though she is in her early twenties, she is very shy—some think stuck-up. Other boys come around vying for her attention, but she is naïve as well. Still, there is nothing Shizuka loves quite so much as to ride in Hitoshi's beautiful Buick along the windy roads that hug the coast.

Bukichi has already approached a go-between to help arrange the marriage. After Miki and Takeshi died, Bukichi held onto life because of Hitoshi. He is happy to see his son grow into such a fine, strong, handsome man. He is happy, too, seeing Shizuka gallivant away with his son to Abbott and Costello movies in Ladysmith. Watching the Buick drive up the road one Saturday night, he whispers after them: "Life is precious, and life is precarious. Make of it all that you can."

In his ten years on the boom before he marries, Hitoshi works and plays hard. There isn't a pinch of fat on his stocky body. He has his father's strong jaw and flat, broad nose. The deaths of his mother and brother trickle away somewhere, creating a distance that seems as unreal as their deaths once had. With its imperceptible passing, time ever so slowly wedges itself between him and those painful memories. He still goes with his family to the cemetery every August to clean up the gravesites and light candles and incense to welcome their spirits home. As the years go by, everything but his mother's gentle voice and his brother's easy laugh fades into washed-out sepia tones.

Meanwhile, his athletic talents come to the fore. When Hitoshi isn't working, he can be found any number of places but home: playing baseball, tennis, sumo, judo, or pool. Then there are the Saturday night treks to Duncan in Takayoshi Kawahara's truck. As assistant scoutmaster to Shige Yoshida's boy scout troop, Hitoshi also finds time for the meetings, expeditions and jamborees. Even though the Okadas aren't as prosperous as in earlier years, neither are they suffering like most. Prosperity aside, the 1930s are the best years of Hitoshi's life. It is a buoyant decade for him, followed by a calamitous, heart-wrenching one.

In 1938, the year before they marry, Shizuka travels to Vancouver where she works toward her diploma from the Academy of Domestic Arts. She lives with her teacher in Fairview and is in her element, creating beautifully designed clothes. She goes home in August to face the biggest sewing project of her life: three wedding dresses for her Shinto-Buddhist wedding. Over the next seven months until the March 25 wedding, Shizuka sits at her treadle sewing machine, pumping through reams of white satin for her traditional wedding dress. Sewing the hem by hand takes an entire day. When it is finally complete, Shizuka begins making her second dress, a floor-length black silk gown with handsewn looped buttonholes down the back. Two months before the wedding, she begins the final garment she will wear in the ceremony, a vibrant blue silk kimono.

Shizuka goes to sleep the night before her wedding listening to rain pound against the window. The torrential downpour is typical for March, with gusting winds churning up the waters at the bottom of Oak Street. She drifts in and out of sleep, waking often to the pinging sound of water bouncing off the boardwalk. By dawn, the rains stop and the wind drops. Shizuka sleeps peacefully through the early morning light and opens her eyes to a calm, grey day.

It is Sadako, her older sister, who wakes her with a gentle rap on the door.

"Morning, Shizuka," Sadako calls, as she pushes the door open and walks to her sister's bedside.

"Morning, sister," Shizuka whispers, rubbing her eyes.

Sadako sits on the edge of the bed while Shizuka orients herself, sitting up to look around.

"There is much to do this morning," Sadako says, watching her little sister comb fingers through her long, black hair. "Mother and I have been up for hours, making *inarizushi, sunomono, yaki manju*, and *kazu noko*. It's all ready now, and the flowers will arrive soon."

Shizuka looks into Sadako's face and offers a wan smile. She has been working hard towards this day, and now that it is finally here, she fights an urge to bury herself in Sadako's lap. But as close as she is to her sister, Shizuka has been raised in the Japanese tradition of keeping her feelings to herself. Instead, she asks the time.

"Just nine o'clock," Sadako replies. "Come. Mother has breakfast ready."

Sadako leaves as Shizuka swings her feet onto the wooden

floor and walks over to her dressing table. She brushes her hair abruptly and studies herself in the mirror, whispering, "Mrs. Hitoshi Okada," over and over again.

Her mother and Sadako fuss over the preparations all morning, flying here and there to look after last-minute details. When the flowers finally arrive from Victoria, they set to work right away, decorating the Japanese hall on Croft Street with bouquets of roses, gladiolas, and chrysanthemums.

Shizuka spends the larger part of the morning grooming herself. With an hour to go, she is pacing her room, unable to settle. Finally she decides to play her *koto* to ease her nerves. It is the closest she will get to her father today.

Hours later, when she and her groom drink sake from the same cup to consecrate their union, Shizuka breathes a sigh of relief. The strict religious nature of the ceremony gives the ritual meaning, but it has also kept her on edge lest she forget what to do. Shizuka needs everything to go perfectly, and so it has.

At the reception in her father-in-law's dining room, Shizuka sits quietly next to Hitoshi, waiting obediently until it is time to depart. The candlelight casts a lovely sheen on her blue silk kimono and her long hair gathered softly above the nape of her neck. Her eyes shine like a black ocean under a half moon, while all about her men drink sake and party. At twenty-four years of age, Shizuka is fulfilling a significant part of her destiny, tidily setting aside her apprehension with the knowledge that all is as it should be.

Her brothers, Norey and Marchi, are outside putting the finishing "Just Married" touches on Hitoshi's Buick when the community follows the newlyweds outside to wave goodbye. It is getting dark, and they have a long drive to the Empress Hotel in Victoria. Hitoshi's father has spared no expense on his favourite son. After their night in the honeymoon suite high above Victoria's inner harbour, Shizuka and Hitoshi catch a steamship to Seattle and ride cable cars in the big American city for hours. Atop its steep forested hillsides, Puget Sound stretches into a gleaming silver oblivion; its horizon corresponds with an expansive inner vision that washes over Shizuka in one warm and lovely moment.

Back from their honeymoon, Shizuka moves into her husband's home in Okada camp, which he shares with two younger brothers and his parents. Hitoshi's stepmother tells Shizuka not to be alarmed when they all get talking. It has been a household of loud, boisterous men for years. Some days she longs for the quiet of her room in Kawahara camp, where she could play her *koto* undisturbed. Here in Okada camp, the living room looks out on the booming grounds where Hitoshi works. Noise and activity is constant.

Bukichi and Rakuju return to Japan after Hitoshi and Shizuka marry in 1939. Their pioneering years are behind them. Bukichi has succeeded where others have failed: he has broken the cycle of poverty for himself and his children. Granted, he paid dearly for it, but the new generation is well established. It is time to go home. Hitoshi drives them to the docks in Vancouver, where they are boarding their ship.

They stand by the gangplank as people file past and others, like them, huddle awkwardly to say farewell.

"Goodbye," Bukichi says, gripping Hitoshi's shoulder and staring into his face as if to memorize it.

"Goodbye, father," Hitoshi replies. Swallowing hard, he turns to his stepmother. "Goodbye, mother."

Rakuju smiles wearily and turns to join the crowd pressing up the gangplank. This will be her third voyage across the Pacific. She is grateful it will be her last.

Hitoshi waves to Bukichi as he turns to follow Rakuju.

"Take care, father. And write. Write often."

Bukichi nods and waves back, then disappears into the

throng. Hitoshi scans the promenade deck for another glimpse, and just as the ship pulls out, he spots his father, waving.

He never sees him again. Pearl Harbor makes sure of that.

On April 26, 1941 Shizuka gives birth to a fine baby boy in the Chemainus hospital. Richard is a healthy nine-pound baby, but he tears his mother badly when he arrives. Two months after he is born, Shizuka still has not healed. She finally goes home from the hospital though, home to her mother and the beautiful bed Risaburo had made more than a decade before. She still has not fully recuperated when Japan bombs Pearl Harbor in December, twisting her life like a toy top spinning and crashing into walls.

She is in her mother's kitchen measuring out rice for the noon meal when a neighbour comes by with the news. She grabs a chair at once and sits down. Richard is playing on the floor by her feet. Her brother, Marchi, was working the late shift at the mill the night before. She can hear the floorboards creaking above her head as she slides off her chair onto the floor. When Marchi comes into the kitchen, Naka is hovering over her daughter.

"What happened?" he asks.

"Some bad news. Japan bombed Pearl Harbor this morning. Shizuka fainted when she heard," Naka says, fanning her daughter's face.

Marchi looks past his mother and shivers. Without a word, he carries Shizuka to her bed and leaves to fetch Hitoshi. She is sitting up, drinking green tea in bed when her husband arrives.

"If they invade us next, what will we do? I can't run," Shizuka asks Hitoshi. "And if you try to help me, surely you'll be caught too."

Hitoshi tries to calm his wife, but he feels her fears are valid. Right now, he cannot think clearly either.

"I don't know what we'll do, Shizuka," he begins, "but don't worry. We'll think of something. Try to get some rest."

In the kitchen, Naka smooths the black drapes tighter into the corners of the window frame, hoping the Japanese navy will not find their little seaside village and her family at all.

The fear of a Japanese invasion soon becomes the much more real threat of a *hakujin* uprising. The Japanese community reels with each successive government decree that curbs their civil rights, but they believe they must be obedient and law-abiding no matter what. First come the orders to evacuate the Japanese-born men to road camps, then the orders to evacuate the entire town in early March. Everyone dutifully finishes packing the belongings they are leaving in the care of the Custodian of Enemy Property. When the evacuation orders are postponed until the end of March and then again until late April, people begin to feel like a packet of marbles being tossed about in a malicious game.

Before he begins packing his family's belongings, Hitoshi says goodbye to his three half-brothers on the Esquimalt & Nanaimo train platform in Chemainus. Because all three are Japanese-born, they are among the first to go. Ryoichi, Haruyuki, and Osamu join the other Japanese men from the community who are being relocated to B.C. interior road camps. The government order wrenches husbands, fathers, and brothers from their families with a callousness that few can fathom.

The morning after they are gone, Hitoshi steps onto his front porch and walks down the steps towards the booming grounds. His boots feel heavier than usual as he clumps along the shore. Anxiety cuts the air like a sheer cliff, suffocatingly close and insurmountable. It is shock seeping through closed doors in Okada camp, where young mothers and old women carry on their routines in a void. Hitoshi recalls the night the

Indians held a vigil on the beach following the death of a young boy. Although his people don't wail outwardly against cruelty, a silent wailing is summoning a force that drifts over the water with the same heavy hurt.

The week before they leave, Hitoshi is extremely busy. The mill has hired replacement workers to work on the booming grounds. The booming contract his father negotiated with the mill in the mid-1920s fell into Hitoshi's hands when his father retired in 1935. Now he is training others in the skills he has acquired since a teenager. Haley Jackson, a team-mate on the all-star team, gets his job.

Hitoshi's crew has a system for everything they do on the job, but Haley and his men will have to wing it. There just isn't time to teach them the intricate tactics the Okada crews developed over the years. Hitoshi hopes that by the time they get back to Chemainus, Haley's men will still be trying to catch up. He will need his job back.

Meanwhile, Shizuka, still recuperating at her mother's, is embroidering hankies as an *okaeshi*, or return gift, for those who gave presents when Richard was born. Her family's custom was to reciprocate on the child's first birthday, but Richard will turn one in Hastings Park—five days after they are evacuated and the community is scattered. Not well enough to walk any distance, Shizuka sends Hitoshi around the neighbourhood delivering the delicate hankies. He squeezes the task in on the few days when he isn't training the new work crew, packing and boarding up windows or taking his 1937 Buick to Victoria, where he is storing it until they return. When he thinks back on that week, he wonders how he fit it all into the daylight hours before the seven o'clock curfew.

Shizuka can't even help with the packing. She is still not well enough to lift anything heavy and has to rest often. When Hitoshi finishes all that has to be done in Okada camp, he walks over to Taniwas to give his in-laws a hand. He finds

Marchi and Norey boarding up the community hall windows. Grabbing a hammer, he joins in. No one speaks. Almost everything is ready. They only have a day to go.

On April 21, 1942, the SS *Princess Adelaide* finally arrives at the docks to evacuate the Chemainus Japanese community. Japanese communities from the Cowichan Valley to the south are also bused to Chemainus, swelling the numbers of people caught in the chaos to 470.

Hitoshi carries his family's luggage onto the passenger ship. His wife is not well enough to hold their one-year-old son, so her sister, Sadako, does; his mother-in-law carries the diapers. Despite Hitoshi's strength, he finds the luggage unbearably heavy. As the steamship pulls away from the mill wharf, he does not glance back at the row of houses where he grew up: their windows boarded up, their contents sealed.

In Hastings Park, Shizuka has difficulty breathing. She sends a note to Hitoshi in the men's dormitory.

"It is bedlam here. Tired children crying, the noise of people talking in this huge building with no walls to cut the sound. The terrible odour of animals mixed with disinfectant desperately trying to make it smell better. I can hardly breathe."

Propped up on his army cot in similar conditions, Hitoshi feels despair creep into his heart. There is nothing he can do for his wife.

The next day another message arrives. Someone has come to visit. Hitoshi goes out into the compound and looks around. A guard points to the fence on the eastern edge of the grounds. His friend, George Ridgway, is waving.

Hitoshi asks the guard for a pass. When he won't give him one, he asks permission for George to come inside. The guard says no. Hitoshi kicks a rock at his feet and stumbles toward George.

They can't even grasp hands through the wire fence.

"How are you?" George asks Hitoshi.

"Rotten," Hitoshi replies. "This place stinks like hell. We're trying to make the best of it, but it ain't easy."

"Why won't they let me in?"

"Who knows," says Hitoshi. "Maybe they think you're going to slip me a hand grenade."

They both laugh. The notion is as ridiculous as their predicament. For a moment at least, the absurdity of it all seems funny.

"You know that's the first good laugh I've had in months," Hitoshi says.

"No kidding," says George. "Hey, these guys ain't worth losing laughs over. This has got to be a temporary thing just to scare you. It can't last."

Hitoshi peers into George's eyes. "You really think so?"

George looks down. He doesn't want to be the one to tell Hitoshi about the vandalism going on. He has walked along the beach that was Okada camp. A sou'easter was blowing, breaking up the boom in the bay and howling through holes punched through doors. All along the boardwalk the wind lifted stuff that was strewn everywhere, old rags and dishpans, Brownie box snapshots, an empty can of shoe polish, and a child's stuffed bear. Anything of value not stolen by vandals has been taken to storehouses for auctioning. George is disgusted by the greed. He can't bring himself to tell his friend.

Shaking his head, he says, "I just don't get it. I never thought Canadians could be so pig-headed. I just can't believe they won't wake up soon and let you come home."

Changing the subject, Hitoshi says, "Hey, remember when we sat on top of the ball park and watched the mill burn down? We kids thought it was spectacular, but our parents thought it spelled the end of everyone in Chemainus."

"That's right, now. They did, didn't they?" George says, the corners of his mouth turned up ever so lightly. It hurts to see his buddy treated like a criminal; it enrages him that there is nothing he can do.

The Okadas are interned in the Slocan at Bay Farm, one of the smaller camps. Shizuka finally gets better after a doctor in New Denver stitches her up. For a while, they share a fourteen by twenty-eight-foot shack with her brother, Norey, and his growing family. Hitoshi works as a swamper on the garbage truck for two dollars a day, but it isn't enough to live on. They make up the difference by living on the savings they have brought from Chemainus. The B.C. Security Commission does not give welfare to people like the Okadas; people with money in the bank pay for their own internment.

Shizuka gives birth to a baby girl in 1945, just months before the war ends. Karen is one year old and Richard is five when the family sets out on the long trek across Canada to find a new home. After a year in an isolated bush camp in northern Ontario, they finally settle in Fort William in August 1947. People are afraid to trust them, which makes it hard to find work and somewhere to live. But they finally meet an old woman willing to rent her upstairs, and they stay there while Hitoshi finds work in the steel construction industry. They begin setting down roots in the Canadian Shield, determined that even the frostbitten land will come to accept them.

In 1949, the government lifts the ban prohibiting them from returning to the west coast. The war has been over for four years, and the property Hitoshi inherited from his father has been sold, his belongings auctioned or stolen.

When the American government interned its citizens of Japanese descent, the Canadian government followed suit. Prime Minister Mackenzie King bowed to pressure from right-wing British Columbian politicians, not because he believed citizens of Japanese descent were a security threat, but because he hoped it might win him political favour in the west.

When the war was over, however, Canada didn't duplicate American policy. Even before the war ended in 1945, Japanese Americans started going home. In the United States, Japanese Americans had homes to go home to.

Almost forty years after gaining the right to vote, Japanese Canadians scored another victory. In 1988, Prime Minister Brian Mulroney agreed to compensate Japanese Canadians interned during the war. Shizuka and Hitoshi were among those who received $21,000 cheques and an apology from the government. Money could not buy back the past or replace what was stolen, but the apology signified the promise of a new era. It confirmed their innocence on national television; it released them from the inner struggle of having to prove they are Canadian, not Japanese.

F O U R

MATSUE TANIWA

MATSUE TANIWA IS SIPPING COFFEE at her kitchen table, gazing at the birch tree outside her Thunder Bay home. She runs her weathered, elegant hands through her wiry white hair and thinks about getting a perm. Two great-grandsons are chasing each other in and out of the kitchen, squealing at the top of their lungs when the phone rings.

"Quiet, you two," Matsue shouts, picking up the receiver.

"Hi, Mom. How are you doing?"

"Stanley! How was your trip?" Matsue asks. Her son is calling from his home in rural Manitoba, so she doesn't hear from him often.

"I just got back yesterday. Something incredible happened in Chemainus."

"Oh?" Matsue says.

"You won't believe this, Mom. I asked some people on the street what they knew about the Japanese community. I explained that I was just a baby when everyone was evacuated and I wanted to find out where I was born. They told me to talk to the people in the murals' office."

"The murals' office?" she asks.

"Well, apparently the town was in a recession after the saw-mill shut down in 1983. Someone came up with an idea to paint the town's history on the walls of stores and offices."

"So?" Matsue is puzzled.

"The idea was to attract tourists and it worked. People started coming from all over, and the economy boomed. They've been painting murals since then, and lately they've been talking about painting one of the Japanese community."

"Well, isn't that something," she says.

"Yeah. Anyways, I introduced myself to the lady in the murals' office. She showed me a bunch of old pictures. There was one of the baseball team with Dad, Uncle Hitoshi and Uncle Marchi. I recognized them right away. I kind of fell apart seeing it, especially Dad."

Matsue waits for him to continue.

"I think it was fate, my going there then. I mean, I only went to Chemainus to see where I was born, and I find out that the town wants this mural. Actually, they want one of a fellow who formed a Japanese boy scout troop in Chemainus."

"That would be Shige," Matsue says.

"Yeah." They are going through all these old pictures, try-ing to find one with him and his troop. They're having trouble coming up with one that everybody likes.

"Anyways, when the woman in the office found out that I am an artist, she said I should send them my portfolio. If they like my work, there's a good chance I'll be painting the mural across the street from where Dad grew up and where you lived in that store."

Matsue sits down, not knowing what to say.

Stanley is forty-nine years old and a lot like her renegade husband—complex, talented, clever, and good-looking. He was only fourteen when his father died, and younger still when Norey deserted the family. Of all the kids, he needed more answers. Not that it was easy for any of them; it was just that Stanley inherited some wild, restless seed from Norey. For both, it created a frustrated driven destiny that had caused a lot of misery. But life had taught Stanley a few things. He was less likely to blame others now and looked inside himself for solutions. Norey never got so far.

"Well, that's a real coincidence, isn't it?" Matsue finally replies. "When will you paint it?"

"I haven't got the job yet, Mom."

"No, but you will, won't you?"

Stanley laughs. "Oh, yes, I will. It'll be next July, in time for the reunion in August."

"Reunion?"

"Oh yeah, didn't I say? Everybody who used to live there is invited back. Maybe you'd rather not go, but think about it, okay? I have to go now, but we'll talk about it again."

After hanging up, Matsue shuffles into the living room and eases herself onto the couch. At seventy-four she is finally able to relax and enjoy life. It has been a long time coming. Her children know what she has been through, and her grandchildren have some vague understanding of her past. But her great-grandchildren are too young to take any interest. She thinks it best to let bygones be bygones anyway. Life is too short to stay bitter, and she is proud of the family she has raised.

Matsue leans her head against the back of the couch and stares at the family portrait on the facing wall. She knows how important it is for Stanley to reconcile his past, but Norey brought her nothing but heartache and trouble right from day one. She was twenty, working in a yardgoods store in Steveston when a friend of her father's introduced them. Her memory of the occasion is as vivid as if it were yesterday.

"Matsue, this is Norimichi."

"Call me Norey," the man says with a smile.

"Hello," Matsue replies, briefly daring to look up. He is very handsome, but much older than her.

"Would you like to go to a show?" Norey asks. "I hear Charlie Chaplin is playing up the street."

Matsue smiles and nods her head.

"I'll come back for you when the store closes," Norey says.

She feels uneasy after they leave. She likes the boyfriend she has now, but she doesn't know how to say no to this strange man. Her mother, Tazu, has already told her that the go-between was going to introduce her to someone more suitable.

"But what about my boyfriend?" Matsue had asked her mother. "I really like him. Maybe he'll ask me to marry him."

Tazu was firm: "If you marry Norimichi and things don't work out, you can always come back to us. But if you go marry the guy you like and anything happens, don't come back to us crying."

Matsue is afraid to go against her mother's will. She is expected to obey her parents and always has. Besides, maybe they are right. Parents know what is best for their children.

A fisherman's daughter, Matsue worked hard throughout her adolescence. She went fishing with her father and did the bulk of the housework from age twelve on. They were poor, but almost everyone was. Her childhood was crowded with happy memories of Steveston, crabbing and fishing with other kids. After grade school, she worked in farm labour pools, which she hated, and in fish canneries, which she liked. Once she worked in a North Vancouver cannery, earning seven cents for each tray of cans she filled with salmon. She lived in a dormitory with other working girls, and it turned out to be great fun. At nineteen, she worked as a domestic for a high class family in Vancouver, just to get away from home. In between her various jobs, she went to dressmaking school.

When she got the job in the yardgoods store, she was ready to come home for good. Now she is about to marry a strange man and move to Vancouver Island. She shivers at the thought.

On April 4, 1937, three months after her twenty-first birthday, Matsue Hikida marries Norimichi Taniwa in the Shinto-Buddhist church in Steveston. She is wearing a white satin gown with a six-foot train and carries a full bouquet of red roses and forget-me-nots. Her fair skin glows in the candlelight as she and her thirty-year-old groom sip sake to consecrate the marriage. In his black tuxedo, Norey bears the fine-grained good looks of a movie star. They take a splendid picture.

After the ceremony, the wedding party boards a tugboat. Matsue's bridesmaids carry her train as she parades down the wharf and steps onto the deck of the tug. Luckily, it is a fine sunny day with only a gentle breeze. To protect her dress and hair, she stays below for the journey across the Strait of Georgia. Everyone else squeezes in too—her parents, the go-between, bridesmaids, flower girls, Norey's best man, and Norey. The knot in her stomach feels thick and gnarled like the tug's bow line. She is especially nervous about meeting her in-laws for the first time. They will be waiting for her arrival in Chemainus, where they are holding the reception. Thinking about it, Matsue feels faint.

Norey loves an audience and entertains everyone with stories. She begins to relax. But when the captain pulls up to the Chemainus government wharf and shoves the gear in reverse to dock, her insides go into reverse too. As she steps onto the wharf and looks up, her worst fears are confirmed. Scores of people stretch the length of the street, hoping to catch a glimpse of Norey's bride.

She holds her bouquet as if it were her lifeline, trying unsuccessfully to stop shaking. The bridesmaids pick up her train and, with Norey at her side, they walk the gauntlet of curious

strangers to the community hall. It is the most unnerving fifteen minutes of her life, but Norey is in his element.

Matsue regains some composure as she climbs the steps to the
reception hall where her in-laws are waiting. She knows they
may treat her like a slave, as is often the case for women who
marry the oldest son, but they welcome her kindly. She sighs
with relief as she enters the hall, thinking the worst is over.

More than ten years earlier, Matsue's father-in-law, Risaburo,
talked the other community leaders into raising funds for this
hall. It hadn't taken much to convince them that the town
needed a proper Japanese language school, as well as a place
for community functions. In addition to judo tournaments,
community musicals, and funerals, Risaburo reasoned that the
hall could host wedding receptions too. Men like Harunobu
Higashi, with his reputation for violent-tempered binges,
worked alongside men like Chiyoki Yoshida, a gentle man
renowned for his skills as a craftsman carpenter. The community pooled its resources to build a hall that celebrated Canada's Diamond Jubilee in 1927, providing a focus for activity
from then on.

Sitting quietly after her gruelling entry to Chemainus, Matsue knows none of the history of the community hall or its
occupants. Hers is not the first wedding party here, but the
reception is typical of the others: men drink sake, get happy,
and sing; women visit friends and neighbours. Matsue perches
on the edge of her chair, bewildered and unsure where to turn.
Norey is drinking with his father and friends. He hardly
seems to know she is there.

A few months earlier, Norey helped Risaburo build a confectionary store on the northwest corner of Oak and Croft Streets.
Although he works hard as a millwright in the sawmill across
the street, Norey gambles his paycheque away. Risaburo
thought a wife and a store might keep his eldest son occupied

during his off-work hours, away from Chinatown and out of debt.

To keep peace with his parents, Norey agrees to the plan. Then his friend Hitoshi offers to bring his pool table from Okada camp and set it up in the back of the store. Following a soak in the communal bath at the end of his shift, Norey goes home to supper and a night of pool with his friends. Circumstances always seem to turn to his advantage.

Matsue gradually feels her way into the community and makes friends with neighbours. She often surveys her world from the upstairs window, trying to fit this piece of her life into place. The sawmill whistle echoes across Horseshoe Bay every morning, noon and night. She has been told that activity in the harbour has dropped off dramatically since the Depression, but sometimes she catches glimpses of Penelakut and Chemainus Native stevedores at work. The population in Kawahara's camp has declined too. Norey tells her that the bunkhouse housed sixty sawmill workers at one time. Only a handful of bachelors are left. The streets are quiet, except that children going to and from school show up like clockwork.

Some days she studies the indigo silhouette of the island where the Indians go to school. Occasionally, she sees them pile onto the ferry at the Chemainus wharf, identifying with the slump in their demeanour as they leave. It is more than loneliness; it is a disquieting fear of having lost something critical en route to a stranger's world.

A month after the wedding, Matsue becomes violently ill. She is pregnant and can't look at food, let alone cook or eat it. She tries carrying on as usual, cooking for her husband and fixing sandwiches for customers in the store. But the sight and smell of food sends her retching to the back room. She is losing weight and miserable. Norey agrees to send her home for a while.

Matsue stays with her parents in Steveston for two months.

Her mother sits by her bed in the morning, telling stories of her childhood on a rice farm near Kyoto. Matsue gradually gains strength and goes out for long walks by the sea with old friends. The worst of the morning sickness subsides, and she says goodbye to her parents again.

In February 1938, she gives birth to a girl. Her labour is not complicated, but the nurse orders Matsue to stay in bed for a week after Susie is born. Matsue watches the Indian women get up and walk around the same day they have their babies.

"Why can't I walk around?" Matsue asks.

The nurse tucks in her sheet and smiles. "Indians are different," she says. "They are just like animals. That's why they can do that and we can't."

Matsue mulls this over. It's true that the Indians are strong. They live in the bush and paddle to town in big canoes. Maybe the nurse is right. The Indian mothers are long gone by the time she is discharged two weeks later.

Everyone pampers Susie at home, especially Risaburo. He cradles his granddaughter while Matsue prepares supper. Every so often, she stalks over to peek at Susie. Her eyes shine like Orion in a winter sky. Risaburo rocks back and forth, whispering *haiku* in her ear in the falling light.

A year and a half passes. Risaburo gets lost mushroom picking one fall day in 1939, and everything takes a turn for the worse. Norey's search party finds him the next day, shivering with cold. Not long after, he goes back to Japan. Susie misses her walks with her grandfather. Risaburo was like a magnet to every kid in the neighbourhood. She loved it when they all came rushing towards her, clinging to her carriage until they skirted under the wharf to the rocky beach.

Kenny follows Susie in April 1940, and then Stanley arrives in September 1941. When Kenny is old enough to walk, Susie grabs his hand and waltzes off to the beach where she went with her grandfather. She remembers the thrill of having his undivided attention as they explored the tideline. Now she shows Kenny the miniature crabs scrambling for cover under the over-turned rocks. Matsue minds the store and waits for them to saunter into view, all wet and mucky but still hand in hand.

Matsue and Norey are relatively happy together. She doesn't have time to be lonely any more, what with laundry, knitting, sewing, cooking, minding the children, and tending the store. Occasionally, Norey goes gambling in Chinatown, but most nights he comes home after work and plays pool, giving her a break from the store if not the children. In the summer he plays baseball after work, bringing his buddies back for a soda pop and a game of pool. Matsue enjoys the baseball season too. It is an outing for her and the children, who love being in the midst of the roaring crowd. Besides, Norey works hard providing for the family. She does not begrudge him his fun.

Whenever the community stages plays at the hall, Norey is sure to be involved. He is a born actor, thriving on drama in real life as well. Onstage he gives his own children such a fright that they run crying to their mother. Afraid of the zealous old man with wild grey hair who rants through his marauding act, they don't recognize him. But to the adults, it is quintessential Norey, his enigmatic character on dazzling display.

He underestimates his own need for stability, however. When the humdrum events of their lives are catapulted skyward, real-life rage begins to consume him.

The day after Japan bombs Pearl Harbor, Norey comes home from work to find Matsue changing Stanley's diaper.

"Where's my supper?" he demands.

"It's on the stove, Norey," she says. "I'll be there in a minute."

"You better be," he yells, pounding his fist on the wall. "I want my food on the table when I come home."

Matsue pins Stanley's diaper into place as quickly as she can. He is ten weeks old and a real little wriggler. Norey is tapping his fingers angrily on the table when she walks into the kitchen. She lays Stanley on his blanket and serves her husband's dinner without a word. Norey has always been demanding, but never threatening.

Matsue has no idea where Pearl Harbor is and doesn't really understand what all the fuss is about. After all, they were born and raised in Canada, albeit with strong Japanese influences. As far as she is concerned, they are just ordinary, quiet people minding their own business.

But when the RCMP escort Otoji Okinobu out of Gihei Kawahara's bunkhouse, she begins to fear more than her husband. They arrive without warning for the fifty-one-year-old labourer on December 8, 1941. He isn't given much time to gather any personal effects but manages to sign a cheque over to Tomoki Kawabe. As secretary of the *jijikai*—the association that looks after affairs in the Japanese community—Otoji clears out the *jijikai* account for his colleague to give to the Canadian Red Cross.

The police never find any evidence of espionage, but everyone knows he is a vocal, ardent supporter of Japan. Otoji accepts his fate without protest and vanishes. After the RCMP take him to the lock-up in Vancouver's immigration building, he goes to Petawawa and Angler, the only two POW camps in Canada. A year later he is released to work for a logging company in northern Ontario. No one in Chemainus ever hears from him again.

Like most of her peers, Matsue does not know Mr. Okinobu well. But the news of his apprehension frightens her just the same. She wonders who will be next, and nearly faints when the Mounties show up at the store one day. She forgot they were coming for their radios and hunting rifles. Norey hadn't. He hid a small radio under his mattress so he could follow the news. When she goes to bed at night, Matsue finds him listening to muffled broadcasts under the sheets.

Norey continues working at the mill for awhile, but the Mounties force them to close the store. Matsue learns that all Japanese-born men are being shipped to road camps and immediately thinks of her father in Steveston. But she has no quick way of communicating and waits months before she learns of his whereabouts. Next comes the news that they will be evacuated, and she begins to pack their belongings.

When she learns that they can only take one piece of luggage each, Matsue throws up her hands in disbelief. She can't possibly fit enough diapers and clothes into a few suitcases. She consults a neighbour and learns that the sawmill company store is selling canvas duffle bags, which hold a lot more than an average suitcase. The cash register is ringing constantly when she gets there, Stanley perched on her hip. After grabbing two duffle bags, she joins the line-up. An old man in front of her is shaking his head back and forth, whispering *shikataga-nai* under his breath.

Norey boards up the windows the week before they are supposed to leave. But the ship is delayed a month, so Matsue struggles on in their upstairs living quarters without daylight. Thankfully, Susie and Kenny play hide-and-seek among the cartons piled up everywhere. Their antics and laughter help her stay sane, just as meeting their needs forces her to keep depression at bay.

One day in March she hears Norey arguing with someone downstairs. "Who was that?" she asks later.

"It was the driver from Nanaimo Bottling Works trying to collect thirty-eight dollars I owe them for stock," Norey says.

"Did you pay him?" Matsue asks, worried that they might not have enough money for food with Norey not working.

"I told him I'd pay him half if he'd settle the account. He phoned his boss in Nanaimo, but the idiot said no. His boss told him that I was trying to take advantage of the situation. What a joke! I gave him five bucks and four dollars' worth of pop and told him to get lost."

Norey kicks a box on the floor, swearing. Stanley wakes up wailing. Matsue holds her head in her hands and presses as hard as she possibly can.

On April 19, she scrounges through her kitchen and manages to bake a cake for Kenny's second birthday. He claps his palms together and giggles with delight at the candles. Susie blows them out for him with one huge puff and gives him a finger full of icing. She is three-and-a-half, not oblivious to the stress at home but excited about going on a boat ride in two days.

Susie and Kenny walk to the steamship holding hands on April 21. It is a beautiful spring day, with the scent of lilacs in the air. Down on the docks, Matsue cradles Stanley while Norey heaves the duffle bags on top of the growing pile. Norey sees Shige Yoshida by the ship's gangplank and squeezes his way towards him. Matsue can see Shige waving his arms about, pointing here and there. Virtually everyone is vying for his attention.

Almost seven months old, Stanley is getting heavy in her arms. Eyes wide, he is fascinated with the hub-bub. She nuzzles his cheek and looks up to see her fifty-four-year-old mother-in-law carrying bags of diapers down the dock. Hitoshi is following her, juggling three suitcases. Shizuka's sister has her nephew Richard in her arms, plus her own three children in tow. Shizuka follows, holding tight to the railing, pale as a frayed bedsheet. Matsue turns to call Norey over to help them, but all she can see is an ocean of black hair, bobbing up and down like apples in a barrel of water. Voices shout over the tops of heads. A few *hakujin* kids search for school buddies in the chaos. Kenny and Susie cling to her skirt and she breaks down, joining the collective wail of women of all ages.

At twenty-six, Matsue leaves Chemainus the same way she arrived five years earlier: inside a boat, facing the unknown without choice in the matter. Life as she knows it will never be the same, but she proves herself a survivor. The indignity of Hastings Park and the difficulties of internment camp life aside, it is Norey who is nearly her undoing. Whatever shenanigans he might have been up to in Chemainus, he always came home and provided for her and the children. His wrath changes all that. Powerless to wrestle with the authorities, he abuses Matsue emotionally, a subconscious salve perhaps to his own humiliation and pain.

During their years in Lemon Creek, rumours abound that he is unfaithful to her. When he isn't home by midnight one summer night, she summons the courage to confront him at the shack where others have seen him. Matsue runs the long streets, a fleeting shadow in the black, balmy night. Pausing to catch her breath in front of the hut, she searches for a glimpse of her husband. The lights are on, but no one moves inside. Pulling her sweater tight across her shoulders, she tiptoes toward the door. Matsue raises her hand to knock, but nerve fails her. She knows he is there; she knows he will deny it tomorrow. Hurt follows her back to her bed, where she lies listening to the darkness between her and her sleeping children.

Despite her husband's philandering, Matsue bears three more of his children in Lemon Creek. Norma is three, Norman is one, and Raymond is still a baby when they leave the internment camp for Long Lac, Ontario in 1946. The family survives two winters in the northern bush without electricity or hot running water. In 1948, Norey injures himself on the job and leaves to look for other work. That summer the family moves again. A few weeks after they arrive in Fort William, Matsue has her seventh and last child, a boy named Wayne. Two years later, Norey walks out of their lives, leaving her to feed, house, and clothe the children on her own.

She finds a job in a Chinese restaurant, earning eighty dollars a month. Seven nights a week, she washes up the supper dishes and stokes the stove with wood and coal before heading off to work. Her neighbours check on her family while she puts in her hours at the restaurant, falling into bed after her shift ends at two a.m. All too soon, she is up again to get the children ready for school.

Over the years, she finds other jobs and manages to get a day off every week. In the summer, she takes her children on picnics and meets new friends. Life isn't easy, but it isn't hell any more either.

In 1955, Matsue learns her forty-eight-year-old husband is dying of stomach cancer in a Vancouver hospital. Unable to afford to take her children to see him before he dies, she tries to help them understand. One night news of his death awaits her when she gets home from work. Widowed at thirty-nine, she collapses in a heap, pounding the floor in one mixed-up rush of grief and anger.

The next morning, she dons her waitress uniform and walks to work in the rain.

FIVE

SUNAO, KANAME AND CHIYO IZUMI

KANAME IZUMI LOOKS OUT his Hamilton apartment window, watching thunder clouds roll over the Niagara escarpment to the southeast. In the forty-seven years since he relocated here, he has witnessed a good number of thunderstorms rage over Lake Ontario, drenching the earth for miles around and bringing temporary relief from the unbearable summer humidity. Now dollops of rain begin to assault the window, obscuring his view of the storm.

His wife is out teaching a dance class. Kaname sinks into his favourite armchair and broods in the late afternoon shadows. Perhaps it is a residual loneliness, left over from the day he and Shunichi Isoki took the train from Hastings Park to Lemon Creek in 1942. That was forty-eight years ago, but his memory of the storm en route is often triggered when thunder erupts nearby.

The pounding rain is hypnotic, and Kaname dozes off. He dreams he is sitting on the hard, wooden bench next to Shunichi as the train heads into the mountains. Suddenly he is sitting next to his brother Haruo en route to Hamilton in the fall of '43. Haruo keeps disappearing. Kaname strides up and down the aisle, searching the faces of hostile strangers, and finally finds his young brother on the platform outside the coach. He reaches for Haruo's shoulder, but his hand falls on Shunichi's arm instead. Now huge claps of thunder are echoing across the Selkirk Mountains in southeastern British Columbia. Kaname is trying to shake the image of his wife waving goodbye from Hastings Park.

Her face is fading into the mountainside when his dream shifts to Haruo again. He is shivering so hard his teeth are clacking.

"What are you doing, Haruo?" Kaname asks.

"I've been walking the aisles from Medicine Hat to Winnipeg, and I can't walk any more," he replies, rubbing his arms. "This is the only place on this god-awful train where soldiers aren't staring me down."

In the brisk October wind rattling through the steel platform, Kaname joins his brother. Railroad ties blur beneath their feet as the train races ahead.

Kaname falls off the platform onto the seat beside Shunichi. Thunder rumbles and cracks like artillery on a battlefield. Forks of lightning slice open the dark, troubled sky. The train carries its passengers through the storm impassively, without stopping to let anyone on or off. They are about to enter a tunnel when he wakes with a start. His wife Chiyo is shaking him.

"Kaname, wake up. You're having a bad dream," she whispers.

He looks up at her pretty, freckled face and sighs. "What time is it?" he asks.

"Five o'clock."

"I've only been dozing for fifteen minutes, but it seems like hours. I was on the train with Shunichi going to Lemon

Creek, but it kept getting mixed up with the time Haruo and I came east. It was awful."

Chiyo sits down beside him. "What made you dream about that?" she asks.

"The thunderstorm, I guess." Kaname looks out the window. The sky above the escarpment is aquamarine. The storm passed as quickly as it came. "Look how beautiful and calm it is out there now," he says.

The phone rings, interrupting the quiet.

Chiyo picks up the receiver and hands it to Kaname. "It's Shunichi."

"You're kidding," he says, reaching for the phone.

Half an hour later, Kaname hangs up and saunters into the kitchen where Chiyo is preparing dinner. He puts his arms around her trim waist. "We're going back to Chemainus again," he says cheerfully. Twirling her around, he asks: "Remember when we went back in '65?"

"And we waded through all those weeds, looking for your mother's grave to put flowers on," Chiyo replies.

"Yes, and when we couldn't find it, we just scattered the flowers around," Kaname says.

"I didn't think we'd ever go back after seeing those headstones in that pile outside the fence. It was disgusting, what they did."

"Well, the drunkards who did it are getting their comeuppance now."

"What do you mean?" Chiyo asks.

"Shunichi just told me that the Anglican minister in Chemainus is helping a Shinto-Buddhist group organize a memorial monument for the cemetery. They are going to secure those headstones to the monument so an earthquake can't budge them," Kaname explains.

Chiyo looks up. "That's the best news we've had since we won redress."

"And when we finally got the right to vote. Those were

important, but this means more to me than anything any politician ever gave us. Anyways, the minister will dedicate the monument in a special ceremony, and Shunichi hopes we'll be there."

Chiyo squeezes his hand. "When will it be?"

"Next August. I'm going to phone my sister and tell her the news. Maybe her and Michiharu will travel back with us."

As soon as Sunao hears her brother's voice, she suspects something is up. When Kaname tells her, she gasps.

"Are you sure? Kaname, if this is another one of your pranks, I'll . . ."

"Of course it's not," Kaname replies, laughing. "Would I tease you about something like this?"

Sunao pauses. "Well, no. I don't suppose you would."

"Shunichi was in Chemainus this summer and met the minister. They plan to dedicate the monument during next year's *O-bon* festival. You and Mich should come back with us. What do you think?" Kaname asks.

"Oh, yes," she replies. "I'm sure Mich will agree to go." Sunao hesitates. "Wouldn't Papa have been surprised?"

"I thought about that too. This would have made him so happy."

Sunao clears her throat. "Yes, well, I better go now. Talk to you soon."

After hanging up, she wanders about her apartment in a daze. The day she learned that the Japanese graves were desecrated she felt flattened, as if on the receiving end of a ten-pin bowling ball. This is a different kind of shock. Although it isn't devastating, it is no less stunning. The thought of her father missing this event stirs an uneasiness in her gut, made more vulnerable by her daughter's death in recent years. She recalls an old friend comforting her one day, saying, "The world is not evenly divided." Its meaning was not lost on tiny Sunao. Tragedy was a constant in her family, but she did everything in her power to rise above it and find the good in life.

Sunao and Kaname's father, Goshichi Izumi, was an adventurous eighteen-year-old when he emigrated to Canada in 1900. His older brother accompanied him from their village in Kumamoto on the island of Kyushu to the docks in Yokohama. When he boarded the cargo ship, Goshichi knew he would not see his brother again. Sad and a little afraid, he waved goodbye and ran to the bow of the ship to face the future alone.

Like most immigrants, he didn't know a word of English when he disembarked in Victoria. Luckily, the owners of the Osawa Hotel helped him get established. He found work as a houseboy and on farms around Victoria, gradually working his way up island to the Cowichan Valley. Getting accustomed to life in this foreign frontier was difficult, but he had a goal: to break free from the desperate cycle of poverty his family suffered in Japan.

When he learned that a woman he knew in Kumamoto had left her drunken husband in Canada and returned home, Goshichi sent for her to join him. He was about to start over in Genoa Bay, and he needed a wife. Towa was waiting for him at the Victoria docks a few months later. Leaving Japan again had not been easy, but at least she knew where she was going. Having been married once already, Towa knew she could not reject his proposal. It was highly unlikely there would be others.

It is a golden day in September 1913 when she arrives in Genoa Bay. The isolated sawmill town on the east coast of Vancouver Island is built on forested slopes that plunge into a deep harbour. Descending the trail to the shack where she will live with her new husband, twenty-eight-year-old Towa braces herself against the base of an ancient Douglas fir. A mere four feet nine inches, she has no delusions about this rugged land. Goshichi stops beside her.

"Are you all right?" he asks.

"Oh, yes. I just need a moment." She lifts her hem and yanks on a stray thread. Goshichi waits patiently, which confirms her earlier instincts. "Life here may be my undoing," she thinks, "but at least this man is kind."

Goshichi is unsuccessful securing a job at the sawmill, so he delivers firewood in a horse-drawn cart to the homes haphazardly scattered above the bay. The couple manage on the pennies he earns, but poverty is grinding down the resolve Goshichi cultivated across the Pacific. He shares his hopes and fears with Towa, gaining strength from her steady, plodding will to carry on.

In 1914, they bury their firstborn in the Duncan cemetery. Although Towa never speaks of her infant daughter again, she visits her grave during *O-bon* every August. Kaname is born in May 1916. A firstborn son does not enter the world without responsibilities. Named after the part of a fan that holds it together, Kaname signifies importance. Five more children follow him over the next eight years. In 1925, when Haruo is one, the sawmill in Genoa Bay shuts down.

The Izumis join the exodus from the area in 1926, moving north to the more prosperous town of Chemainus. Goshichi gets a job as an oiler at the sawmill. The pay is better, but not good enough to support his growing family in comfort. Kaname is ten and Sunao is six when they settle into one of the poorer homes in Okada camp. Over the next four years, Towa bears three more children. One, a baby boy, dies on March 13, 1928, three days after he is born. Towa and Goshichi bury Nobuyuki on a wet March afternoon and carry on as if his birth and death were an aberration, their grief mitigated by the absence of another mouth to feed.

As the oldest daughter, Sunao stays home from school to

help with household chores while her mother recuperates. She will be nine in three months and enjoys her brief holiday from school, never imagining that housework will all too soon become a way of life.

One of about twelve families in Okada camp, the Izumis live in primitive conditions and think little of it. Raw sewage floats in the bay where kids swim and fish among the booming grounds outside their door. Water from a nearby spring is their only means of refrigeration, so cold that jello sets in it.

The neighbourhood is spotted with small vegetable gardens and wells. The community bathhouse is kiddy-corner to a hard dirt playground, where the Izumi children mingle with the Okada, Otsu, Sakata and Shigetomi children. Among them, Kaname is possibly the wildest. A prankster extraordinaire, he often entices his two brothers, Mitsuo and Satoshi, to join in the fun.

Sometimes they are simple gestures that do little harm. Many times, they traipse to a farm on the outskirts of town to pick apples. If the cows are being milked, Kaname stands where the farmer can squirt it into his mouth directly from the cow's teat. His brothers double over with laughter as Kaname hams it up all the way to the apple orchard. Windfalls are all they can afford, so Kaname instructs his brothers to cover the good apples with a layer of bruised ones. When the farmer opens their sacks, he says, "Oh, windfalls, eh. That'll be twenty-five cents." And off they go.

Once he and his brothers get caught fishing out of season. The fishing inspector takes them to the police station in Ladysmith and gives them a lecture. Ironically, the time they are caught is the time they hadn't known they were doing anything wrong. Nervous of being thrown in jail, Kaname tries to think of an explanation his parents will accept. But after chastizing them, the inspector releases them to walk the fifteen miles home.

Another brush with the law has a funnier ending, at least for Kaname. He is with some *hakujin* boys stirring up trouble in Chinatown. A Chinese man calls the police to get the boys out of his yard, but when the police officer arrives, the boys lead him on a wild chase through backyard vegetable gardens. It is dark, but the boys know their way like rabbits in a warren. They are particularly careful to avoid the barrels of urine recessed into the ground, which the Chinese use as garden fertilizer. Hiding nearby, Kaname roars with laughter when he hears the cop swearing. He is pulling himself out of a barrel, dripping. The chase is over.

Then there is Hallowe'en. Moving outhouses and throwing dirt into the community bath are commonplace pranks that Kaname often instigates. But he can't resist the spontaneous urge to be more creative, like lifting a fence from a front yard and tying it onto the school flagpole. In the morning, someone's fence is hoisted up for all to see—the irate owner in the principal's office demanding the culprit be punished.

If Kaname isn't making trouble, he isn't happy. During cold winters, he and his friends climb the hill to Chinatown with buckets of water to throw down the path. Workers coming home from the mill find the only way up the icy hill is on their hands and knees—with the boys pelting snowballs at them from the bushes and the men swearing back in Chinese.

One summer Kaname watches his brother Satoshi plant a patch of watermelon. After he's gone, Kaname sifts through the earth, replacing the watermelon seeds with cucumber seeds. When the plants first sprout up, they look just like watermelon. Satoshi tends them every day, pleased with their progress. One day he comes home from school and the flowers are out.

"That's cucumbers," he says, eyeing Kaname.

"Are you *sure* you planted watermelon seeds in there?" Kaname asks.

"I'm darn sure I planted watermelon!" Satoshi quips, angrily.

"How come cucumbers are coming up then?" Kaname asks.

Satoshi grunts and slumps away. He suspects his brother is the culprit but has no proof. Grudgingly, he harvests a bumper crop of cucumbers over the summer.

Sunao, who isn't party to Kaname's pranks, idolizes him. Satoshi could fill her in if she'd listen, but she believes her oldest brother can do no wrong.

Kaname hates school with a passion. He spends a good deal of time in the corner, often as punishment for taking a bathroom break against the teacher's orders. He is ecstatic when he finally finishes grade eight and begins working. With a big grin, Kaname drops his wages into Towa's hands at the end of a day. He only earns ten cents an hour to weed fields on local farms, but every bit helps. Money aside, he never comes home empty-handed. The farmer tells him to help himself to whatever crop he is growing, and Kaname takes full advantage of the offer.

"How about your animals?" Kaname asks one day, keeping a straight face.

"No, no. I didn't mean animals. Vegetables or fruit—you're quite welcome," the farmer replies, shaking his head and chuckling.

Sometimes he splurges and dashes into Okada's store for gum and candy. Stuffing them into his pockets, he runs to the beach and jumps into a skiff that he rows to Kuper Island. Although the nuns at the residential school won't let him ashore, they have little power to stop his dinghy rocking near the beach. Seeing him approach, hordes of students dressed in dirty rags race to the shoreline. They scramble over each other, desperate for the candy he lobs at them from his skiff. Kaname feels sorry for these children from the local Cowichan tribes. Few families are more poor than

the Izumis, but at least they aren't wrenched from h
imprisoned in horrid schools.

His friends on the Westholme reserve take him spear fishing when the salmon spawn up Chemainus River. He can't see
the sockeye from the bank at all, but in no time his Indian
tillicum dangles a fish on his spear. Kaname rubs his belly,
knowing he will eat well tonight. Then there is the elder from
Westholme. Kaname sits with his Japanese and Indian friends
on the railroad tracks, listening to the old man tell stories. One
day he tells them that Chemainus is their word for a bag of
clams. The idea that they are living in "a bag of clams" sets
them off, and the little group on the tracks rocks back and
forth laughing.

The Sun-now'-netz people, who live on the beach nearby,
offer Kaname his first taste of the surreal. Whenever someone
dies, they dance, wail and beat drums around a fire until
dawn. Occasionally, he wakes in the night to the haunting
rhythm of the vigil echoing across the bay. He listens in the
dark, a little in awe of the colourful, crazed world around him.

Sunao finishes grade five the summer that Kaname goes to
work in the logging camp at Paldi. It is 1933, and the cut in
their father's wages has created more hardship. So when
Kaname gets a job as a faller, they celebrate. At seventeen, he is
beginning to live up to his name.

He knows nothing about falling huge Douglas firs, but he
soon learns. The only Canadian of Japanese descent among a
camp of Japanese immigrants, he is treated like a favourite son.
The men return from their gambling sprees in Duncan with
more chocolate bars than he can eat in a week. He doesn't go
home that first month, waiting for his paycheque and occupy-
ing himself on weekends by looking after the cook's little baby.

The last weekend in July, Kaname gets a ride out of camp
to Duncan. He boards a bus for Chemainus, his first real pay-

cheque hot in his hands. It isn't a lot of money, but it is more than he has ever earned. Proud of every penny, he is itching to turn it over to his mother. He has been a bit homesick too, and thinks of his brothers and sisters as the bus chugs along the winding, bumpy road. Almost more than anything else, he looks forward to a game of baseball. He shakes his head, wondering how he'll survive a summer without baseball.

The bus lets Kaname off at the Horseshoe Bay Inn, and he runs down the hill to the cluster of homes along the shore. He is hot and thirsty when he finally strides up the back steps into the kitchen. Towa is stirring the laundry over the stove with a big stick, her forehead dripping. Kaname's youngest sister Toyo is climbing over the rough kitchen benches and squeals when she sees him. He tweaks her cheek and tickles her belly, then walks over to Towa.

"It's good to see you, Kaname," she says. "We missed you."

"I was homesick, Mama, but it was worth it," he replies, grinning as he holds up the cheque. Drying her hands on her hips, Towa takes it from him gingerly and bursts into tears.

Less than a month later, she is dead.

Kaname is lying in his bunk at the end of his shift one August afternoon, feeling disgruntled about missing the baseball season. He is watching shadows from the forest play on the ceiling when several co-workers file into the bunkhouse. Kaname knows they were at someone's funeral earlier and thinks it odd when they suddenly stop talking. Then he overhears a whisper: "We ought to tell him. We really should." Looking up, he sees Mr. Kawabata shuffling over.

"Your mother got sick at Mrs. Nagano's funeral this afternoon. She might be in the hospital in Duncan, so you better go and see her."

"What happened?" he asks.

"It's best if you go now. Plenty of time to get to Duncan before dark."

Kaname frowns and jumps off his bunk. After throwing a few things in an overnight bag, he hitches a ride on the road. He arrives at the hospital to find his father sitting by his mother's bed.

"What happened, Papa?" Kaname asks.

"Your mother fainted at Mrs. Nagano's funeral, so we brought her here," Goshichi replies. "She is breathing, but she won't open her eyes or talk to me."

"Did you talk to the doctor?"

"Yes, but I don't understand him."

Kaname nods and puts a hand on Goshichi's shoulder. "I'll be right back."

Kaname finds a nurse and learns that his mother has had a stroke and is in a coma. He returns to her room.

"It's not good, Papa. Mama had a stroke."

Goshichi looks up at his son. His eyes are clouded. He shakes his head and stares at Towa again.

Kaname observes her left leg moving a little and looks at her passive face. He has never thought of his mother as a beauty. Taken individually, her features are strong, but her forehead is too short and her eyes too narrow for her broad cheeks and full lips. None of that ever mattered. A kind, loving woman, she gave all for her family. At forty-eight, she is spent.

Nothing is changed when Kaname joins his father beside Towa's bed the next morning. The doctor enters and confirms their fears. "I don't know when she will die, but there is no hope," he says.

Goshichi nods, forcing a smile. Kaname begins to translate, but his father puts a finger to his lips. He already knows. Suggesting they leave the hot, stifling room for a while,

Kaname leads his father into the shade on the back steps of the hospital.

"It's just a matter of time, Papa," he says, sitting down beside him.

Goshichi stares ahead. A widower at fifty-one with a family of eight, he must take the tragedy in stride. But there is a frailty about him that concerns Kaname. He seems hollow, like an empty clamshell rattling in a rock crevice, vulnerable to the next rising tide.

His wife has already begun her journey into the spirit world when they return to her room. Kaname wants to cry, but no tears come. He thinks perhaps they will come later, when the world takes shape again and feeling returns.

The family holds a vigil in their living room that night. Towa lies in the open coffin that local carpenters hammered together earlier. Sunao sits in a corner, watching people come and go all night long, their shadowy forms tinged by candle-light as they drift through blue incense smoke. The candles light the way for Towa's journey through the afterworld. Over the next forty-eight days, the Izumis will light many more to guide her soul toward its destination.

A Shinto-Buddhist priest from Vancouver conducts the funeral in the Chemainus cemetery the following afternoon. Stone-faced, Goshichi places a simple wooden marker next to the grave of his three-day-old son.

Towa's death does nothing to ease the family's financial burden; it just adds grief to the mix. Although loathe to leave, Kaname boards a bus for Paldi. Goshichi returns to his job at the sawmill, rising at five o'clock every morning to grease the machinery before the early shift begins. His fifteen- and sixteen-year-old sons take farming jobs and whatever else they can find. Now thirteen, Sunao slips into Towa's shoes, mothering, cooking and cleaning for the entire family. Her four younger siblings range in age from ten to two. Every morning she faces an endless pile of dirty work clothes and diapers. Although she isn't especially fond of school, she never imagined she'd have to quit for this. No amount of tears changes a thing. Adolescence bypasses Sunao.

The first year is the worst. By the time she turns fourteen, turmoil is beaten out of her. The transition to adulthood took its toll, but now she accepts the unrelenting pace and labours under the yoke of domesticity like other women in the neighbourhood.

Several times a day, she crosses a trestle near the mill's train tracks to get water for laundry. Unaware that her future husband has his eyes on her, she struggles with the buckets, water sloshing over the edge as she trundles along the tracks.

Kaname continues working as a faller through the autumn and winter months. But one day in early spring he slips and cuts his knee badly. He waits for the logging train to take him out of the bush on its late afternoon run to the sawmill. By the time he gets to the hospital he has lost a good deal of blood. His friend Hitoshi Okada comes to visit after he gets stitched up.

"Don't go back to Paldi," Hitoshi says. "Come and work with us on the boom."

"It's a deal," Kaname says, beaming. "That's the best news I've had in years."

"Well, we know what your family is going through. They need you around," Hitoshi says. "I remember how awful it was after my Mama died, and Papa does too. Work on the boom has slowed down, but we could still use an extra hand. Besides, we need you on the ball team this summer."

"Watch out, then," Kaname shouts. "I'm going to play ball like you've never seen," he adds, grinning.

Hitoshi laughs. "Chemainus just isn't the same without you around, Kaname. Nobody knows how to make trouble like you."

As soon as his knee heals, Kaname is on the boom, learning

his job from one of Hitoshi's older half-brothers. Osamu is tough and fearless, but Kaname has no trouble measuring up. Working the boom without a life jacket forces a certain respect for the unpredictable sea, but his body reacts instinctively to the slippery rolling logs under his feet.

"Gee, Kaname, you're not bad for a beginner," Osamu says.

"Must have been all those times I ran the boom to fish under the train trestle when I was a kid. But, have you ever worked in the bush?" Kaname asks.

Osamu pulls his tobacco and rolling papers out of his shirt pocket. "You know, I never have. Here, want one of these?"

Kaname isn't a smoker, but after a few days on the job he figures he may as well join in. It is a choice between standing around and smoking or working while the others goof off. "Sure, thanks," he says, piling tobacco onto the paper.

"Well, falling big timbers isn't easy. In fact, it's downright dangerous. But you know there's something to be said for having both feet on the ground while the earth shakes around you," Kaname says.

"This is the only work I've ever done, so I wouldn't know," Osamu replies, looking out to sea. "We'd better get back to work, buddy. Clouds moving in."

Kaname looks up. An angry black mass is rolling high up in the sky. "Right," he says, grabbing his peavey pole. "Let's get going."

An hour later, Kaname looks at the bank of trees on the hill behind his house. Huge limbs are thrashing about wildly and two trees crash to the ground. The boom is rolling in the swells underfoot. He should have packed it in already and looks up to see Osamu waving him in from the wharf. Falling in now would be just as precarious as riding the boom in the dark, when a cable pulls it towards the mill before shutting down. He'd never be found alive if he falls. Osamu paces as Kaname scurries back to the wharf, unharmed.

Kaname isn't fearless, but he likes the job and the camaraderie of being one of the boys on the boom. Before long, his brothers Satoshi and Mitsuo are working on it too. Sometimes they get mischievous, forcing too many logs onto the cog that feeds them into the mill, causing the chain to break. One of the millwrights has to come and weld a new one on, so they take a smoke break and swap tall tales. Osamu gets fed up letting his partner bum his tobacco. Finally, Kaname starts buying his own.

On her trek to fetch water, Sunao trips along the mill's train tracks above the shore. She often sees her brothers huddling out in the bay, clouds of smoke mingling with the damp, grey mist that hangs in the air. Despite the penetrating chill, she wishes she were a boy.

After hauling her buckets back home, she sets a big tub on the pot-bellied stove and pours the water in. She punches down the dirty work clothes with a big wooden stick and carves shavings of Sunlight bar soap into the mix. After boiling it awhile, she scrubs it on a scrub board until her fingers are raw. Her childish hands are not big or strong enough to wring the water from heavy work clothes and bed sheets. Kaname does it willingly when he comes home from work and often helps prepare supper too.

One night he boils some burdock root and everything in the pot turns black. He finds Sunao changing Toyo's diaper in the next room.

"I've ruined dinner, Sunao."

"How?"

"You'd better come see."

Toyo follows her big sister into the kitchen, and Kaname picks her up. Sunao lifts the lid on the pot.

"Oh, Kaname, you have to soak burdock, but don't worry. It just looks bad. It'll taste okay."

Soon everyone sits down to dinner, facing bowls of black

vegetables. Goshichi digs in and says, "Oh, this is good, Kaname. You're a good cook."

He winces. "You never complain, Papa."

After supper Kaname daydreams about the Thanksgiving turkey dinners he once enjoyed at Shige Yoshida's home. He remembers the trek along the road past the cemetery, down to Mr. Howe's farm on the outskirts of town where Shige's family lived. Satoshi, Mitsuo, Kaname and Sunao ran through piles of autumn leaves en route, the pungent smell of burning leaves filtering through the crisp, cold air. As they approached the Yoshidas, the smell of roast turkey sharpened the ache in their bellies.

Turkey was a short-lived, almost unimaginable luxury, but the sea offers an ongoing supply of fish and clams. Sunao especially likes going digging for clams in the winter, when their flavour is enhanced by the cold. At low tide on moonlit nights, the Izumis join other Japanese and Indian families in the bay. Their shadows lengthen over the bubbles in the mud as they set down coal oil lamps and buckets and dig in. Pockets of half-bent bodies are silhouetted against the silver sand, while the squishy sound of mud sucking boots echoes across the bay.

Time passes and the family gradually overcomes its grief, settling into routines that include as much recreation as they can squeeze between the long hours of work. Kaname and his brothers play baseball and fish in the summer. Everyone goes swimming and on picnics to Bare Point, where the world floats before them like a saucer of slippery mercury. Sunao takes up tennis with friends at the rough courts the Halheds let them use at the back of the bay.

Sunao still does most heavy household chores, but her sister Misao is old enough to take care of the children now. So when Michiharu comes calling, Sunao drops everything. Nothing beats riding in the back of Takayoshi Kawahara's pickup truck on Saturday nights. She cuddles up close to Michiharu as they laugh down the road, believing this strong, warm body next to hers is nothing short of heaven-sent.

Oddly enough, Sunao's mother was the first person Michiharu met when he came to Chemainus, earlier the same year she died. He was a timid seventeen-year-old away from his isolated home in Tofino. Towa, holding her youngest child on her hip, introduced herself. "Welcome to Chimunesu. I'm Towa Izumi and this is Toyo."

"I'm Michiharu. I work in the mill with my brother-in-law."

"Have you come a long way?" Towa asked.

"I'm from Tofino, on the west coast of the island. It is wild there."

"Is that so? Well, I hope you will like it here."

Overcome with her warm welcome, Michiharu confessed, "You are such a nice mother—and the first stranger to speak to me."

Towa studied his face. "My oldest daughter is Sunao. Please, look after her for me."

Surprised, Michiharu stuttered some reply, and they went their separate ways. She could not have known that he would marry Sunao eventually, thousands of miles from Chemainus and their shacks on the shore. But she saw that he was kind, which was all that mattered.

Many years before Sunao marries Michiharu, Chiyoko Hashimoto marries into the Izumi family. She knows Sunao better than Kaname from the year her family lived at the back end of Chinatown, next to Hong Hing's pig pen. Chiyo and Sunao were friends in grade one that year, but she lived most of her childhood in Steveston, Victoria and Duncan.

When she is thirteen, her parents send her to Americamura in Japan to be with her grandmother for awhile. Her grandmother intends to teach her about life and marriage.

"You must marry before you are twenty-one, or you will be an old maid for the rest of your life," she says.

"I don't believe you, *Baa-san*," Chiyo replies. "I'll get married when I want to."

"Listen. Do as I say or you will be sorry."

She impresses this old-fashioned superstition on her pretty granddaughter with such fervour that Chiyo decides she will not marry until she is twenty-one. With equal fervour, she is also determined not to marry the oldest son in a big family. But like most young women of her generation, she will learn that the decision is out of her hands.

Five years later, Chiyo is back in Duncan when the go-betweens, the Okadas and Shiozakis, introduce her to Kaname. A vivacious eighteen-year-old with a mind of her own, she has no advance warning.

"This is the man that you are supposed to marry," says Chiyo's mother.

"Oh," she replies, stunned.

"He's a nice fellow. He's going to look after you."

"Really?" Chiyo asks, full of doubt. The tall, slender man frightens her, but she turns to him and smiles weakly. "Hello," she says.

"Hello," Kaname replies, shuffling his feet.

After they are engaged, they still don't know what to say to each other. Chiyo has never heard his easy laughter or notorious jokes. He is too uptight to reveal his marvelous wit and warm sense of humour. Like most men of his generation, Kaname grew up with stringent, implausible expectations of women. Suddenly he realizes how little he understands the opposite sex. The prospect of marriage is every bit as daunting to him as it is to Chiyo.

One day, Chiyo says to her mother, "I know I'm going to

have to marry him, but he's such a scary person to live with all through my life. And he's got so many brothers and sisters. I always used to tell myself never to marry the eldest son."

"The eldest son in a big family is the best person to marry, because he will be very understanding and kind," Koto replies.

"Oh, what's the point, Mama? You know it can be dreadful, marrying the eldest. Why don't you tell the truth?"

Koto throws her daughter a look. Chiyo sighs and goes to her room. She will do as she is told.

On November 9, 1940, Chiyo marries a man she is afraid of in a gold-trimmed pastel orange kimono she doesn't want to wear, nowhere near the charming white United Church of her dreams. Instead, Bishop Aoki performs the Shinto-Buddhist ritual in the Izumi household on a clear day. Outside the living room window, steam rises off the booming grounds as cold air meets salt water warmed by the Japanese current. She is nineteen; her groom is almost as naïve at twenty-four.

After the reception, Chiyo and Kaname drive to Nanaimo to spend the night, hoping to catch a boat to Vancouver the next day. But they can't find anywhere to stay and drive back to Chemainus in silence. They are within walking distance of home when they book into the Horseshoe Bay Inn. With lukewarm enthusiasm, they decide to make Victoria their destination in the morning.

The newlyweds wake to falling snow. Lying in bed, they watch the flakes drift soundlessly past the hotel room window. About four inches cover the ground when they board a bus to Victoria a short hour later. Travelling south, Chiyo admires the evergreen forest through the flurry. Branches laden with wet snow arch toward earth, and soft drifts nestle into amber crooks of Arbutus branches. She sighs. The cool caress of silk against flesh comes to mind as snow blankets the woods.

The honeymoon is fun, if short-lived. They go sight-seeing

in Victoria, and discover the Takata Gardens on the Gorge waterway. An amusement park with a Japanese tea garden, it isn't as popular as it was when Chiyo was a child. They stroll through the Japanese garden, stopping to admire exotic fish and ducks in the pond. Gazing at a gentle waterfall upstream, she surrenders herself to the future.

But after moving into the Izumi household, Chiyo is miserable again. She spends her first three days going door-to-door with Osamu Okada's wife to introduce herself to the women in the community. At each household, Chiyo makes a formal request for co-operation, followed by a good deal of bowing. At the end of each day she cries, for she is neither Chiyo Hashimoto nor Chiyo Izumi. She is Kaname's wife. Right now, she would rather be an old maid.

Winter and spring pass. Chiyo is settling into her new identity and home, while Kaname is getting accustomed to his role as husband. The summer after their wedding, they take a bold step together. On July 1, 1941, the couple goes to a sawmill-sponsored dance in the company hall. Canadian dancing is strictly against the wishes of the *issei*, who consider the close body contact in public immoral. Fed up with these old-fashioned ideas, Chiyo and Kaname decide to go anyway. They are the only couple of Japanese descent in the place.

A live band is playing "In the Mood" when they walk into the dance hall. Some *hakujin* people jeer at them, but Chiyo notices welcoming smiles from others. After all, it is the first of July, a time for community spirit and celebration. Kaname leads Chiyo to a table at the back, where they scan the crowd for familiar faces. Tapping their toes, they wait for a second wave of courage to pluck them from their seats and push them onto the dance floor. It finally comes when the band plays "Blueberry Hill," one of their favourite songs. Some hours later, they stroll home hand-in-hand, every dance spent.

During the following weeks, *issei* talk about their immoral behaviour and peers are reluctant to speak up on their behalf. Kaname responds by organizing a dance with his friends. The *issei* reluctantly agree to allow it, providing they close down precisely at midnight and don't smoke or serve liquor. The night of the dance, several *issei* peer through the windows. Whether out of curiosity or hoping to nail them with transgressions, Kaname never knows. He and Chiyo kick up their heels along with scores of friends. The Chemainus Japanese community is finally coming of age in Canada.

Five months later, Kaname attends a wedding that sears his memory for the event that it precedes. On December 6, 1941, one of the community's judo experts marries the barber's daughter in a simple ceremony in the groom's home. Mitsuyuki Sakata takes Masaye Nishimura as his wife the day before an era closes.

The morning after the wedding, Kaname and Chiyo are finishing their breakfast when Noboru Yoshida bursts into their home.

"Did you hear?" he asks. "Japan bombed Pearl Harbor this morning."

Kaname doesn't believe his friend. There has been a lot of talk in the commmunity lately, but he is skeptical of claims that Japan is winning the war in Asia. He has had arguments with some *issei*, but his own father is quiet. A peace-loving man, Goshichi doesn't want any part in war or talk of it.

Kaname switches on the radio. Listening to the news, he draws a deep breath. Something akin to an icy fist lodges itself in the pit of his stomach.

Within the month, Kaname and several friends receive conscription notices. Although they don't have the right to vote, they are willing to fight for their country. After passing their physicals, they go to the recruiting office in Victoria.

"Who sent you here?" the recruiting officer asks disdainfully.

"What do you mean?" Kaname snaps back. "Here are our notices."

"Sorry, boys. We don't need you now," the officer replies curtly.

Kaname wants to punch his pug face, but turns abruptly and storms out with his friends. Enraged and humiliated, they return to Chemainus on the same train that will take their fathers to road camps in two months.

No one celebrates the arrival of the New Year in 1942. January 1 has always been a day of open houses and much drinking of sake. When he was little, Kaname tingled with excitement as the big day approached, dreaming of all the special treats women were preparing. His family could not afford special treats at any time of year, but the community was generous to everyone, and those less fortunate took full advantage of an opportunity to eat until they were full.

On January 1, 1942, Kaname goes for a walk to Bare Point, leaving Chiyo and Sunao to brood at home. It is a New Year's to remember for its leaden silence. In other years, Okada camp was a flurry of people going to and from houses, stopping often to exchange hearty wishes. But Kaname has no sense of renewal today. Standing at the edge of Bare Point, he studies the horizon. Space melts: grey sea with grey sky, then, nothing.

The day the RCMP come for Goshichi, Sunao is sitting in the living room. She can just make out the shape of her brother's deft movements as he works the boom in the bone-chilling damp. She is thinking how calm the sea is when she hears the knock. Everyone in the family has known it might come any day, but she has persistently refused to acknowledge it. Losing her father revives all the hurt of Towa's passing nine years before. Waving goodbye, she aches for protection from harm. The sense of security she seeks is universal. Unwittingly perhaps, the *hakujin* community is shoring up its needs at her expense.

As Goshichi leaves, Chiyo urges him to take care of himself in the road camp.

"Don't do too many hard jobs, because you are getting old, Papa," she says.

"I'm not old," Goshichi retorts, insulted. A few weeks later, he turns sixty in one of the Rocky Mountain road camps.

Months later, the rest of the family is settled in Lemon Creek. Kaname learns his father is on a bus to New Denver. When he finds him, Kaname sees a man ten years older than he was some eight months earlier. Goshichi lost little in material goods when the RCMP led him away, for he had little to lose. But his pride diminished with his stamina until he rattled inside, a distant shadow of the teenager who fled Kumamoto bursting with dreams of wealth and adventure in a faraway land.

When the Izumis leave Chemainus on April 21, 1942, they walk out of their home as if they will be back later that day. Everything is intact. Dishes and bags of rice remain inside cupboards. The homemade hemlock table is ready for setting. Clothes hang in closets, along with boxes of photographs. A *butsudana* sits on Sunao's bedside table. It was her mother's small but elaborate Buddhist shrine, with which she had worshipped her ancestors when she was alive. Sunao could not fit it in the suitcase. She tiptoed toward the closet and stopped, holding it to her chest as she glanced around the room.

"Don't hide it," she whispered. "Leave it to protect our home from harm while we're away."

Muttering a quick prayer, she set it on the beside table and left. She never saw it again.

Decades later, Kaname searches for his roots in Japan. A relative of Chiyo's drives them up mountainous, winding roads near Kumamoto. After making a few inquiries, he learns a cousin is living nearby. Akino Sakai has never met them and does not know to expect them.

She is bent over her terraced fields when they arrive.

"Hello, cousin," Kaname begins. "I am Goshichi's son, from Canada, and this is my wife Chiyo."

The woman looks up and bursts into tears. "You must be Chiyoko, the beautiful bride in the picture. I'll never forget that picture. Oh, you haven't changed at all," she says, hugging them both. "You must come in. I never make pastry, but this morning something told me I was going to have visitors," she mutters, dabbing her eyes with a handkerchief.

They follow her into her humble home and sit on cushions on the floor. Soon the conversation turns to the past. They learn that Akino-san was pregnant when her husband was conscripted into the Japanese navy. He never returned, leaving her to raise their only son.

Before they leave, Kaname asks if there are any family graves nearby.

"Oh, yes. Come with me," Akino replies. She pulls up some flowers in her backyard and traipses through a neighbouring field. Kaname and Chiyo follow, not exactly dressed for trekking through the bush. Kaname is brushing aside a cobweb just as they reach a little cemetery.

Akino takes them to the Izumi section and lays the flowers down. Kaname tries to read the names, scraping off a plush layer of moss from the headstones. He runs his fingers over the calligraphy. There, basking in the sun on a mountainside, are the graves of his grandparents, uncles, and aunts.

The next day, they switch trains four times to visit Akino's brother in the north. Now in his eighties, Kaname's cousin is very feeble, but his wife is thrilled to meet them.

"We heard about you during the war, you know," she begins. "Everyone said all these families were coming back. We thought you would too, so we kept some of our rice rations aside."

"But you needed that rice yourselves," Kaname exclaims, feeling flushed.

"It was just a little every day. We sent you a letter, but fifty days later it came back. We thought, 'Oh, they must be all killed in the war.' We kind of gave up."

Kaname takes a deep breath and mumbles, "We never realized you would be worried about us." Wiping his eyes briskly, he exchanges glances with Chiyo. How could he have possibly anticipated his Japanese relatives would care?

On the island of Shikoku a few weeks later, Kaname's old booming ground mate hears he is around. Osamu Okada, one of the unfortunates to be repatriated after the war, searches every hotel in the city. In his shirt pocket, he carries an old picture of Kaname, leaning on his peavey pole, smoking a soggy cigarette and grinning. Osamu is about to give up when he finds them. He is so happy all he can do is cry.

S I X

MATAHARU OTSU

MUTT OTSU WATCHES THE AFTERNOON SUN filter through the sheer curtains in his Toronto living room. A slight breeze flutters across the sheers, rippling the lace border. Mopping his brow, he longs for the temperate saltwater breezes of his youth.

The dappled light on the walls is dancing in waves before his eyes. Combined with the stifling heat, the movement coaxes him to drift off. He dreams of his three sisters in Japan, whom he has never met. In his dream, Mutt is looking for them on the beach at Okada camp where he grew up. He does not know what they look like, so he calls their names as he strolls along the shore by the booming grounds.

"Shizue, are you here? Yoshiko, Mitsuko, where are you? I am your brother. Please come to me. We must talk."

He calls their names over and over. No one else walks the beach. It must be Sunday, the only day in the week when the mill is not running. Still, it is unusual that no one is around. Glancing up the embankment toward the train tracks, he sees human bones and the tops of skulls protruding from an Indian midden. Mutt picks up his pace.

It is urgent that he find his sisters. He needs to explain why his mother never sent for them. They must not blame Tsune for abandoning them. It was not her fault, just her fate. Despite the fact that her parents owned an orchard in Japan and were quite wealthy, Tsune left the Tokyo suburb of Hakone with her husband in 1914 and crossed the Pacific in search of a better life. But working conditions and wages in Canada shattered Shinjiro's dreams of returning to his family a wealthy man. In Genoa Bay, three more children were born while Tsune clung to the memory of her daughters in Hakone. She wrote home often, promising to send for them as soon as she could. But stomach cancer killed Shinjiro in 1923, the same year that her family was displaced during an earthquake in Tokyo. Destitute and pregnant again, Tsune lost track of her daughters in Japan. A canyon of unimaginable proportions cut her off from them and the wealth she had known in her youth.

Tsune never spoke of Shizue, Yoshiko, and Mitsuko, harbouring her pain silently for over thirty years. After the war, she relocated them and wrote many times before receiving an angry reply. She had disgraced them.

When Mutt finally learns he has sisters in Japan, he is stunned. With the help of his wife's friend in Japan, he tracks them down. Now that Tsune is gone, it seems even more critical to coax forgiveness from the silence, for children abandoned by their parents suffered in Japan.

But they are not here; no one is. The deserted beach stretches before him. The sea is flat calm, lifeless but for a gull that screeches across the harbour, plopping excrement. Mutt shivers and turns to go, but his house isn't there. All the neighbours' shacks are gone too, along with the Okada's store and the public bath. Terrified, Mutt scans the embankment for something, anything, to redeem his past. A wavering mirage halts along the railway tracks: tiny, shy Sunao is carrying her buckets to the well. Mutt calls her name, and she pivots in slow motion, gazing at him mournfully. He runs toward her, shouting, "Let me help you get water, Sunao. You shouldn't work so hard." But his feet feel like lead. It takes forever to reach the railway tracks. When he does, she shimmers into oblivion.

Mutt opens his eyes. His wife Mikiko is standing above him with a tall glass of water.

"You were dreaming. I heard you calling your sisters."

He props himself up on an elbow and reaches for the glass. "Yes," he says, taking a drink. "It was the strangest dream, Miki. At the same time that everything was so familiar it was like I was on another planet." He lifts the glass to his lips and stares across the room.

"You've been thinking too much about your sisters ever since Shizue declined to meet you," Miki says.

"Yes, it hurts. In a way, I understand why they don't want to stir up the past. They are old now, but I can't shake this feeling that a chunk of me is missing." Mutt pauses. "Maybe it's the idea of going back to Chemainus next summer, too. I want to see all my old friends, but there are so many ghosts in B.C."

"What ghosts?" she asks.

"The same ones that you left behind, dear. The very same ones."

Mataharu Otsu was born in Genoa Bay on September 19, 1920, Tsune and Shinjiro's firstborn Canadian child. He is three when his father falls ill and loses his job at the mill. He dies shortly before Yasuyo is born, without leaving so much as a simple memory for his oldest son, let alone the other children.

Tsune decides to pack up and move to Chemainus, where there is a larger Japanese community, where there are no memories of Shinjiro or his pain. They move into Okada camp, next to the Izumis, who are every bit as poor. Tsune goes into debt putting food on the table. Once Mutt sees his mother crawl on her hands and knees, begging for a bag of rice from the Okadas. She has accumulated close to a $100 debt, an astronomical amount of money no average working person could hope to repay. She also orders food from the travelling Vancouver merchants who work the island communities, until that debt outgrows their trust too. Tsune does what she can to bring in a few extra pennies, laundering work clothes for bachelors and making tofu. Every Saturday, Mutt and his brothers take turns pulling a wagon stacked with a pan of the slippery white bean cakes. They traipse over to Kawahara camp, where they sell it for five cents per square. Tsune gives these pennies to a neighbour who places orders for her when the merchants come around.

After several difficult months, Tsune remarries. It is not an arrangement that frees her from poverty or from shame, but the Otsu children are lucky. Tairyu Fujimoto loves them as if they are his own.

Mutt doesn't go to school until he is nine because of severe eczema, which school officials fear is contagious. For years, Mutt and Tairyu share a bedtime ritual. Tairyu winds strips of a torn bedsheet around his stepson's arms and legs to stop him from scratching the sores. The young boy co-operates, enjoying the gentle strength of his stepfather's hands. But when Mutt wakes in the morning, the sheet often sticks where his scratching has broken the skin and drawn blood.

Mutt observes a morning ritual as well. Wrapping himself in a blanket on the veranda, he watches his younger brothers join friends on their way to school. He feels sorry for himself and daydreams the hours away. Sometimes he schemes how to get his brothers in trouble, often provoking them into fights at night when they are all in bed together. His brother Yoshiharu is a calm, mild-mannered soul, but Mits is different—easily riled and often wrangling for a fight himself.

Mits is short for Mitsuharu, and about the same time he inherits that nickname from the neighbourhood boys, the name Mutt sticks to Mataharu. Their brother Yoshiharu and little sister Yasuyo have already taken English nicknames to help them assimilate into mainstream culture, but Mutt and Mits have to find other ways to forge a link with the dominant culture.

Somehow Tairyu's meagre salary is never enough to stretch through the month, due in part to merchants trying to collect old debts from Tsune. His job requires him to stand for long hours at a time, preventing waste lumber from piling up too high on the conveyor belt going to the burner. Mesmerized by the repetition, he knows no escape from this jumble of waste ends rolling through his life. To compensate, Tairyu expects his slippers at the door when he arrives home. Sometimes only one is there, so he kicks it into the kitchen where Tsune is cooking. Expressionless, she fetches the other slipper and goes back to work.

Sunday picnics at Bare Point break the monotony. The family lives for summer days at the point, a forty-five-minute hike away. Wanting an early start, Tsune is the first to drop her feet to the floor. But unlike most days when she pushes her weary bones into action, she steps lightly into the kitchen to prepare their picnic lunch.

The Otsus are the first to arrive and the last to leave. Tairyu carries the daughter Tsune has given him, as well as the picnic hamper. Once there, he spreads a blanket on the golden grass and lies on his back with little Akiko at his side. He points to the *kami*, or nature spirits, in the billowy clouds flying overhead, and whispers their Japanese names in her ear. They watch lions and elephants transform into emperors and lords high in the sky, content and warm in the summer sun.

The other children trail along with their mother. Struggling with a cardboard box en route, Mutt is impatient. "Come on, you guys," he yells at his brothers. "Beat you to the Point."

He races his brothers to the bluff and jumps on the flattened box. "Yippee!" he hollers, flying over grass that is like polished hay. Soon a horde of young boys join them. Before noon, dozens dot the hillside as they scream towards the sea on cardboard toboggans.

Tsune sits on the picnic blanket in a rare state of uninterrupted calm. Gazing along Stuart Channel, she puffs on her homemade cigarettes, reaching absently for a rice ball or pickle every now and then. Peace invades her body, and she surrenders herself with grace. She daydreams about her daughters in Japan, flinging silent blessings into the play of shadow and light combing the grass. *Kami* breezes caress her brow. As the day progresses, the auburn glow of Arbutus branches reaches deeper into the royal blue water. She tucks the silken dignified beauty into her mind's eye, sustenance for the undignified week ahead.

The horizon was shimmering like silver when they arrived, but now afternoon is sliding below the bluff. The setting sun washes the sky in translucent lilac, and they trudge home, weary in the best possible way.

Tsune sweeps the fir floor, stooping to pick out dirt between the boards with a hairpin. Her daily routine is a litany of such chores. No matter that they live in a two-room shack. No one can say it isn't clean: immaculate is more to the point.

It is September 1929, and Mutt is getting ready for his first day of school. He buttons his shirt as he strolls to the outhouse over the creek, which they share with neighbours. His eczema is getting better, but Mutt is preoccupied. He has waited so long to join his brothers and friends at school. Now that the time has come, he is nervous and insecure.

The outhouse door swings shut behind him as he walks up the back stairs into the kitchen. Tsune is setting steaming bowls of rice on the table as he climbs onto the wooden bench.

"Mama, I'm not very hungry," he says, eyeing the rice.

"You, not hungry? What's the matter?" Tsune asks.

"I don't want to go to school."

"What? You've been moaning about not being able to go since you were six."

"But I'm going to be three years older than everyone in my class. Mits is only seven, and he's already a grade higher than me. Everybody's going to make fun of me," Mutt says, pouting.

Mits walks in, chanting, "Old sickie, old sickie. . . ."

"Hush! Don't talk that way," Tsune says, glaring at Mits.

Mutt is close to tears, and Mits gives him a shove as he sits down beside him. "You rat! I hate you, I hate you," Mutt screams.

"Stop it, both of you. Mits, go see what Yasuyo wants. I can hear her calling," Tsune orders.

Scraping bits of butter and sugar onto several slices of white bread, she turns to Mutt. "You know better English than your brothers did when they started school. You'll be the smart one in your class."

Mutt watches her make their lunch. "If I don't like it, can I come home, Mama?"

"Don't worry. Just obey your teacher. You will be okay."

Doubtful, he picks up his bowl of rice and begins eating. His brothers join them while Tsune packs their sugar sandwiches. They can't afford baloney or other fancy fixings, so she substitutes sugar. None of the Japanese Canadian children eat Japanese food at school, knowing they will be ridiculed. But bread costs more than rice, so Tsune often packs them lunches to eat at the Japanese community hall. On the first day, however, they will have sandwiches to eat next to their *hakujin* classmates.

As the boys push out the door, Tsune waves each one good-bye. "Remember, do as you are told," she calls out. They run ahead, barely paying attention. Mutt is the only one to turn and wave, feeling a weird mix of excitement and dread.

It takes them almost an hour to reach the other side of Kawahara camp. They play tag through the mill site and out onto the streets, where they join boys and girls from Kawahara camp ambling toward the school playing field. Mutt is having too much fun to worry by the time the bell finally rings. His years as a student begin in earnest. As Tsune predicted, he does just fine.

Later that fall, Tairyu falls ill and can't work. Food grows more scarce in the Otsu kitchen again. Tsune sends Mutt to catch fish, and she harvests vegetables from the garden. But she grows anxious again, wondering how they will manage if Tairyu doesn't get better. The pain is so bad he has to go to the hospital, where the doctor explains he is dying of stomach cancer. At least mill employees do not face hefty medical bills for hospital treatment. It is one of few ways in which the mill takes care of its workers, regardless of race.

Tairyu sends for his lifelong friend, Iwajiro Imagama, who is living in one of the Chemainus bachelor camps.

"I am dying, Iwajiro," he begins.

"Yes, I know. Can I help?"

"There is one thing, a very big favour," Tairyu whispers, fidgeting with the edge of the sheet. "Tsune cannot manage on her own. She is a good woman, but she needs a man to help raise the children. Will you promise to look after them when I am gone?"

Iwajiro meets Tairyu's gaze. "Yes, I will do as you ask. I do not have your patience with children, but I will do what I can."

"Thank you, Iwajiro. Before you know it, the boys will be old enough to look after their mother themselves."

"I suppose. Well, I should go. You are weary."

After Iwajiro is gone, Tairyu sinks further under the bed-covers. Having taken care of his family, he waits for death to free him from pain.

An hour later, Mutt and his brothers arrive for lunch. Tairyu cannot eat what the nurse brings, so the boys divvy it up among themselves. His bed is in a small cottage built for tuberculosis patients, although none convalesce there now. Screen windows allow fresh air and sunshine to circulate, and tangy, saltwater breezes temper the sour smell of sickness.

Mutt hates to see his stepfather so sick, but he eats his share of the lunch while Tairyu tosses about, moaning. Perched on the edge of his bed, they tear into sandwiches with meat and gulp down mouthfuls of soup.

"Do you think he knows we are here?" Mits asks when they are done.

"Shh. Maybe, maybe not," Mutt whispers. "Let's go."

They tiptoe outside. "Race you back to school," Mits says. "We've still got half an hour to play."

They run with full bellies, masking their sadness for a while. They do not speak of Tairyu's sickness, or of his death when it comes, but each boy grieves. He was a good father for four years, and they miss his loving, if sometimes stern, ways.

Mutt is nine and Tsune is forty-six when twenty-year-old Iwajiro makes good on his promise and moves into the Otsu home. Although a resourceful man, he does not have a job at the mill. A two-horsepower outboard propels Iwajiro's row-boat around islands in Stuart Channel, where they search for cascara trees. There is a market for the medicinal properties in the bark, but most of the trees grow on private land. To avoid getting caught, they go early in the morning.

Mutt enjoys these outings, putting through the velvety wa-ters of the channel past island outcrops and rocky reefs where large brown sea lions loll about. All eyes are on shore as they circle an island, looking for the distinctive silhouette of the

cascara sagrada. When they find some, they scramble ashore
and peel the bark before the landowner spots them. Mutt likes
the thrill of taking risks and the gypsy-like camp life on these
excursions, for they do not go home until their bags are full.
Once home, they dry and chip the fragant bark before sending
it to Vancouver.

The boys help Iwajiro harvest and sell firewood as well.
Tsune continues doing laundry and making tofu to bring in a
little extra. Somehow they manage, helped along by harvesting
as much food as they can from the sea. During the extreme
tides of the winter months, Iwajiro wakes the boys up at midnight to go clam digging in the bay.

"Tonight's the night. Let's go," he bellows. Half asleep,
Mutt puts on his pants and sweater in the dark room where
everyone sleeps. He stumbles to open the door, and the
penetrating damp rushes through him. Even though the
moon is full, he grabs a coal oil lantern. The tide is halfway
out the bay, and they walk for half an hour before digging,
their shadows like sticks crossing silver-streaked rivulets on
the beach. The boys make a game out of who can fill his
bucket the fastest. Digging through the mud is hard work,
but carrying the heavy buckets home is even harder. After
they have had their fill of clams, Tsune salts and dries what
is left.

Digging for horse clams is fun too, although it doesn't require the extreme low tide or the midnight excursion. The
Otsu boys watch women grabbing the penis-like muscle before
the clam can retreat into the mud. Husbands and friends tease
them, while children stand around giggling at this unusually
uninhibited public display.

As the Depression worsens, the Otsus live on the edge. They
are not alone. Mutt's friends are equally poor, especially Kiyoshi Nishimura, who lives on the back end of Chinatown.

They ogle Hitoshi Okada when he walks past one lunch hour, eating a sandwich filled with sliced egg.

"Did you see that?" Kiyoshi says, turning to Mutt.

"See it! I can smell it. Phew."

"Hey, Hitoshi. Got any more?" Kiyoshi yells.

Hitoshi ignores them and keeps walking.

Mutt changes the subject, wanting no extra reminders of the gap in his stomach. "Want to see if any Japanese ships are at the wharf tomorrow?"

"Sure," Kiyoshi replies.

Indian longshoremen are packing the hold of a cargo ship with lumber for Japan when the boys arrive Saturday morning. This is a favourite pasttime; just being near the ships is great fun. They go aboard and visit the Japanese crew. The sailors listen to their stories, but not for long.

"Do you boys have any sisters?" one sailor asks.

"Oh, yes. And we have a shortwave radio too," Mutt replies. "Want to see?"

The sailors look at each other. Ready for any excuse to go ashore, they follow Mutt and Kiyoshi to Okada camp. They crowd around the shortwave in the Otsu's kitchen and listen to news from home, while the boys vie for their attention all morning long.

As Mutt nears the end of grade seven, he knows his years at school are drawing to a close. One day, Iwajiro tells him there is a job at the mill.

"I want to finish my grade eight first," Mutt pleads.

"Well, if it's that important to you," Iwajiro replies, shrugging his shoulders, "I won't stand in the way of your schooling. We can manage one more year."

Mutt is stunned. Feeling cocky just the other morning, he had mouthed off when Iwajiro ordered him to do his chores. Iwajiro reached for the iron on the cookstove to hurl at Mutt, but the iron was hot. Burning pain fuelled his rage even more. Like countless times in the past, Mutt fled outside to hide for hours while Iwajiro's temper subsided.

"Do you really mean it?" Mutt asks.

"You've got my answer, now go."

Mutt wanders off, shaking his head in disbelief. He had been afraid to ask, fully expecting Iwajiro to blow up and order him to get a job.

A year later, Mutt regrets the decision. There is nothing at the Chemainus sawmill, so he gets his first job falling timber in the MacKay Lake area for Mayo Singh. Almost seventeen, he begins working with tough Japanese immigrants much like his guardian—volatile and short-tempered.

He hasn't been on the job long when he has his first fight with his co-worker.

"Go stick it," Mutt shouts, fed up with being ordered around.

"I'll kill you, you creep," he says, picking up his axe.

Mutt drops his gear. They are deep in the bush, and the undergrowth is thick, but Mutt outruns his co-worker back to camp. Terror of the axe propels him over huge fallen logs and through chest-high salal. The next day, they work together again, Mutt having apologized for his remark. But on another occasion, the same faller saves his life.

"Clear away," he shouts.

Mutt leaps sideways instantly. Broken limbs, ten feet wide, rebound from a tree they just felled and crash where he was standing. Mutt's heart is racing. He has narrowly escaped one of the most common causes of death in the bush.

A week later, another fellow is not so lucky. Mutt drops what he is doing when he hears the whistle some distance away. Vaulting over logs, he crashes through the brush to the edge of a ring of loggers sawing like madmen. A bucker is pinned under a forty-foot log.

It is pouring rain, muffling the slippery frenzy of saws cutting wet fir. Mutt looks around. No one speaks. He stares at the stricken face peering out from the end of the log and feels sick. Little rivers of rainwater skirt around his feet. Life in the forest is momentarily halted, replaced by an eerie silence that rings much louder than the normal clamour of a working crew.

The men free the bucker, but it is too late. When their straw boss sits him up, blood trickles from his mouth.

"Heart is still beating, but it's almost gone," the boss announces. Five minutes later, he is dead.

Mutt didn't know the man, but that night at dinner he and his friend, Michio Inouye, don't have their usual appetites. The only other logger Mutt's age, Michio is also Canadian-born. They often eat a dozen bowls of rice before leaving the mess hall, sometimes well after other workers drag themselves back from the public bath to bunk down. But not tonight.

The incident has a sobering effect on everyone in camp. Sometimes accidents are unnecessarily fatal, due to the length of time it takes to get from the bush to the hospital. Thinking about it, Mutt feels weary. In two weeks he will go home for his monthly visit, a short-lived reprieve that always seems an eternity away.

The worst thing about going home is the stinging reminder of all he is missing: girls, baseball in the summer, friends his own age, to name a few. The six-day work week at Mayo drags on him. He doesn't begrudge his earnings to his mother, but he berates himself for not taking the Chemainus job when he had the chance. As the logging progresses, the camp moves further into the bush. The landscape is a bleak mix of clearcuts, railway tracks, and makeshift camp buildings. To make matters worse, he contracts asthma. It will plague him for the next thirteen years. The men do their own laundry, cut their own hair, work, eat, and sleep. Mutt keeps a diary on the monotony for something to do.

On his way back to camp one Sunday afternoon, he gazes out the window and mopes, knowing his friends are playing ball. Then he remembers the package of cherry Jello he tucked into his bag. He holds onto the thought of smooth, cold jelly sliding down his throat and feels better. As soon as he gets to camp, he mixes it with cold water and sets it under the bunkhouse to gel. Even that simple treat eludes him, however. Every day for a week, he lifts the bowl out to find it is still a bright red liquid. He pours it out in disgust and never tries again.

Mutt nears the end of his first year in Mayo when a job opens up at the Chemainus sawmill in 1938. He is on the site the next day, learning how to lubricate all the machinery from Goshichi Izumi and Yoshi Higashi.

Yoshi, nicknamed Gene after Gene Autry, was born a week later than Mutt in 1920. The oldest in a family of eleven, Yoshi can hold his own with his abusive father now, as can Mutt with Iwajiro.

The young men get along well at work and become good friends. On Saturday nights, they visit "the girls," talking and joking until one or two o'clock in the morning. Neither has a girlfriend as such, but they are well liked by the young women in town.

Early one Sunday morning in July, Mutt and Yoshi are walking down the alley in Kawahara camp after leaving Tosh Yoshida's home. The air is balmy; constellations are lucid in the black sky.

"Shall we go to work for an hour and get our job done?" Mutt asks.

"Yeah, then we can play ball tomorrow afternoon," Yoshi replies.

Ten minutes later, they punch in. Yoshi sets off for the south end of the complex, while Mutt starts where Tairyu used to sort waste lumber on the conveyor belt. Everything is still. In order to oil the bearing on the drum, Mutt steps onto the conveyor belt and reaches over a ten-foot drop where the belt winds toward the wood burner. But he slips over the edge, banging his head on the drum as he grazes past, his freefall cut short by the lower level of the stationary belt. Later, he doesn't remember any of this; he has no memory of anything beyond reaching for the bearing. If it hadn't been for his groaning, Yoshi might not have found him.

A week later, he is still unconscious in the hospital, causing fears that he might not live. Friends visit without his knowledge. He wakes to an ice pack on his throbbing head. For the first time in months, he does not write in his diary.

Mutt works another three years at the Chemainus mill. In 1941, he returns to Mayo, where he can boost his wage by five cents to forty-five cents an hour. The mill's reasoning that Orientals don't need equal pay to Caucasians because their standard of living is lower infuriates Mutt. As a Canadian, he wants to better himself as much as the next man. For its part, the Caucasian community resents Orientals working for less. Naturally, the mill brass hire cheap labour—especially cheap, industrious labour—whenever they can, denying white men those jobs. Racial intolerance deepens because of economics and the ongoing struggle to survive.

Mutt doesn't return to Mayo as a faller but as a rigger, which is slightly less dangerous if just as demanding. But he isn't there long when Japan bombs Pearl Harbor. He and his counterparts are ordered back to their hometowns almost immediately. Despite all the upheaval in his young life, Mutt cannot fathom the turn of events that follow.

As the evacuation date approaches, Mutt and his brothers spend hard-earned cash on heavy Cowichan sweaters. Learning that it is cold where they are moving, they buy the sweaters for everyone in the family. Tsune is almost sixty, ever so proud that her sons can afford this luxury. She focuses on the little things that make her feel good, but her world is shrinking: the blackened windows at night, the finger-printing, the curfew, the rounding up of *issei* men, including Iwajiro. For almost twenty years, the shack facing the booming grounds has been home. Her youngest daughter, Akiko, was born here, and it is here also where the children have grown into fine, respectable people. Life has only just begun to smooth out its sharp, jagged edges when it opens its unseemly maw again.

Walking down the wharf toward the SS *Princess Adelaide*, Mutt battles rage. Like corrosive acid, it stings, tempered somewhat with the more subtle ache of worry. The uncertainty is a terrifying void. He sees tears in his mother's eyes and his own burn with anger. The all-powerful God he worshipped at the Anglican church suddenly strikes him as a very bad joke. It is politicians and hateful people who wield power, not a benevolent God. This is what he learns as he turns his back on home, where ashes from his diaries lie in a soft heap.

Chaos comes in large doses in Hastings Park. People are flung together like animals herded into pens. Allowances for individual idiosyncracies give way to bitter feuds, creating hostile factions and tense enmity. Those suspected of pandering to the authorities are threatened and sometimes beaten. Those who follow orders are shunned by men who passively but firmly refuse to co-operate, choosing to be prisoners of war rather than acquiescent victims. Rumours are rampant, including one that young men being shipped to Ontario road camps will be sent overseas as cannon fodder.

All of it drives Mutt crazy, along with the tick mattresses that aggravate his asthma. Within days of arriving in Hastings Park, he boards a train heading toward Jackfish, a road camp northeast of Lake Superior. Accompanied by his brothers and two Chemainus friends, Mutt weeps as the train chugs out of the station. He watches Tsune and his sisters, Yasuyo and

Akiko, shrink into a tiny huddle on the platform as he wrestles with the oppressive sensation of going nowhere fast.

Soon, Fraser Valley farms roll by. Mutt knows that Japanese families cleared and cultivated the land for over forty years. Now it is falling into the hands of *hakujins*, possibly the kin of soldiers guarding his journey east. Guns and cold eyes impress on him the nature of his crime: to be born of Japanese parents.

He arrives in Jackfish on May 1, 1942, not long after spring break-up. Mutt hauls out the camera concealed in his belongings. Photography has been his favourite hobby since he bought the camera with coupons when he was fifteen. Rather than hand it over to the authorities, he smuggled it out of Chemainus in his duffle bag.

The landscape in Jackfish is far from inspiring, but Mutt wants to document where he is. He climbs a nearby bluff and snaps a wide shot of Canadian Shield country. The hollow where the camp lies has been clearcut and is as inviting as Mayo on a bad day. Having just crossed mile after mile of prairie, Mutt surveys the great span of rock and forested bluffs. It is bleak, to be sure, but at least it isn't flat. Then he shivers, longing for the rush of waves breaking on shore some 3,000 miles due west.

Life quickly settles into a lackadaisical routine. The work is light but boring, as is camp life in general. One day a train passes by en route to Petawawa with Japanese Canadian prisoners of war. The men drop their tools and wave, but the POWs spit at them vehemently. They are *gambari-ya* or diehards, who consider the road crew soft "yes" men because they do as they are told. In defence, Mutt and his companions accuse the *gambari-ya* of being unpatriotic toward Canada. The hard feelings will last long after the war is over.

Back in camp at the end of the work day, Mutt takes off with his camera. The possibility of a moose or bear wandering up by the lake takes his mind off these unsettling times. Being in the outdoors gives him a sense of freedom, and he heads for it whenever he can.

The following week he convinces a buddy to hide with him under a piece of cloth in the garbage dump to get a picture of one of the black bears that rummage through there regularly. To his horror, an approaching bear doesn't start eating garbage. Slowly, it rumbles closer to them, its nose twitching and sniffing along the ground.

"Maybe the bear is going to attack us," Mutt whispers. "We better go. Let's run."

His friend nods, eyes big. They fling off the cloth and race for cover. The bear, equally scared, lumbers off too. The camp cook greets them with jeers and laughter. Breathless, Mutt collapses onto a bench and smiles. "Whose cockeyed idea was this anyways?" he asks.

"Yours, yours," a chorus of men replies, slapping their thighs and doubling over with laughter.

Mutt laughs too. "Guess I'll leave that shot for another day."

As summer progresses, Mutt and Kiyoshi Nishimura go from Jackfish to Black camp, then Empress to Schreiber, the most westerly camp on this stretch of the Trans-Canada. Black flies are like the boredom: incessant.

Empress camp is the exception. A nearby French-Canadian community welcomes them to their regular dances. The first time Mutt goes with his friends, a local official spots them walking along the railway tracks.

"You guys got no business walking on the railroad," he yells, shaking his fist.

Mutt turns and stares. "We're not doing any harm, sir."

"I don't want no backtalk from a Jap," he shouts. "And I don't want no Japs walking this rail line, you hear."

They turn back to camp, moaning about the long road into town. It winds through many more miles of country than the railroad, so they wait for dark and walk the tracks again, passing unnoticed. After that, the young men wait until sundown before setting out for a town dance.

The trek is worth the trouble. This community loves to shake the hall down, often with only an accordion and a guitar. More than the music, there are girls. Mutt and his friends have not seen women for months, let alone dance with them. Anita, Lucille and Mary swing like fashion models in their arms. Mutt is baffled by the warm welcome, and asks Lucille why they are all so friendly.

"Well, why not?" she replies, her blue eyes quizzical.

"Because no one else is. Not regular whites anyway," Mutt says.

"Oh, they're brainless scaredy-cats," Lucille says. "Don't pay them any mind," she adds, swinging blonde curls across her shoulders. "*Viens*, let's dance."

Walking home under the stars much later, Mutt mumbles Lucille's words over and over: "Don't pay them any mind." He is euphoric from dancing with her all night and blissfully free from worry. Lucille's smile swims before him, a warm, happy memory for keeps.

Life in the road camps is relatively short-lived. Mutt, Kiyoshi Nishimura, and Mitsuo Izumi are the last three to leave Schreiber when the camp closes down that December. Rather than work in northern pulp mills, the young men get permission to work for a lumber company in Toronto. The train jostles them toward their destination, stopping at Petawawa to pick up a Japanese Canadian POW. He wears baggy overalls with a red circle in the middle of his back and slumps between his escorts, quite ill. Mutt shudders, unable to reconcile the war criminal label attached to someone so sick. Despite the resentment he feels about the gang spitting at them in Jackfish, Mutt knows that the man is no criminal—only that his stand on civil rights has exacerbated the racism. He suppresses an urge to extend a comforting hand and stares out his window. The scenery is even more bleak than the day he arrived.

Two days before Christmas in 1942, the young men arrive in Toronto. They track down McCaul Street in the Jewish community, one of few neighbourhoods where landlords won't slam the door in their faces. After finding a room to rent, they plant their belongings on the floor and look around.

"Well, at least we've got a roof over our heads," Mutt offers.

"Yeah," Kiyoshi mumbles absently.

"Not much to look at, is it?" Mitsuo says.

"No better, no worse than what we've ever had, I suppose," Mutt says.

"Oh, better for me," Kiyoshi says. "Anthing's better than waking up to Hong Hing slaughtering his pigs next door."

"I guess!" Mitsuo says. "But camp was better in one way."

"What's that?" Mutt asks.

"We got fed."

Road camp wages didn't amount to much after board was deducted, but they pool what they have and walk over to the neighbourhood store. Two days later they eat canned chicken noodle soup for Christmas dinner, perching on the edge of their beds.

"What're you thinking about?" Mutt asks Mitsuo, breaking the awkward silence.

"I'm wondering what Mama is cooking right now."

"In those shacks they wrote about?" Kiyoshi says. "Not much, I bet."

"Yeah, you're probably right," Mitsuo says.

"At least they're together," Mutt says.

"We're not there." Mitsuo replies.

"No, but everybody else is. Being so far away and thinking of them holed up in shacks somewhere, not knowing what's gonna happen next. . . . It's awful," Mutt says.

"Yeah," Mitsuo whispers.

"From what I hear on the radio lately, we may not get back together for years," Kiyoshi says.

Mutt gets up and washes his bowl mindlessly. He misses the cockroach skittering along the baseboard as he strolls toward the window. He sits on the sill and watches snow falling from a black sky, not thinking, not speaking.

After two years working for the lumber company, Mutt and his roomies inquire about a better paying job in a Standard Sanitary factory. Night shift jobs paying fifty cents an hour are available, five cents an hour more than they are earning now. They quit their lumbermen jobs and arrive at Standard Sanitary with a bag lunch for the four p.m. shift, only to learn that the entire foundry is threatening to strike if "Japs" are hired. They walk home and eat their baloney sandwiches on the front steps of their boarding house.

Obliged to report to the job placement officer who keeps track of where they are, Mutt and his friends are sent to pick peaches in St. Catharines the summer of 1944. Mutt suffers with his asthma, swearing he'll never pick fruit again. He resorts to soaking in a hot bath at night, where he can rest without worrying about waking his co-workers with his almost constant wheezing.

Back in Toronto at the end of the summer, Mutt takes a job the placement officer finds him at a machine shop. When the war ends a year later, he is free to go as he pleases and choose his own line of work. He begins applying for jobs in the clothing business, a radical departure from anything he has ever done.

In 1946, Mutt sees his sister Akiko for the first time in four years. He is gazing out his window when she walks by. An innocent sixteen-year-old when he left the coast, Akiko is a young woman now. Her thick black hair is all done up like a fashion model. Wearing a short skirt, she strolls along looking at street addresses, stopping in front of his boarding house.

Mutt's fingers slide down the window pane, smearing the glass. "Oh my God," he mutters. "What happened to my sister?"

Down the street, Iwajiro, Yasuyo, and his mother are traipsing along. Tsune is a bit slow on her feet, but otherwise looks healthy and in good spirits. He flies down the stairs and out the door.

"I can't believe you're all here!" Mutt shouts, grinning. He suppresses an urge to twirl them round, one by one, right there on the street. He is even happy to see Iwajiro.

"Yes, son. We're here," Tsune says. "To stay."

In 1947, Mutt meets a seamstress named Mikiko Ohashi at Ontario Boys' Wear. She is sweet and kind and teaches him all the tricks of the trade. Life is more stable now, and they can laugh again. After dating for a while, they decide to marry. But Mikiko's father is a devout Buddhist, and custom dictates that the marriage be performed in the religion of the bride's family. Baptized in the Anglican church in Chemainus, Mutt will have none of it. They talk about eloping, but finally Mikiko's father gives in. Unhappy but resigned, he allows his daughter to marry in the neighbourhood United Church in 1949. Mikiko joins the Otsu household, raising a family and looking after her in-laws. In 1956, Iwajiro returns to Japan and marries; eleven years later, Tsune dies at the age of eighty-four.

Meanwhile, Mutt works his way up to a supervisory position with Tip Top Tailors, overseeing the production of suits. After retiring in 1985, he and his wife join the annual winter trek many eastern Canadians make to warmer climes. Over the years, their itinerary includes Florida, South America, Fiji, Australia, New Zealand, Hawaii, and Japan.

Sadly, he never meets his Japanese sisters, but he always comes home with a tan that glows.

SEVEN

TOSHIYE KAMINO

Tosh kamino steps outside her Etobicoke townhouse and squints at the sun. She reaches for the garden hose by the back door and waters the plants and flowers. Leaning forward, she thrusts her nose into a cluster of sweet peas. Bathing in their fragance, Tosh recalls the sweet peas from her childhood in Chemainus. Her stepmother used to plant them in the garden plot that Mr. Kawahara provided for his tenants. Tosh remembers the rush of perfume as she raced past them to play hopscotch with friends.

A Siamese cat rubs against her legs, and she stoops to pick him up. Standing in the sunlight with the cat purring in her arms, she sways gently to and fro. A smile creases her lips.

Vivacious, pretty, and petite, Tosh has been widowed for seventeen years now. She counts her blessings that their three children were grown when Yasuo died. It was sudden, his going. But just like the evacuation in 1942, all the signs were there. Somehow, despite all the black blotches in her life, Tosh always finds something to smile about. Now sixty-seven, she knows that troubles come and go in every life. Hers is no exception. The important thing is that they go.

The upcoming Chemainus reunion is a good example. Tosh is thrilled about it, but she is troubled by those who don't share her enthusiasm. Many do, of course, but some are turning their backs on it, the bitterness is buried too deep.

It isn't that she doesn't understand how much it hurts to return. Certainly they were shafted on a grand scale, but many Chemainus people were friendly enough, one on one. She still corresponds with Vera Fraser Grant, a friend from her first year in public school in Chemainus. They never really talked much about the evacuation, then or now. The *hakujin* community seems rather torn about the whole affair. Maybe they didn't know what they were doing at the time; perhaps they were both victims and perpetrators of the hysteria. Now they all have to live with the shame, even those who won't admit that what they did was wrong. Tosh knows that times change as life puts history in perspective.

Tosh thinks of her father, Tomekichi Yoshida, and sets the cat on the ground. He wouldn't have gone to the Chemainus reunion if he were alive, but she imagines a smile lighting his eyes when she tells him about the murals. The fact that the government didn't apologize when he was still alive nags her some days. At least her tall, gangly stepmother lived long enough to get redress. Now in her nineties, Hina spends her days enjoying the company of other *issei* in Nipponia Home. But Tomekichi died without the opportunity to heal those old wounds. He sacrificed so much to offer the family a better life, and then, like so many, got trapped by the hateful mood of the times.

Tomekichi Yoshida was one of the youngest of ten in his family in Hiroshima. Born in 1881, he fought in the Boxer Rebellion in China when he was in his late teens and again in the Russo-Japanese War when he was twenty-three. A descendant of the Samurai class, he then learned the craft of making Buddhist shrines and married a young woman from the country surrounding Hiroshima. In 1908, Okiye Matsuo gave him their first son, Tomiharu, followed by another boy in 1910. Tomekichi's decision to go to Canada the year Eichi was born came down to economics and class. Before the Emperor Meiji came to power, Samurai families were looked after by the lords they protected. When that class system was disbanded, men like Tomekichi's father were suddenly forced to support themselves. Canada offered Tomekichi a quicker and easier route to prosperity, or so he thought. But instead of returning to Japan a rich man two years later, he sent for his wife. Tomiharu was four and Eichi was two when their mother left them in their grandparents' care. She never saw them again.

Tomekichi's younger brother, Matakichi, had already emigrated and established a grocery store on Vancouver's Powell Street when Tomekichi arrived. Dreams of getting rich went underground as the young immigrant struggled to adjust to the language, customs, and landscape. Tomekichi tried his hand at fishing, worked in a restaurant, and helped his brother fill food orders for the Japanese logging camps up the mainland coast. For months he managed to save a little towards his wife's steamship passage across the Pacific. When she joined him in 1912, he was still struggling to find work that would bring some security to their lives. He decided to try his luck on Vancouver Island, moving from job to job in Victoria, Duncan, Genoa Bay, Mayo, and finally, Chemainus. Tomekichi had been in Canada twenty years when he found a job as a millwright at the Chemainus sawmill. By then, the Depression squashed any remaining notions of securing a fortune with which to return to Japan. In the long term, he felt that Canada held more promise for his family anyway. Now it was home.

His third daughter, Toshiye, is born at night in Genoa Bay without an attendant midwife or doctor. In the morning her mother wakes to the golden light of autumn shimmering in the sea below their shack. Born in September 1923, Tosh is Okiye's sixth and last child. Two years later, diabetes kills Okiye, leaving Tomekichi a widower at forty-four with children ranging in age from two to eleven. In 1927, his first-born son emigrates from Japan to help out. Now seventeen, Tomiharu has not seen his father since he was two.

A year after Tomiharu arrives in Genoa Bay, Tomekichi books his passage to Japan to marry again. A wedding has been arranged with a woman who left an unsuccessful marriage. A burden on her family, she succumbs to the pressure to marry a widower eighteen years older and move to an isolated village 4,000 miles from her home near Hiroshima. Only nine years younger than his stepmother, Tomiharu goes on his own after she arrives in 1928.

Hina switches her talent for sewing geisha dresses and actors' costumes to falling alder saplings with a bucksaw on the steep slope outside her new home. The sawmill closed down three years before, so she never knows the luxury of having Goshichi Izumi deliver scrap firewood in a horse-drawn cart. Tomekichi is working in a lumber camp and only comes home weekends. When he steps in the door that first weekend, Hina is waiting for him.

"*Anta*," she begins, eyes downcast. "Please. I chop wood for the cookstove, do laundry, look after the children and cook and clean, but those trees. . . ."

He follows her eyes to the forest outside.

"Those, I cannot cut down. You must do for me."

Tomekichi still has his overcoat on. Without a word, he strides back outside and falls two alder while Hina watches from the kitchen window. She smiles at him when he comes in.

"Thank you," she says, and he nods.

There are three ways out of the tiny village. One route involves a long, winding road via the next bay to the north; another is to hire a rowboat or canoe to Cowichan Bay; the third possible exit is to climb the 1,610-foot trail up Mount Tzuhalem. In the months she lives in Genoa Bay, Hina goes nowhere. But within a year of her arrival, the Yoshidas move to Mayo. They are the last Japanese family to leave the deserted sawmill town in Genoa Bay.

Tosh is too young to take many memories with her, but her older sisters won't forget the picturesque bay. Fishing one fine afternoon off the wharf, they catch so many perch that they cannot carry them all. Fukuko climbs out of her petticoat and lays it on the wharf. Yukiko watches her slide the slippery fish onto the freshly laundered cotton eyelet, which she then curls into a bag and slings over her shoulder for the hike home.

"Mama is going to be mad at you, Fuku," Yuki says.

"Well, how else would we get them home? We can't carry them all," Fuku replies.

"She'll never get the fish smell out, you know," Yuki says.

Fuku just shrugs her shoulders. "Maybe not, but we'll have a feed of fresh perch tonight."

Yuki grins. "Race you home, smarty."

Later in the week, Yuki spends an afternoon on top of a bluff daydreaming. Her happiest memories of Genoa Bay were here, watching huge schooners sail in and out of the bay. It doesn't seem that long ago when the cove was dotted with ships waiting to dock for shipments of lumber that would go clear around the world. Tall masts swayed and rigging clacked in the wind as Yuki dreamed about sailing to ancient cities.

But it is nothing so exotic that takes the family away. Despite the bay's spectacular deep sea docking facilities, the sawmill had ongoing problems with water supply. It could not support the bustling port indefinitely, forcing people to relo-

cate to other industry towns. After it shuts down, the landscape slowly reclaims itself until nothing of the former sawmill
can be gleaned from the site.

By 1929, the Yoshidas resettle in Mayo, another sawmill
town near Duncan named after mill owner Mayo Singh. Tosh
starts grade one in the predominately East Indian and Japanese community that year. She has been speaking English with
her older brother Noboru since she can remember, and English is common among her Mayo playmates. When she starts
grade two in Chemainus the following year, the teacher is
impressed with her ability to read a long passage.

"Are you sure you haven't read that before, Tosh?" Miss
Vye asks.

"No," Tosh replies, surprised the teacher took notice. Then
a classmate in the desk behind pokes her back.

"Oh, gee, you're good," Mits Otsu whispers.

Tosh searches her classmate's face. She is baffled by his
earnest admiration. She thinks her English average, but life in
Kawahara camp changes that. Before the year is out, she
speaks Japanese at play like all the others, and her English
begins to suffer too.

In 1931, a year after the Yoshidas move to Chemainus, Hina
gives birth to a son. Tosh, who has been the baby in the family
until now, is eight when Yuji is born. Her oldest sister Yuki is
working as a domestic in Duncan, and their sixteen-year-old
brother Noboru works in the mill to help support the family.
Before long, Fuku also finds work as a domestic. Tosh is Yuji's
only sibling still allowed the luxury of childhood, although
they aren't playmates. Differences in age and personality set
them apart.

Tosh is so easy-going that life's bumps don't seem to affect
her. Yuji, on the other hand, feels every bump intensely. He is
a determined, enthusiastic, and happy youngster who plays as

hard as he tumbles. Tosh seems to sail among the apple, pear and cherry trees in the compound, deceptively free of troubles as she mingles with her friends. It isn't that she avoids problems at school or injuries in play. One day, her teacher straps her for giving the wrong answer to a math question. Her hand smarts and her pride is hurt, but Tosh just carries on. Soon enough, she is laughing with abandon again.

Tosh makes friends with some *hakujin* girls at school during her first weeks in Chemainus. She plays hopscotch and jumping rope with blonde Doreen Scoffield and quiet, skinny Vera Fraser. One day, Doreen asks Tosh to bring lunch to school so they can spend the hour together.

The next morning Tosh asks her stepmother to make her a sandwich for school.

"Why?" Hina asks. "You walk home for lunch."

"A friend asked me to stay, that's all."

"Oh well, I guess so," Hina says, afraid to admit that she doesn't know what to put in a sandwich.

Swinging her lunch bag en route, Tosh is soon skipping to school. Inside the classroom, she shoves it in her desk as nearby classmates whisper.

"I wonder why Tosh is carrying a lunch," Mits says to his chum.

"She always walks home, doesn't she? Maybe teacher has given her a detention," Kumeo replies.

Tosh ignores these rumblings, shaking her head at such silliness. When the lunch bell rings, she runs outside with Doreen and they plop themselves in the middle of the playground. About to ask Doreen what kind of sandwich she has, Tosh stops short when she pulls two pieces of buttered bread from her bag.

"Oh, my stepmother," Tosh says, embarrassed.

Doreen glances at the bread. "Doesn't she know how to make a sandwich?"

"No, I guess not," Tosh replies, taking a nibble.

It is their one and only lunch together.

As the year progresses, Tosh leaves Kawahara camp less and less to play with her *hakujin* friends. Running down her front steps and across the alley, she skips past the community bath-house to the dirt playground where she joins the other children. From May until September, she melts into the hubbub and plays for hours on end. For the most part, school is the only reason she steps outside her neighbourhood.

One day, sweet young Chizuru Isoki asks Tosh if she would like to go to Sunday school.

"Sure," replies Tosh, always game to try something new. The next Sunday she puts on a hat and her best dress, a white cotton one with swirls of sky-blue flowers. It seems to take forever to get to Saint Michael's and All Angels Church in the south end of town past the mill. Reverend Robathan greets them at the door of the quaint nineteenth century church, leaning down to say hello to Tosh. He has soft brown hair and even softer brown eyes behind his horn-rimmed spectacles.

Inside church, Chizuru and Tosh tiptoe along the aisle and slide onto one of the polished hemlock pews beside two brothers from another Yoshida family. They wait quietly for the swish of Reverend Robathan's long white gown to approach the altar and begin the morning Anglican service. Soon they are all on their feet singing "Onward Christian Soldiers." By the time she is whisked off to Sunday school in a back room, Tosh is dying to get her scratchy hat off. A blonde girl with ringlets is standing next to her when she lifts the hat and sighs with relief.

"I hope I'm not in Mrs. Robinson's class," the girl whispers into Tosh's ear. "When she talks, she spits at you!"

Astonished, Tosh stares at her. "Oh my God," she says, edging closer to Chizuru. In her experience, people don't say mean things, and Sunday school is the last place she expects it. Soon the teacher seats them around a table to study the Bible, and Tosh's attention is elsewhere—daydreaming. Mostly because it gives her and Chizuru time together, she suffers through boring Bible study a few more years.

Meanwhile, her stepmother is becoming active with two women's clubs in the community. The *fujinkai* is mainly fun, organizing and performing plays in the hall, as well as preparing food and decorations for special occasions in the community. One afternoon, Mrs. Nakatsu brings a cake to the meeting. Pretending to be very solemn, she sets it in front of the ladies and bows. "Make the *fukeiki* go away," she says. Everyone giggles. *Fukeiki* is their word for the Depression—and the pretend ritual, their way of making light of hard times.

The other women's group has a more serious intent, which is to discuss concerns regarding their children's progress in school. One afternoon, Tosh bursts into one of their *hahanokai* meetings.

"Mama, you won the pool," she says.

"What?" Hina whispers, putting her finger to her lips.

"You know, Mr. Taniwa's World Series pool. Remember, you bought a ticket last week. He was selling them in the road in front of his store, catching all the men going to and from work."

"And I won?" Hina asks, blushing. She quickly loses interest in discussing her children's homework habits and excuses herself with a curt bow.

They march over to Taniwas to collect her pool. Humming under her breath, Hina clutches a hot two-dollar bill in her hand as Tosh skips down the alley and sprints up the stairs to broadcast the news at home.

Tosh blossoms in her early teens. Aiko Higashi is a year younger than her, but they are best of friends. She lives on the other side of Mr. Kawahara's bunkhouse on the backside of Tosh's home. A dark beauty and a daredevil, she buttresses herself against the harsh realities of life with long, arching dives off the wharf into Chemainus harbour. More timid, Tosh usually jumps in after her friend, whispering her trademark "Oh, my God" in mid-air. They watch baseball games together, and cheer on their brothers and boys whom they fancy. They hike to Bare Point to pick bouquets of delicate wild lilies and admire the fabulous view on warm spring days. They share their secrets and face the world, giggling.

One of Tosh's other good friends is Kaz Kawabe. The Kawabes live a few blocks north of Kawahara camp in their own house. In addition to the sunporch where Kaz's father nurtures a colony of chrysanthemums, the garden he created out front is an inviting sanctuary. A little rock bridge crosses a pond where brilliant orange carp skim near the surface under the decorative shade of ornamental maple trees.

A prominent man in the community, Tomoki Kawabe employs dozens of men for his lumber piling contract with the sawmill. His daughter Kaz enjoys the distinguished status she has among her peers, but Tosh pays no mind to Kaz's uppity ways and likes her for her strong personality and quick wit.

Tosh and her friends ride the bus to high school in Ladysmith every morning. Aiko and Yasumi Nishimura walk down the alley to Tosh's house, and the three girls carry on to Maple Street, where they turn to pick up Kaz. Inevitably, they find her shaking the dust mop out the side door when they arrive. It doesn't matter how much they tease her, Kaz won't leave until the floor is dusted.

On a hot summer day the year before she graduates from high school, Tosh stands outside the Japanese community hall with six of her girlfriends and Kumeo Yoshida for a special graduation picture. Few teenagers are still going to public school or

Japanese language school in 1940 because most are working. But every day after school for ten years, Tosh trudged along to the community hall for two hours of Japanese language and history instruction. Among her teachers, Mrs. Sugaya stood out, for she encouraged them not only to be proud of their heritage but also to be good Canadians. Now those lessons are behind her, and with them, her adolescence.

As high school graduation approaches, Tosh watches her dress take shape in Sadako Hayashi's hands. The seamstress has a knack for working with fine fabrics, such as the dusty rose chiffon Tosh chose for the floor-length gown. At her last fitting, Tosh fingers the puffy sleeves and smiles sweetly at Sadako.

"I'm so pleased with these sleeves, Hayashi-san. Mama didn't like the idea, but I think she'll change her mind now," Tosh says.

"I'm sure she will. The dress looks lovely on you, Tosh," Sadako says.

Tosh blushes. "Thank you," she says, the whisper of fine chiffon brushing her legs. "This is the most special dress I've ever had. I'm going to keep it forever."

The next day Hina nods her approval when Tosh models the gown, and they go shopping for petticoats and shoes to match. When the time comes to dress for the evening ceremony, Tosh is in a liquid mood. Her fingers skim the fabric as she lifts the chiffon gently over her head and lets it tumble to her feet. Standing before the mirror in the falling light, she brushes her hair until it gleams. Tosh tiptoes closer to the mirror and applies a creamy layer of dusty rose lipstick. Stepping back, she studies her reflection with satisfaction and moves to the window. Mr. Kawahara should arrive any moment in his taxi.

When his black Chrysler rolls around the end of the alley, Tosh slips over to her dresser and gathers the pink roses from the vase. She slides a doily over the stems to complete her bouquet and checks the mirror one last time. Floating downstairs into the soft June dusk, she hesitates on her front porch. Neighbours are stretched along the boardwalk, waiting for her to appear. Smiling and waving, Tosh drifts down to the street and steps into the waiting taxi. The evening has just begun, and life hugs her with promise.

Tosh celebrates her eighteenth birthday in September 1941 after enrolling in the Kawano Sewing School in Vancouver. She is staying with her brother Tomiharu and his family on East Georgia, happy with life in the city and her new-found freedom.

Three months later, she is oblivious to the gale blowing down Stuart Channel, churning the sea into a frothy mass against the Chemainus shoreline. In Vancouver, the howling wind is accompanied by heavy rain, so she is glad it is Sunday and she doesn't have to go to school.

Hina is helping clean the community hall on December 7 about the same time Tosh and her brother hear the news on the radio. Mr. Okinobu comes round to the hall to tell the women that Japan has bombed Pearl Harbor. Hina finishes quickly and goes home to find her husband and stepson Noboru listening intently to the radio. Meanwhile, Tomiharu is beside himself, pacing the living room floor. His wife is upstairs napping with their toddler, and he doesn't want to disturb them. Finally, Tosh can't stand her brother's pacing any more.

"I know it's awful, *Nii-san*, but you shouldn't be so upset," she says.

"Look, Tosh. This is the beginning of the bad news," Tomiharu replies.

"What do you mean?"

"I don't know what they'll do to us, but you can be sure they'll think of something."

"Who are you talking about?" Tosh asks.

"Politicians like Ian Mackenzie, the MP, and the White Canada Association. I bet they're knocking on the Prime Minister's door right now."

"But what can they do?"

"Push through their campaign to get us out of B.C., for starters. Have you ever heard these guys talk?" Tomiharu asks.

"No."

"You've been living in Chemainus too long, Tosh."

She shakes her head and goes to her room. Tomiharu's fears might be exaggerated, but she can't ignore the queasy knot in her tummy. Staring out her window at the rain, Tosh feels homesick for the first time since leaving Chemainus.

When Tomiharu learns that all Japanese-born men will be sent to road camps, he packs up his wife and child and moves to Kamloops. Within a few months, Tosh's father is in a Rocky Mountain road camp. Hina, Noboru and ten-year-old Yuji join Tosh in Tomiharu's house, but with no income they cannot stay. In May they swallow their pride and enter Hastings Park.

Tosh leaves her sewing course on uneasy terms. Her teacher argues that she hasn't paid her full fee, and it upsets her that she can neither pay nor finish the course. But soon after arriving in Hastings Park, she sees Aiko Higashi moping around. Suddenly sewing school doesn't seem so important after all.

"What's wrong, Aiko?" Tosh asks her friend, who is sitting outside the huge dormitory, her eyes a bloodshot mess.

"I'm allergic to that god-awful hay in our mattresses," Aiko replies tartly. "But more than anything I'm so mad about not finishing high school that I could scream."

"I haven't really talked to anyone yet. We just got here yesterday."

"Awful, isn't it?" Aiko says, screwing up her nose.

"Yeah, it's pretty bad. So tell me. What happened with school?" Tosh asks.

"Well, we asked the RCMP for permission to stay behind long enough to write our exams. Our principal, Mr. Spargo, he was on our side, you know."

"Really?"

"Yeah, he tried to convince them we weren't a threat, but the police just ignored him."

"That's awful, Aiko."

"I won't forget Mr. Spargo, though. One day back in January some grade ten kid called me a dirty Jap in the hallway. I whammed the top of his head with my textbooks. Trouble was, Mr. Spargo saw me."

"Oh no," Tosh says.

"So he called us into his office and asked me why I hit that boy. I told Mr. Spargo that he called me a dirty Jap.

"He didn't get mad or anything. He just told us both to go back to our classes and behave ourselves. I thought, 'A lot of good that's going to do.' But the next day he called an assembly and told everybody that we weren't the enemy, that we hadn't anything to do with the Japanese who bombed Pearl Harbor. He said we were Canadian citizens just like everyone else."

"Mr. Spargo said that?"

"Afterwards, a few *hakujin* students told us they were sorry we couldn't finish the year, but none of it made any difference in the end. It's so unfair," Aiko says, narrowing her eyes and staring ahead.

Tosh is quiet, remembering how much her graduation meant to her. Lately, she has been at a real loss for words.

Tosh and her family leave Hastings Park in September to join her father, who has been transferred out of road camp to help build a few thousand shacks in Tashme. The largest of all the internment camps, Tashme has the unfortunate distinction of being hundreds of miles from the camps clustered throughout the Slocan Valley. With the exception of Sandon, a remote ghost town in the Slocan, Tashme is the most gloomy place to be. The nearest town is Hope, where the landscape leaves the fertile Fraser Valley behind and launches itself toward the rugged Fraser Canyon. Aged, foreboding mountains close in on the settlement at the valley bottom. Cutting winds funnel through, creating huge snowdrifts in winter and carrying torrential rains in the fall. The shacks are so thinly constructed, icicles form on inside windows during winter nights.

For young people like Tosh, the opportunity to meet new friends compensates a little for all the upheaval. On her arrival, Tosh meets her first friend, a young man named Juji Matsui. Climbing out of the livestock trucks into the bedlam, Tosh sees him standing about and smiles.

"I haven't seen a women in three months," he says to Tosh, "and you guys come in slacks!"

Tosh laughs. Coincidentally, Juji is one of two young men who will share the cramped quarters of the Yoshida's tarpaper shack. His own family needs his bed for a younger sibling, so he sleeps in a spare one that Tosh's family makes for him. But then he falls ill with meningitis, and his mother gives up her bed to nurse him back to health.

Not long after, Tosh visits him. Sitting at his bedside, she forces a smile. He is a shadow of the energetic twenty-year-old who greeted her just a few months before.

"Tosh, say the Lord's Prayer for me, will you?" Juji asks.

Tosh hesitates and whispers, "I haven't said the Lord's Prayer since grade school, but I'll try."

Juji repeats it after her, over and over again. Early the next morning he is dead.

They cremate him in an open field by the creek, where his family and friends mourn his death under the mountains that hold them captive on earth.

Tosh makes the best out of a bad situation. She has a job in the B.C. Security Commission general store, earning twenty-five cents an hour. When she isn't working, she joins friends for as much recreation as she can fit in her day. They find a lake to skate on in the winter, and hike nearby mountains in the summer. Whenever they reach the mountain summit, they reflect mirrors down at the camp to show how high they have climbed. Seen from below, the silver flashes from the mountain top defy their internment.

On many of these outings, Tosh laughs alongside her new boyfriend, Yasuo Kamino. In addition to skating, hiking, and fishing for trout in the creek, Saturday night dances bring the young couple together. In the bleak upset that is her life, nineteen-year-old Tosh is falling in love.

In the summer of 1944, Tosh leaves Tashme with her sister Yuki. It is Yuki's idea to go east, and she invites Tosh along. Not one to consider what obstacles they might encounter, Tosh agrees without hesitating. Her boyfriend and his sisters have already gone east, giving her added incentive.

Their father disapproves. "People will laugh and talk because you have left your aging parents behind," Tomekichi says.

"But Fuku and Yuji can look after you, Papa," Tosh replies.

"That does not matter. We should all stay together."

"Papa, we do not know what is going to happen. I am young. I cannot stay here forever. I am going."

That September she turns twenty-one, waiting on tables at the Toronto YWCA. Over the next year, she works at everything from housecleaning and sewing alterations to assembly line jobs in sunglass and greeting card factories.

Ironically, it is Yuki who breaks free from the menial jobs that characterize the working lives of so many. Tosh got her high school education, while Yuki didn't return to school after their mother died in 1925. Most of the household chores fell on her when she was only eleven. Hina's arrival a few years later changed that, but she started working as a domestic when she was sixteen, moving from Duncan to Vancouver. Before the war, she took odd jobs in drycleaning and dress-making shops.

Even when the war is over there is little reason to get an education. Professions such as medicine, social work, teaching, and law have racist policies that make it excessively difficult, if not impossible, to secure a job. In addition, the concept of a career was foreign to most women of Yuki's generation, particularly when they were raised in rural Japanese communities. But when she secures a clerk's job with the National Film Board in Ottawa in the late 1940s, she seizes the opportunity to cultivate inherent talents. By 1975, she is a technical producer in Studio D, a women's production unit. It is the international year of women, and Studio D is the NFB's response to a federal directive to boost women's profiles. When she retires in 1978, Yuki Yoshida is part of the team that wins an Academy Award for a series released that year called "I'll Find A Way." They are children's films that portray the diversity of life in Canada. Yuki can't help but bring the diversity of her own childhood to bear on the production. Out of her burdened past, she wrestles a precious victory. Nothing from her early years on Vancouver Island suggested meaningful work would enrich her life. Nothing, perhaps, except ambition toughened through hardship.

Before Yuki's career begins to unfold, Tosh opts for tradition and love. In May 1945, she moves out of the housekeeping room she shares with Yuki and marries Yasuo Kamino. Fearing more disapproval from her father, she does not wait for her family in Tashme to arrive. When they do come east, Tosh realizes she needn't have been so stubborn. Her father could be difficult, but often it is because he can't let go of the old ways. Nonetheless, it pleases him to see his daughter happily married.

Tosh continues working for a Jewish woman in a dressmaking shop until her son is born in 1946. Busy with life as a young mother, Tosh is surprised when a letter arrives from an old Chemainus friend a few years later. It is Meiko Sumiye, whom she has not seen since her family went to Japan in the 1930s. But the news is not good. Her sister Hisako was burned in the Hiroshima bombing and suffered a long, agonizing death. Still in grade school at the time of the bombing, Hisako was a baby when the family left Chemainus. Tosh remembers her, but only vaguely. She closes her eyes, and Mrs. Sumiye's cheerful, round face appears, cooing to her baby as she strolls along the boardwalk one fine afternoon.

In the early 1950s, Tosh has a girl and a boy, while Yasuo works hard to provide for them. She has almost thirty years with her husband, building a new life out of the old. When Yasuo dies in 1973, Tosh is fifty. Childhood dreams of becoming an actress are passed down to her daughter Brenda, while Tosh spends her remaining working years as a floral designer.

Troubles come and go. Yet she laughs often, her eyes shining like polished black diamonds.

Shizuka Okada, Hitoshi Okada, and Kaname Izumi laying wreaths at the Chemainus memorial monument, August 9/91.

Author Catherine Lang with Takayoshi Kawahara in front of the Chemainus building where his father's store had been, August 1991.

Stanley Taniwa painting "The Lone Scout" mural, August 1991.

Takayoshi Kawahara at the reunion, August 1991.

205

Cy Shillito, pitcher for the Green Lantern baseball team, and
Hitoshi Okada, reminiscing at the mural unveiling, August 10/91.

Joyce Kamikura in front of her mural "The Winning Float," July
1991.

Kaname Izumi, reminiscing under the entranceway to the former Taniwa's store, August 9/91.

Matsue Taniwa at the mural unveiling, August 10/91.

Artist Stanley Taniwa and subject Shige Yoshida in front of "The Lone Scout" mural, August 10/91.

Scoutmaster Shige Yoshida being made an honourary member of the Cowichan Valley Baden-Powell Guild, August 10/91.

Mitsi Kuwahara (nee Yoshida), eldest daughter of Shige and Sumiko Yoshida, who was age nine when evacuated, at the reunion, August 1991.

Mataharu (Mutt) Otsu after the *O-bon* service, August 10/91.

Memorial monument at the Chemainus cemetery, incorporating
headstones bulldozed in 1942 and discovered amid debris in 1988.

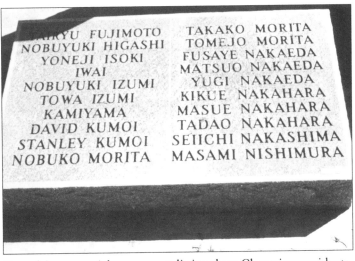

FUJIMOTO   TAKAKO MORITA
NOBUYUKI HIGASHI   TOMEJO MORITA
YONEJI ISOKI   FUSAYE NAKAEDA
IWAI   MATSUO NAKAEDA
NOBUYUKI IZUMI   YUGI NAKAEDA
TOWA IZUMI   KIKUE NAKAHARA
KAMIYAMA   MASUE NAKAHARA
DAVID KUMOI   TADAO NAKAHARA
STANLEY KUMOI   SEIICHI NAKASHIMA
NOBUKO MORITA   MASAMI NISHIMURA

Part of the memorial monument, listing those Chemainus residents
buried in the cemetery who were either Japanese immigrants or of
Japanese ancestry.

Unidentified man at the Chemainus cemetery following the *O-bon* service, August 10/91.

E I G H T

SUMIKO AND SHIGEYUKI YOSHIDA

SUMIKO YOSHIDA PUTTERS ABOUT HER KITCHEN, mixing batter for tempura and slicing sweet potatoes, carrots and green peppers that will surface golden and sizzling hot. She hums a soft melody while slipping the vegetables and prawns into a pot of hot oil. Her Toronto apartment kitchen is tiny, but Sumiko mastered the art of making fabulous meals in cramped quarters long ago.

Preoccupied with the task at hand, she jumps when the doorbell rings. It must be Ida, her sister-in-law. They have invited her to dinner to celebrate the news about the Chemainus reunion. Her husband, Shige, answers the door.

"Hi, Ida," she calls.

"Hello, Sumi. Smells wonderful in here."

"It'll be ready soon," Sumiko says, checking to make sure the tempura is bubbling gently. She sets last-minute condiments on the table while Shige and Ida chat on the couch. Listening to him tell his sister about the mural, Sumiko wonders how he will make it through the coming year. He is like a

211

kid wielding a prize trophy when his boy scout accomplishments come under the spotlight. She is his ballast on such
occasions, her calm, assured manner a steadying influence on
the heady mix of ego and vindication of past wrongs.

The tempura sweetens the air. Sumiko smiles her unassum-
ing smile and notices the afternoon light fall across her husband's thin shoulders. Shige is too busy talking to catch her eye.

"The murals' society has chosen a picture of me in my scout
uniform," Shige says, his eyes as bright as the day he formed
the 2nd Chemainus troop.

"Is that so?" Ida says, watching Sumiko set a steaming tray
on the table and motion her over. Pushing herself up off the
couch, she adds, "We're all proud of you, *Nii-san*. And after all
these years. . . ."

"Yes, it's really something, isn't it?" Shige says, chuckling.

After dinner, Shige buries himself in his study, perusing his
scouting paraphernalia. In addition to trophies, flags, badges,
and certificates of merit, he compiled three large albums from
material gathered during his years as a scoutmaster. The albums contain an autographed photograph, telegrams and letters from Lord Baden-Powell, the founder of the scout movement, and news clippings hailing the accomplishments of his
troops. Among many photos is one dating back to the first
gathering of his Chemainus troop on June 23, 1930.

Examining the picture, Shige swells with pride at the boys'
earnest enthusiasm. Although he alone was responsible for
creating the troop, Shige relied on *issei* leaders to support his
goal and form the troop's executive. Looking stern but proud,
they surround him in front of the community hall.

All but one are *issei*. Sitting at Shige's feet is the president,
Reverend Eric Robathan. Studying his face, Shige recalls the
Anglican priest's gentle, loving manner and outspoken sup-
port during years of intense racial hostility.

He turns a page and notices an article the reverend wrote

for the newspaper in 1931. Lifting his magnifying glass to read the fine print, Shige scans the familiar history of the movement. Robathan noted that twenty-five boys attended the first camp on the Dorsetshire coast in 1909, a year after Shige was born in Victoria. In just over two decades, the movement spread to 42 countries with an enrollment of nearly two million boys, promoting international brotherhood, comradeship, peace and love.

Shige vaguely remembers the reaction to the article. Not everyone in Chemainus was pleased that Robathan had pointed to the only Japanese troop in Canada as a model of the scouting spirit, but the boys were ecstatic. Praising Shige and his patrol leaders, the priest reported that the troop was "making splendid headway. The boys are putting forth every effort to make their troop 'second to none' and a credit to the community."

Shige reads on, recalling the scout meeting when everyone came with a copy inside their shirt pockets. They took his words so seriously back then, and discussed his ideas among themselves.

"What part will these scouts of the 2nd Chemainus troop play in world affairs when they have grown into men?" Robathan asked. "Will they lose sight of those ideals upon which their characters are being built up at present?"

An optimist, Robathan predicted that "the responsibility of bringing about a closer and more intimate relationship between East and West" might fall to them. "Nations have been drawn closer together by modern methods of transportation, radio, etc., but these methods are of no avail unless hearts as well are bound together in a mutual sympathy and understanding of each others' aspirations, ideals and needs."

In conclusion, Robathan impressed his young subjects with the ultimate responsibility of scouting. It was a message they could hardly ignore.

"The true spirit of the scout comes from another world than

that in which men push and strive for themselves; it comes
from a world where honour, truth, unselfishness, and brotherhood rule, the world whose name is the Kingdom of God. All
scouts are trustees of that spirit."

Shige sets the magnifying glass down and stares at the case
containing his memorabilia. He had forgotten what Robathan
wrote so long ago, but the message is part of him yet. Almost
sixty years later, the irony of the reverend's sentiment does not
undermine Shige's heartfelt belief in the same ideals. After all,
he has sacrificed a great deal to prove good can prevail over evil.

Shige's father is a handsome, adventurous twenty-year-old in
1899 when he leaves Enzan, a village in Yamanashi. Searching
for wealth and prestige in America, Shigetoki Yoshida finds
work in the vineyards of Fresno, California. His fun-loving
and carefree ways notwithstanding, he is a well-educated,
clever man who becomes a straw boss to a crew of immigrant
labourers. Eight years later, he returns to Japan to marry
Kume Ogiwara. A woman from a wealthy family with delicate features and soft, imploring eyes, she is in her early twenties when she reluctantly leaves her homeland with a man she
barely knows.

Shigetoki's plans to return to Fresno are foiled, however. In
1907, the couple disembark in Victoria after American
authorities refuse them entry because Kume has an eye infec-
tion. The city is a bastion of British colonialism, striving to
dominate both the physical landscape and nearby Asian and
Native Indian enclaves. Fortunately, Bumpei Kuwabara acts
as an unofficial interpreter at the customs office and introduces
them to the small Japanese community scattered about town.
After showing them where to buy food and rent a room, he
leaves them to figure out things most take for granted. Neither
has seen a flush toilet, so they use it as a wash basin on their
first night in the Osawa Hotel.

Shigetoki soon learns that work is not easy to come by here. Immigrants take whatever jobs they can find: gardening, working as domestics for the wealthy, or as bellhops in the Empress Hotel. Some manage to buy or lease land to farm or to start a small business, but there are no major employers looking for pools of cheap labour.

His savings are running out when he learns that coal baron James Dunsmuir is hiring men to clear land for his castle at Hatley Park. Soon he is on the job, learning how to fall old-growth timber in the wilderness west of Victoria.

When he gets paid, Shigetoki rents a small flat in Victoria's Chinatown and moves his pregnant wife out of their tent on the Dunsmuir lands. On May 16, 1908, Kume delivers her first child in their Fisgard Street flat, thankful a midwife is at hand. But she is an unhappy new mother, pining for the comforts and companionship of life in Japan. Tiny Shigeyuki brings her some solace, and acquaintances with *issei* women in the neighbourhood help her cope.

After finishing up the Dunsmuir job, Shigetoki takes whatever odd jobs he can find. Kume bears two daughters in their primitive home, while Shigetoki saves his pennies. In 1912, he opens a pool hall in Ladysmith, unaware that a coal miners' strike is imminent. It proves to be one of the most bitter, protracted strikes in the region's history, devastating the economy. Forced to shut down the unsuccessful venture, the Yoshidas move south of Chemainus in 1914, where an Englishman hires Shigetoki to clear portions of his land.

A good-hearted employer, Matthew Howe offers them an unused barn on his property. Shigetoki builds an outhouse and partitions off the hay loft, creating one main room for living and eating, another for sleeping. Matthew helps him install a sawdust burner for heating and cooking, while Shigetoki carves rough furniture and builds a Japanese-style bath out of waste lumber.

A year after settling in the barn, Kume goes into labour with her fourth child. Midwives are not readily available in such remote locations, so Kume expects the local doctor to attend the birth. When he does not arrive, Shigetoki panics and drives into town for help. Naka Taniwa and Miki Mizuta are not midwives, but they agree to come. Some hours later the inexperienced team delivers a healthy girl, and Shigetoki finally stops pacing. In three years, Kume relies on her husband alone to coax their fifth child into the world. In 1918, Shigetoki cuts his son's umbilical cord with shaky hands, wishing he were outside falling timber instead.

Living away from town is lonely for Kume, but their arrival marks a new beginning for the Howe's only son, Jackie. When he learns the Yoshidas have a six-year-old son, he is at their door the next morning.

Shige opens the door to a skinny boy with a wide grin.

"Want to go fishing?" he asks.

"Why, sure," Shige says. "I have to ask first, though." He turns and Kume nods her approval.

Jackie leads his new friend down to the creek. Dappled light bounces off polished rocks as rainbow trout slither downstream. The boys look at each other.

"Let's go dig up some worms," Jackie suggests.

"Where?"

"Up by my place. C'mon."

They race each other back to Jackie's house and dig up a can of earthworms in some freshly turned soil. Jackie runs inside and comes out with bits of string and two safety pins.

"Here, tie these strings together," he says, giggling. His mother steps onto the porch, where the boys are poking safety pins through the string. She can't remember when she saw her son having so much fun.

Shige grabs the can of worms, and they are off. By noon,

they have caught enough trout for everyone's dinner. They haul their catch back up the hill and stop outside the barn.

"Can you play this afternoon?" Jackie asks.

"Maybe after I do my chores," Shige replies.

Jackie continues up the path to his house. Halfway there, he turns to wave. Shige is waving his arm high above his head, his other arm heavy with a string of fish gleaming in the sun.

That afternoon Matthew drives them to the beach in his 1911 Hupmobile Roadster. As the landscape unfolds, Shige can't believe his eyes. "We could roam here for hours, Mr. Howe," he says, "and look at all the sheep and cattle up on the bluff. Can we go see them?"

Jackie turns to his father. "Can we, Dad?"

Matthew smiles. "Don't get too close. Those cows will be calving soon."

The boys jump out and scramble up the hill. Matthew watches them go, chuckling under his breath.

In time, Jackie becomes good friends with Shige's sister, too. The second oldest Yoshida child, Kanako listens for Jackie calling her English name when she steps outside in the morning.

"Connie," he calls, wistfully. " Connie, are you ready?"

She looks up the path toward the Howe's house. Jackie is on his veranda, waving his bony arm. "He looks so cute," she says, hopping on her bicycle. In no time they are cycling along the dirt road toward town, hair flying as they race down the hill, over the railroad tracks, up past the cemetery, Chinatown, and the mill grounds until they reach the public school on Cedar Street, breathless.

Kanako likes school because she gets to play with other children. But one day at recess, she finds Shige fighting with Takeshi Okada on the grounds. Her brother's hot temper often gets him into trouble, but this is more serious than usual. Everyone is huddled around the muddy field where the boys are scrapping.

The recess bell rings, but the boys ignore it. Soon Mr.

Pritchard, the principal, wades through the ring of onlookers, muddying his galoshes and pants. Kanako watches him pull Shige and Takeshi apart, both of whom have bloody noses. With a hand firmly on the shoulder of each boy, he turns and orders everyone back to class.

Kanako shuffles indoors and slides behind her desk, head hanging. She is a grade below Shige, but three grades are all in one classroom. When Shige and Takeshi walk in five minutes later, only Takeshi slips into his seat. Miss McInnes is approaching Shige with a cat-o-nine tails in her hand. He is standing in front of the class, hands behind his back.

"Young man," the teacher barks, "put out your hands."

Shige obeys and fixes his stare, determined not to cry. He will not give his teacher or Takeshi that satisfaction.

Everyone jumps at the first crack, and Kanako starts to cry. Shige winces, then there is another crack and yet another. The ordeal continues, but still Shige doesn't cry. Once or twice, he moves his hands before the strap hits, enraging Miss McInnes further. Finally she stops, and Shige returns to his seat. No one moves. By now, Kanako is sobbing.

The morning inches by. Normally an enthusiastic student, Shige sits still while everyone scribbles in their notebooks. He can't pick up his pencil for a week.

At home, he tells Kanako what happened.

"Takeshi accused me of tripping him when he was running for the football," Shige says.

"Did you?" Kanako asks.

"Of course not. We were arguing about it, and we got so mad that we started punching each other."

"Why didn't Takeshi get the strap too?" Kanako asks.

Shige looks down. "Because I'm older than him, that's why."

Kanako is preoccupied when she walks up the Howes' front steps to help Mrs. Howe make butter on Saturday. Anna

Howe doesn't notice that her shy helper is out of sorts and begins pouring buckets of cream into the barrel on the porch. Wearing a crisp apron over her work dress, Anna smiles and begins churning while Kanako waits her turn. They have the butter separated in no time and transfer it onto a large board, which they carry into the kitchen.

Kanako picks up a rolling pin and smooths out the creamy mass on the board. The memory of Shige's strapping is still vivid, but she feels safe in Mrs. Howe's big, bright kitchen. When the butter is finished, Kanako fetches a bucket and opens a tap for water to wash the floor. The Howes may be isolated, but they are not without conveniences.

Jackie invites her and Shige to play cards in the evening, so Shige leads his sister back up the trail after supper. As they approach, they can see the inside lights. Mr. Howe has created this thing called electricity using water from Fuller Lake. Inside, Kanako can go to the bathroom without fear of being attacked by a wild animal.

Shige is twelve when his leadership qualities come to the fore. On the first day of school in September 1920, ever-punctual Shige strides into the classroom unnoticed. He sits beside Kinjiro Seko, who towers above his classmates. Having just emigrated from Japan, Kinjiro wants to learn English. Shige welcomes him to Chemainus and turns his attention to the teacher, a dowdy woman with a weight problem that prompts some to whisper "cow" behind her back.

Miss Dwyer calls the roll in her strident voice, pausing at Kinjiro's name. When she is finished, she walks in front of her desk to address the class.

"All of the Oriental students will now proceed to room number three across the hall," she announces.

Instinctively, Shige stands up. "I don't think that's right," he says. "I won't stand for that. I'm sending my students home, and you're not going to stop me."

Miss Dwyer is speechless. This boy may only be twelve, but something stops her from bullying him back into his seat. Shige turns to the Japanese students. "Everyone go home," he orders. The eldest of the Japanese Canadian students, he knows they will obey. Without any fuss, they file out the door.

At home that night, Shige explains what happened.

"I knew it didn't sound right. I knew it was wrong right away. They are discriminating against us," he tells his father.

"You acted wisely, son," Shigetoki replies. "Tomorrow I'll send a telegram to the Japanese consulate in Vancouver. We'll have this sorted out soon."

Sure enough, the consulate negotiates with local school trustees, and the students are back in regular class the following week. But it is not so easy for men like Kinjiro, who cannot ignore hostile *hakujin* parents demanding the withdrawal of Japanese adults from their children's classrooms. Foregoing his hopes of learning proper English, he leaves. Like other *issei*, he will learn what he can on the job at the sawmill. Canadian-born Shige, on the other hand, competes for top marks every year with his arch rival, Evelyn Toynbee.

As work on the Howe's property diminishes, Shigetoki gets a job as a jitney driver at the sawmill. Waving and smiling at everyone he passes, he moves lumber about the plant in his Ford jitney. "Here comes Henry Ford," the workers say, laughing as he manoeuvres the little truck like a dinky toy.

Kume's work offers no such perks. She never goes into town, fitting the needs of the children around laundry, cleaning, and cooking. Shige spares her the task of fetching water from the creek, and Kanako and Chizuko tend their young siblings after school. Pregnant again, she sits down to knit and sew after the children are in bed.

A month after Kumeo is born in 1921, his sister Yachiho starts school. While she adores her father, she can't abide the name he gave her, which means "battleship." Perhaps because it matches her stocky build, she is desperate to change it. Even her Japanese friends can't pronounce it properly, let alone the *hakujins*.

On the first day of school, the opportunity to give herself a new identity finally arrives. When the teacher asks her name, she stands up proudly and announces, "Ida Yoshida." It is just a name she likes the sound of. Now it is hers. In her mind, Yachiho ceases to exist.

She is unable to dismiss her father's drinking and driving so easily. Unreserved, boisterous and full of laughs, Ida loves going places with Shigetoki—even though getting home is often a terrifying journey.

One Sunday afternoon, Shige and Ida accompany their father to the Yoshiki home in Hillcrest, a sawmill town north of Duncan. It is a mild autumn day, and Ida sticks her head out the window as they wind around old-growth stumps left behind by loggers. Shige sits in the middle, surreptitiously teaching himself how to drive by watching his father shift gears. He has made a point of it ever since he went through the windshield coming home from the fair in Nanaimo. His father hit a ditch somehow; miraculously, Shige wasn't badly hurt.

Arriving in Hillcrest, Shigetoki rolls to a stop and beeps his horn outside his friend's home. Mr. Yoshiki steps onto his porch and waves them inside. As soon as they are indoors, he brings out the sake, prompting nine-year-old Ida to plead with her father.

"Please don't drink too much, Papa. You're driving."

"Quiet!" Shigetoki scolds.

"Yes, Papa," she murmurs, slouching down at the kitchen table beside her teenage brother.

Several sake later, Shigetoki's stories are getting more and more hilarious. Finally, Shige nudges his father.

"It's time to go. Mama will have supper ready soon."

"Yes, yes. You're right," Shigetoki replies, grinning at Shige. "My son is always right, you know," he says, steadying himself as he pushes away from the table. Ida swallows hard and steels herself for the trip home. Shigetoki weaves toward the truck, trying three times before he manages to haul himself up behind the wheel. With her eyes fixed firmly ahead, Ida concentrates on the resounding thump of hard tires on packed earth. Every time huge stumps loom up before them, she grips the edge of her seat and holds her breath, waiting to crash. But Shigetoki always swerves just in time as he bumps merrily along.

After a near mishap, Shige finally turns to his father. "You better take a rest. I'll drive."

"You never drove before. How can you drive?"

"I've been watching. I can do it. I'm sure."

Ida holds her breath while Shigetoki thinks about it. When their father slides over, Shige tramps around to the driver's seat. Ida clamps her mouth shut, suppressing an urge to shout, "Hurray, *Nii-san*!" He drives the rest of the way home without incident.

It is still daylight when they get back, and Ida has to collect milk from the Howes. She slides the empty lard pail off the shelf by the door and grabs her little brother's pudgy hand. Kumeo loves to walk with his big sister, for Ida tells him stories on the way. Mostly, they are grand make-believe stories, but today's isn't.

"You should have seen him, Kume," Ida says, turning a pretend steering wheel in her hands. "Oh, he is a good driver."

Shige has been expanding various side jobs into full-time work since he finished grade eight when he was thirteen. Every summer he negotiates a berry-picking contract, hiring Chizuko and her friends to pick the loganberries while he makes shipping arrangements. In addition, he sells everything from flower seeds and custom-made shoes to life insurance and newspapers. Money-making ventures aside, he volunteers to serve as spokesman for the *issei*, most of whom don't speak English very well. He attends school board and Red Cross meetings, speaking up for his people and correcting errors of fact in the propaganda war threatening to marginalize them further. Shige proves himself a fighter, believing he deserves no less and no more than the next man.

He also takes a keen interest in boy scouts, reading anything he can get his hands on about the movement. Ever since he heard *hakujin* boys boasting about campouts and jamborees, Shige started eyeing their uniforms and colourful badges. He is sixteen when he applies to join the 1st Chemainus troop, having finally saved enough for a uniform. Some weeks later, the scoutmaster tells him that the troop is full.

Keeping his anger in check, Shige marches off. He knows the rejection is racially motivated and it hurts, but it also fuels his determination to find another way. Soon after, he discovers an ad for the Lone Scouts of America in one of the newspapers he is selling. The Chicago newspaper publisher is the founder of a boy scout correspondence course tailored for American boys in remote locations. Shige applies and waits, bicycling the three miles to the post office on Mill Street every mail day for a reply.

When the first package of material arrives, he beams at the postal clerk. He runs his fingers over his name on the label and hollers "Hurray!" Placing it in his bicycle basket outside, he jostles it about to estimate its weight. Shige pedals home in high spirits, whistling with the wind.

That night he gets to work, sorting out the assignments and books and setting strict deadlines for himself. For the next five years, he studies hard. In 1929, he writes his final exams, achieving the highest possible rank. A year later he receives a warrant from the Boy Scouts of Canada, granting him the authority to form his own troop.

In June 1930, one month after his twenty-second birthday, Shige and his two patrol leaders, Takayoshi Kawahara and Shunichi Isoki, herd eight boys into the Japanese community hall to learn the principles of scouting: to do a good turn every day; to smile and whistle under all difficulties; to be prepared. The first Japanese-Canadian boy scout troop in the British Empire, it swears its allegiance to king and country.

The year before Shige forms his scout troop, Sumiko Takahashi leaves her quiet, isolated life on the Fraser River. Having finished grade eight in New Westminster, Sumiko is going to live with her sister's family and learn dressmaking in their tailor shop in Chemainus. Her parent's only Canadian-born child, she is a shy fourteen-year-old when she says goodbye to their houseboat near the Patullo Bridge.

Her childhood is full of memories from the houseboat deck, watching the Fraser flow past as they moved down river during salmon runs. Sojourns on the river aside, she has never set foot outside New Westminster. Now she is boarding a steamship bound for Nanaimo, with no idea where Vancouver Island is or who will meet her on the other side.

Sumiko doesn't know her sister very well. A marriage was already arranged for Shimo when she arrived from Japan, so she never lived on the houseboat. Sumiko has never met her sister's second husband, Suketaro Ota, but he recognizes her when she steps onto the Nanaimo dock. Two silent hours later, he ushers her into their humble home in the back of his tailor shop on Oak Street. Sumiko stands awkwardly in the middle of the kitchen, fiddling with the edge of a pocket on her dress.

Shimo steps into the kitchen with a baby in her arms. "Hello, Sumi. My, how you've grown."

"Yes, *Nee-san*," Sumiko replies.

"Come. Sit and we'll have some tea."

Sumiko slides into a chair and sighs. While her sister puts water on the stove, she plays with the baby on the floor.

"So, did anyone tell you about all the nice boys we have in Chemainus?"

Sumiko blushes. "No, *Nee-san*."

"Well, we'll have to do something about that, won't we?" Shimo teases, pouring the tea and sitting down to chat.

Before the week is out, Sumiko has a new friend, but it isn't a boy. Chizuko Yoshida often comes by to mind the baby or tend to customers. Her family no longer lives in Matthew Howe's barn but in a house that they bought around the corner on Esplanade. The girls become best friends right away. Like Sumiko, Chizuko spent most of her childhood isolated from friends at school. Happily, that changes for both.

Sumiko meets Chizuko's brother Shige, too. On his day off from his job at the sawmill, he drives up and down island with Suketaro selling made-to-measure suits in various Japanese communities. But neither take much notice of each other when he comes into the shop. Sumiko is too young and shy, while Shige is so caught up in his business endeavours and scouting activities that he hasn't time for girls.

During Sumiko's third summer in Chemainus, Shige's father decides it's time his twenty-four-year-old son got married. One evening in 1932, Shigetoki knocks on the door and asks to speak to Suketaro privately. Sumiko thinks little of it and goes to her room, but when her brother-in-law takes her aside two weeks later, her mind starts racing.

"Mr. Yoshida has asked your father if you will marry Shige," Suketaro begins.

Sumiko says nothing. She is thinking of all the times she has seen Shige: visiting Chizuko in her home, at baseball games, in the tailor shop. She can't imagine him as her husband. The thought never crossed her mind—or his, from what she can tell.

"What did Father say?" she finally asks.

"Shige will make a good husband. He is reliable, hard-working and honest. He doesn't drink or gamble. Your father thinks you should accept."

Sumiko looks out the back window onto the alley that cuts through Kawahara camp. Children run along the boardwalk, playing tag and giggling. She recognizes Shige's two youngest brothers, Kumeo and Noriyuki. At seventeen, Sumiko knows nothing about marriage except that it is inevitable.

"When?" she asks.

Suketaro smiles. "Probably sometime this fall. But you'll go home again first."

On October 26, 1932, Shige dons his navy wool suit and combs his hair with water. He studies his reflection in the mirror, all five feet two inches of it. Fine bones and features belie his tough character. Satisfied with his appearance, he slips downstairs to get his father. It will take several hours to reach the Takahashis' houseboat on the Fraser, so they are getting an early start.

Sumiko is still sleeping when Shige and his father cross a lumpy Strait of Georgia in the CPR steamship. By the time they reach Vancouver, she is setting out smoked salmon and sweet bean cakes. Her mother has invited friends to a small ceremony on the houseboat, expecting Shigetoki will arrange for a minister to marry them in Chemainus later that week.

Strolling into her room, Sumiko lifts a wine-coloured dress from the closet. She jiggles the hanger, watching the satin ripple in waves. The cool fabric sends shivers up her spine as it slips to the floor. Then she brushes her curls and applies red lipstick, pressing her lips together like a movie star. She exam-

ines her face. Although she isn't a delicate beauty, her profile is
strong and her complexion flawless. The sheen from the satin
glows in her large black eyes.

By early afternoon the nervous bride and groom are sipping
sake from the same cup, consecrating the marriage in the can-
dlelit room heavy with the sweet musk of incense. Everyone
gathers round a sunken table following the ceremony, politely
nibbling on *manju*. Always the entertainer, Shigetoki swaps
tall tales and jokes until it's time to go. When the meal is over,
Shige bids his bride an awkward goodbye and leaves with his
father.

Sumiko arrives in Chemainus with her parents two days
later, expecting the wedding ceremony with the minister. But
Shigetoki has arranged nothing, and her parents leave the following day. Saying farewell on the front porch, Sumiko is
glum.

"Mr. Yoshida is *nonki*, Mama. Everyone tells me he means
well, but he is careless."

"We are disappointed too, Sumi," her mother says. "But we
must go now."

Sumiko nods and waves. She watches them round the corner, knowing she probably won't see them for years. Her eyes
fall on the gnarled fruit trees across the street. As much as she
likes her father-in-law, she is upset that he let them down.
When she becomes pregnant four months later, Shigetoki finally arranges for a minister to marry them.

Shige happens to be home on his lunch hour when Sumiko
goes into labour during the Indian summer of 1933. He walks
his eighteen-year-old wife across the street to the Chemainus
hospital and returns to work for the afternoon, confident she is
in good hands. A nurse sits nearby, monitoring her labour.
Sumiko gratefully inhales ether to ease the pain as her baby
girl is finally born.

After a week in the hospital, Sumiko brings Mitsi home to a mostly familiar routine. Her mother-in-law cooks all the meals, while Sumiko helps Kume with housework and laundry. When the day's chores are done, she cradles Mitsi in her arms and strolls down the street to visit her sister and her friend Matsue Taniwa. After chatting for a while, Sumiko hikes back up the hill whispering in Mitsi's ear.

The following spring she plants sweet peas, sweet williams and candy tuft along the front of the house. Although finding the time isn't easy, she enjoys gardening. It gives her a break from household chores, which she and Kume share. Luxuries are non-existent, but it is all she expects from life and is content.

Shige is happy too. Although his job as a jitney driver at the sawmill is steady, he hustles side jobs whenever possible to ease the financial strain. Between work and scouting activities, he is hardly ever home. His brothers Tokio and Kumeo see more of him than his wife: they are scouts.

Scouting gives the boys access to a world normally out of bounds. For Tokio, getting to events is half the fun. Ten years younger than Shige, he is in his early teens in the 1930s when the troop sets out for a conference in Bellingham. Bustling about on a Victoria dock, they pray for the weather to co-operate. A thick blanket of clouds obscure the Olympic Mountains across Juan de Fuca Strait. An hour passes and Tokio stamps his feet impatiently, no longer content to study the tough little tugboat that will ease them around the tip of the Olympic Peninsula and down the coast of Washington State.

Everyone is about to lose hope when the southeast winds blow over and the sky clears. The tugboat captain announces, "Seagulls going out to sea, so I think storm is over. Come on board." Eight boys, two patrol leaders, and Shige spill onto the deck and depart in a cloud of black smoke. Standing on the bow, Tokio sucks in the salt air and thinks of his father venturing across the Pacific. Plying the waters is powerful excitement, heightened by the deafening rumble of the engine at full throttle.

Of the many activities Shige organizes for the boys, the April 1935 jamboree in Victoria is the highlight. On a beautiful spring day on the Willows exhibition grounds, some 2,500 boy scouts, girl guides, wolf cubs, and Brownies congregate to show off their skills and hear the Chief Scout, Lord Baden-Powell, and his wife applaud their achievements.

Before the honourary couple speak, the 2nd Chemainus troop joins a competition to build a suspension bridge. The boys hustle as a team, tying clove hitches and reef knots around saplings that form the planks, circling trees with rope to suspend the bridge, driving stakes to secure the apparatus. When it is complete, Lord Baden-Powell marches to the centre and offers his approval. "Well done," he says, leaning forward to shake Shige's hand.

The scoutmaster beams. Through perseverance and hard work, Shige grasps equality in the white man's world.

A year later, Sumiko gives birth to a boy. Standing proudly over him in the hospital nursery, they name him Shigeru. But months after bringing their frail bundle home, Sumiko begins to worry. No matter how much she feeds and pampers him, he doesn't gain weight. Finally, she consults Shige.

"I've done everything I can think of, but he isn't getting better. What should we do?"

"We will take him to doctors in Victoria," he says. "Don't worry. We'll find out what's wrong."

The specialists in Victoria inform Sumiko she has a "blue baby," which means nothing to her except that he isn't normal. After they return home, his health deteriorates further and they admit him to the Chemainus hospital. Shige and Sumiko sit beside his crib and pray for signs of improvement, but within days six-month-old Shigeru dies.

They stumble home from the hospital, stunned to lose their beloved boy so suddenly. No one warned them he might die. Sumiko shuffles through the front door in a daze. Her three-year-old comes running, and Sumiko crouches down, arms hugging. She carries Mitsi into the living room and sits her on her lap.

"Baby Shigeru is not coming home, sweetie," Sumiko begins.

Mitsi looks into her mother's face. "Are you crying, Mama? Why isn't baby coming home?"

"He's gone to heaven, dear."

"Heaven? Where's that?"

"Oh, it's a very nice place, way up high in the sky."

"Will he be happy there?"

"Oh yes," Sumiko replies, pulling Mitsi against her and rocking to and fro. "He will be very happy."

Shige's father calls on his friend Mantoku Sakata to perform the Shinto-Buddhist rites in their home that night. They bring Shigeru home in a simple wooden casket and place him on a table in the living room. Flowers and candles surround the casket as the smell of incense thickens. Sumiko sits in the corner and stares into the flames. Mantoku's chanting seems so far away. Hours pass. Finally, Shige guides her upstairs, where they both fall into a fitful sleep. The Buddhist blessings of Shigeru's grandparents are guiding him on his journey to the afterworld, even though his parents are Anglican.

The family huddles around his grave in the Chemainus cemetery the next day, lighting candles and incense as Mantoku chants in a low relentless drone. At specified intervals over the next forty-eight days, the Yoshidas light more candles to help Shigeru complete his journey. In the coming years, they tidy his grave regularly, fixing or replacing the wooden

cross as it deteriorates. And every year during the August
O-bon festival, they light another candle to welcome his spirit
home.

In 1989 when a volunteer worker discovers headstones in a
pile of dirt outside the cemetery fence, the wooden cross that
marked his grave is decomposed in a rubble of earth. No one
knows exactly where he lies any more.

The year after Shigeru's death, Sumiko has a healthy baby girl.
Jean is born on a hot day in July, when ocean breezes merci-
fully sweep through the hospital room. Breastfeeding her infant later, Sumiko watches the cotton curtains fluttering. Dusk
is washing the world outside in a lovely shade of lavender.

At twenty-two, she is well-adjusted to motherhood and
happy again. Her memory of Shigeru is fading, and with it her
grief. When Mitsi and Shige arrive to see Jean, Sumiko is
jubilant. The euphoric phase follows her home from the hospital, but it too fades as piles of laundry, housework, cooking,
and caring for the girls occupy her hours. She never complains,
even though she no longer has Kume's help. In Kawabe's
bunkhouse two blocks away, her mother-in-law cooks for
bachelors from morning to night.

Five months after Jean is born, Kume and Shigetoki take
their youngest son about 100 kilometres west of Tokyo to the
prefecture of Yamanashi. They leave Canada on New Year's
Day in 1938, venturing across the Pacific to the heavily popu-
lated islands off the coast of Asia.

The purpose of the trip is twofold: to provide Noriyuki
with a Japanese education, and to provide a childless aunt and
uncle with a son. Although fourteen-year-old Noriyuki takes
their surname, he lives with his parents in the town of Enzan,
close to his father's home village. Shigetoki tutors his son until
he is ready for school. But during the two years it takes to
perfect his Japanese, Noriyuki struggles to gain acceptance.

Strangely, he feels the discrimination here more acutely than anything he encountered in Canada. Even Kume finds she no longer fits into Japanese society after her twenty-one-year absence, so she returns to Chemainus in 1939.

The responsibilities of the Yoshida household fall to Shige and Sumiko. They include keeping Shige's brother Kumeo in high school until he graduates in 1940. The only Yoshida child to graduate in Canada, Kumeo is an A student who loves mathematics. But he is not altogether happy about being a burden on Shige and Sumiko and feels indebted to his older brothers. Tokio started working at the sawmill in 1933, having left school at fifteen to help make the house payments. He cried the day his father told him to leave school and get a job. Dreams of training as a diesel mechanic died when he joined the ranks of unskilled labourers at the mill. As for Shige, he accepted his responsibility as the oldest son at an early age. But had times and circumstances been different, he might have practised more than his boy scout's first aid: Shige dreamt of being a doctor one day.

The Yoshida girls are all married by the time Kumeo graduates, neither contributing to the household nor a burden on it. Kanako was seventeen when she married the son of a fisherman on Saltspring Island in 1927. Ida was next, marrying a man who took her to an isolated logging camp outside Ladysmith in 1931 when she was sixteen. In 1932, Chizuko married and moved to Vancouver at the age of twenty-one.

Dreams of their youth were wrapped up in the pages of Eatons' catalogues, where fantasies about fancy apparel and modern homes lay dormant. Unlike their brothers who sacrificed their education, the girls never dreamed of careers outside marriage.

Shortly after Kume returns from Japan in 1939, Tokio muses about going to Toronto to make money. His mother will hear nothing of it, so he reluctantly abandons the idea. He is a good son who laughs easily and takes life as it comes, but at twenty-one he feels constrained in Chemainus. With or without Kume's blessing, he decides to enlist in the air force in 1940. The possibility for adventure aside, it will also be a chance to prove his loyalty to Canada. With any luck, it might even curtail the racism that has denied him opportunities *hakujin* men take for granted.

One Saturday, Tokio leaves work early and meets his friend Satoshi Izumi by the Horseshoe Bay Inn. They wait for the bus in a light drizzle.

"Imagine flying over Europe, Toki," Satoshi says, dreamily.

"And shooting down Germans. No one will call us yellow then," Tokio says.

"I can hardly wait 'til we join our old *hakujin* classmates in uniform."

"Yeah, won't they be surprised?" Tokio adds, chuckling.

The bus arrives and they hop on. En route to Duncan, they gaze at the ramshackle homes of the Westholme Indians and the farms of the earliest *hakujin* settlers. When the bus rattles into town, they make a beeline for the RCAF recruitment office, blissfully preoccupied as they scurry past NO JAPS ALLOWED signs in the bowling alley and restaurant windows.

Inside the recruitment office, a pleasant young man leads them to a doctor for their physicals. Satoshi's eyesight is failing, but Tokio passes with ease. Afterwards, he consoles Satoshi over a Chinese meal at Konkui House, trying to keep his own high spirits in check.

Back home, months go by without any word. Finally he acknowledges he isn't going to get called up. Closing his eyes, he sees the word JAP in large block letters scribbled across his application. It is the last time he will volunteer to put his life on the line for his country.

In June 1941, Sumiko becomes pregnant again. She is thankful Kumeo can help out with expenses now that he is finished school and has a job. When Shige and Tokio's wages were cut back during the Depression, they got by, but only just. Now that the worst is over, there still isn't any money to spare.

Sumiko isn't worried, though. She feels secure in a world that is anything but. Like most women of her generation, she does not encounter racism very often. Lack of exposure to the wider community screens it from her experience. She is six months pregnant when all that changes on December 7, 1941.

Shige and Sumiko are renovating the living room when they hear the broadcast. Shige slides down the ladder and turns the volume up. Sumiko sets down her pail, and they sink into the sofa to hear the newscast. Shige shakes his head back and forth.

"I knew something was going to happen," he says.

"What now, Shige?" Sumiko asks, rubbing her arms. "Will they invade here next?"

"Who knows, Sumi," he replies. "Anything is possible."

The chaos begins within the week. Shige disbands his scout troop, fearing any association among them will be suspect. But because of his profile as scoutmaster, the police solicit his help. They need someone to deliver messages from the B.C. Security Commission, the government body that administers the orders-in-council that Parliament passes under the War Measures Act. Shige accepts the responsibility without hesitation. His messenger status notwithstanding, police confiscate his car a few months later. That spring, he tallies up a lot of miles delivering their messages on his bicycle.

Although he believes that co-operating with the law is the ticket to proving the community's loyalty, he takes exception to one missive in particular. When the police tell Shige to inform all Japanese-born men that they will be shipped to road camps, he is stunned.

"Those men are the breadwinners in their families, and the women and children have no other means of support," he protests.

"We will take care of them. They will receive welfare," the constable says.

Shige swallows and shifts his weight. He looks at the rain outside the officer's window and thinks about the hill he has to climb to reach Chinatown. It is a challenge to cycle from camp to camp, delivering messages between the end of his shift at the mill and the seven o'clock curfew. His throat and chest are tight as he steps outside and hops on his bicycle. Focusing on the pedals, he works every muscle to propel him uphill.

It is the only message that doesn't affect the Yoshida household, for Shige's father is in Japan. But that does little to ease the stress: communication ceases for four years. In addition to Shigetoki and Noriyuki, Kanako is also trapped overseas because her husband wanted his ailing parents to meet their grandchildren. Kanako and her children barely survive the war years on meagre rations of rice.

Shige's main worry is not his father or Kanako but Noriyuki. After completing university in 1942, he is conscripted into the Japanese navy. Now nineteen, he survives the first heavy bombing, recuperating from burns in a military hospital before returning to duty. The worst comes near the end of the war when he is a fully brainwashed third petty officer. Part of an instalment of 500 battleships near the Philippines, Noriyuki is taking part in early morning training when three submarine torpodeos target his ship. After thirty hours in tropical waters, he is rescued only to be torpedoed again. When the battleship *Yamato* lifts him from waters near the coast of the Philippines, they are attacked by some 2,000 planes. The *Yamato* sinks with its remaining crew the next day, when Noriyuki is quietly en route to a naval base. He is among few survivors who are quarantined for six weeks to keep the news from getting out.

As Shige pedals from camp to camp, he has more than Noriyuki's fate on his mind. The impending arrival of another baby aside, he considers the community's welfare his responsibility. By getting messages out quickly, he does what he can to alleviate fears fed by rumour.

While her husband is out, Sumiko adds packing to her list of household chores. Nine-year-old Mitsi is in school, but Jean is only five and still at home. One day she finds Sumiko packing the festival dolls she and Mitsi received every Girls' Day in March.

"Why are you putting them in the box, Mama?" Jean asks. "Won't they get cold and lonely?"

Sumiko brushes Jean's thick, black bangs away from her eyes. "See, I'm wrapping all the dolls in blankets to keep them warm while they sleep," she says.

"Will they be asleep for a long time, Mama?"

"I hope not, dear. I'm sure they will be really happy to see you when we get back," Sumiko says, setting the last one in the storage chest before closing the lid. The tiny but perfect Japanese empress, dressed in a robin's egg silk kimono, guards the collective beneath her.

Jean never wakes the empress from her slumber, and she never finds out who does. The cedar chest just disappears.

In early March, Shige learns that the evacuation is scheduled for the very week the baby is due. Unsure what to do, Shige decides to approach Miss Esther Ryan.

A United Church missionary who worked in Japan, she is familiar with Japanese culture, fluent in Japanese and an invaluable asset to the community. A few years after Shige formed his scout troop, Miss Ryan invited Japanese Canadian girls to join her cgit group. Shige immediately recognized her as an ally.

After picking up the message from the rcmp, he cycles to her home and knocks on the door.

"I'm sorry to bother you, Miss Ryan. I just found out that the ship is coming for us the same week my wife is expecting her baby. She may not be out of the hospital yet."

"Well, I will stay with her," Esther says. "The authorities will agree. What else can they do?"

Shige fidgets with the brim of his hat. "Thank you. I will write for permission today."

"Bring me the letter when it's written, and I will sign it too," she says.

Turning to leave, Shige mumbles another thank you. "Sumi will not worry now."

As it turns out, the turmoil in communities along the B.C. coast is matched by the chaos in the administration of the evacuation. The ship scheduled for Chemainus in March is delayed a month, making the arrangements with Miss Ryan unnecessary.

Sumiko gives birth to a healthy girl on March 15, 1942. On the eve of the evacuation five weeks later, Shige is at the police station. He is getting last-minute details on evacuees from Duncan, Hillcrest and Paldi, who will be leaving on the same ship in the morning. Insulating herself from uncertainty, Sumiko is nursing Virginia as if all were right in the world. Suddenly, she hears Tokio confront a stranger in their living room downstairs.

"What the hell are you doing here?" he asks.

"Just wanted to have a look around," the *hakujin* announces. "Thought I'd see what you Japs are leaving behind."

"Get out!" Tokio yells, advancing toward the man.

Sneering as he turns to go, he says: "I'll be back after you're gone."

Sumiko puts Virginia to bed and flies downstairs. She finds Tokio on the front porch shaking with rage.

"What was that all about?"

"Some jerk sauntered in as if he owned the place," Tokio replies, punching his right fist into his left palm. "He called me a Jap in my own living room."

Sumiko looks down the street, but sees no one. The curfew is approaching, soon to throw the neighbourhood indoors. She hates the raw, eerie quiet that follows.

"Come inside, Toki," she mumbles, taking his elbow. "I'll make tea."

Shige rises at dawn the next morning. He splashes cold water on his face and dresses, his mind already racing. The morning passes in a blur, like a disjointed dream in which nothing gets resolved. All he remembers later is the heap of luggage gleaming against the royal blue water like an ungainly pack of sea lions basking in the sun.

In keeping with his messenger role, Shige is also responsible for ensuring that everyone get on board. He appoints Kaname Izumi and Mitsuyuki Sakata to help him check off the 470 names as people board the ship. The RCMP stand by like sentinels, on alert for would-be escapees as men, women, and children file up the gangplank onto the floating hulk of the SS *Princess Adelaide*.

Shige's fifty-nine-year-old mother holds hands with her two granddaughters, while Sumiko carries five-week-old Virginia onto the ship. Tomoki Kawabe picked Virginia's Japanese name, Yukuko, meaning "to go" in Japanese. The last baby of Japanese ancestry born in Chemainus, she will be five when her family settles into a home of their own again, some 3,000 miles to the east.

Within a week of their departure, the Yoshidas splinter as the mass dispersal of Japanese Canadians begins. Tokio is the first to leave, signing up the moment he hears the call for road crew volunteers in Jackfish, Ontario. Kumeo is next to flee the stench of Hastings Park, heading for a large dairy farm near St. Thomas, Ontario in early May.

With her husband, youngest son, and eldest daughter in Japan, Kume watches Tokio and Kumeo run almost as far away in the opposite direction. But unlike those in Japan, Tokio and Kumeo can write to her. Ever watchful for subversive activity, Canadian authorities censor their letters—a measure that, like all that is happening, falls outside Kume's comprehension.

The women and children pass the summer idly in a Hastings Park dormitory, while Shige takes charge of the boys' dormitory and runs it like a military barracks. With no household chores, Kume and Sumiko join others on the grounds outside and chat or wander aimlessly about. No one stays inside any more than they have to. Had they a choice, they would avoid the cafeteria-style slop with equal fervour. Spared the indignity, Virginia nurses through the summer months. In the dead of night, Sumiko contributes to the muffled shuffling of mothers responding to cries of hunger in the massive hollow space.

In September they leave for Tashme, the largest of the internment camps. Shige chooses it because it is close to Vancouver, and therefore to home, but Sumiko learns later that her parents are hundreds of miles away in the Slocan Valley. Although anything is an improvement on Hastings Park, Tashme is cut off from the cluster of camps in the Slocan.

As the war progresses, so does the dispersal. Ida leaves Tashme to join Chizuko in sugar beet fields near Lethbridge, Alberta. They pass the duration of the war hoeing rows of sugar beets stretching out of sight. In return for their back-breaking labour, they live in hovels.

Meanwhile, the Yoshidas share a shack with Sumiko's sister and family. Impossibly crowded, the Otas get another shack in due course. Even with them gone, the space is as inadequate as the insulation from winter. But none of it dampens Shige's enthusiasm for creating opportunity. Hired as assistant welfare manager for the B.C. Security Commission, he assists people in need and mediates disputes while the *hakujin* manager does the paper work. Then by coal oil lamplight at night, he leans over his kitchen table and plans his next boy scout troop.

In February 1943, Shige hoists a Union Jack in camp and forms the 1st Tashme troop. A year later the troop celebrates its first anniversary with a torch parade under a star-studded sky. Sumiko bundles up the girls and joins the crowd lining the main boulevard as Shige and his assistants march 110 boys along the streets. Holding their torches high, the scouts wind through deep snow banks, their faces aglow in the bitter cold.

When it celebrates its second anniversary in February 1945, the troop is the largest in the British Commonwealth. All 200 boys are interned Canadians of Japanese descent, swearing their allegiance to the Union Jack.

Thousands of miles away, one of Shige's Chemainus scouts volunteers to prove his allegiance overseas. On February 12, 1945, Kumeo Yoshida joins eleven Canadian Japanese privates enlisting in the army as Japanese linguists in Southeast Asia—not so far from his young brother's treacherous exploits in the Japanese navy. But the war is almost over when Kumeo finishes training with the Gurkha regiment in Poona and Calcutta. As a translator for prisoners of war after Japan surrenders, Kumeo finally realizes his goal. Although not in combat, he proves his loyalty to Canada, an ethic instilled in him at an early age by his big brother, the scoutmaster.

The 1st Tashme troop holds a farewell party for Shige in May 1945. Giving his goodbye speech in the camp hall, "Dynamite

Yoshida" can't contain his tears. Facing the unknown once
again, Shige not only has to let go of his attachment to the boys
but to scouting itself. In his efforts to re-establish a home base
for his family, Shige will never find time to lead a scout troop
again.

Sumiko is bracing herself for his departure. She still hasn't
shaken the image of her sister and family disappearing down
the road for Japan. Knowing she will not see them again, she
fears the worst. Like thousands, they succumbed to government pressure to "repatriate." Some agreed to go because they
were bitter; many were too old and afraid to start all over in
eastern Canada; few expected widespread disease and famine
to greet them.

Two weeks after Sumiko watched the Otas go, Shige
climbs into the same truck caravan and rumbles out of sight
in a cloud of dust. She has no way of knowing when or
where she will see him again. During the two years it takes
Shige to establish a firm home base in Toronto, the war ends
and the government begins closing down the camps. Now
head of her family, Sumiko is the sole decision-maker for
the first time in her life. Shuffled from Tashme to Kaslo
first, the Yoshidas join Sumiko's parents. After some
months, they are sent to the tiny nearby settlement of Rose-
berry and finally to the military base in Moose Jaw, Sas-
katchewan. During the winter of 1946, Sumiko's father
loses his will to live and withers away in the Moose Jaw
military hospital.

In June 1947, Sumiko arrives at Union Station in Toronto
with her three daughters and two mothers, as elated as they
are black with soot. She can still feel the hot expanse of prairie
trailing them as the promise of a real home looms around the
bend. Impulsively, Sumiko flings her ID card onto the tracks
and takes her husband's arm. They disappear inside the station, their family in tow.

Eventually, all the Yoshidas but one are reunited in Ontario. Chizuko remains in Alberta, raising her family of eleven. Shige buys a hardware store in downtown Toronto and prospers. His father returns from Japan a few years before he dies in 1952 at the age of seventy-two. Kume is almost ninety-three when she dies twenty-four years later.

A young woman again in her mind, she is climbing the mountain above Mitomimura to collect firewood.

NINE

SHUNICHI AND HANAYE ISOKI

SHUNICHI ISOKI RISES AT DAWN and slips downstairs without disturbing his wife. An early riser since his youth, he enjoys the solitude and soft light, often using the time to brush up on his Japanese. But this morning he limbers up his hands briefly before opening his writing pad. His arthritis is a bit troublesome, but he still takes pride in his clear, uniform handwriting. He scratches his temple with the end of the pen and begins the letter to his sister and her husband.

Dear Yoshiko and Takayoshi,
    Hana and I got back from the coast yesterday. Chemainus has changed so much I hardly recognized it. We strolled through the old neighbourhood and found the house our family lived in on Esplanade. It is one of very few homes that remains in what used to be Kawahara camp. The old community hall is still there too, but it is a private home now. It looks so small compared to what I remember. Walking those streets after almost fifty years felt strange, but everyone we met was friendly.

There are some wrinkles in the plans for the scout mural, but arrangements are proceeding. After a lot of discussion, we decided on a picture of the troop and scoutmaster—only to find out it has been lost somehow. Our second choice is the picture of the troop and issei *executive in front of the community hall in June 1930, but that isn't finalized yet.*

Things went more smoothly regarding plans for the cemetery monument. Reverend Costerton showed us where the land toward the back of the cemetery dips into a shallow hollow. It seems likely that is where our community's graves were, so we'll put the memorial in that general area. The headstones that the volunteer worker found will flank both sides of a large marble plaque. The names of the deceased, including our baby brother, will be engraved on two additional marble plaques.

I feel strongly that we should all be there to witness the dedication of the memorial monument. Hana and I are driving across and would like you to join us. We hope you will consider it.

Please write soon.

Shunichi sets the pen down and stares at the Toronto suburb outside his living room. Highrises across the street are partially obscured by the Japanese plum tree in his yard. The morning sun is filling the corners of his lovely home, drawing his attention back indoors. The brass clock chimes are about to strike seven. Hana will be up soon.

The steady ticking of the clock has a calming influence not unlike the calm he once felt at sea aboard his fish boat. He closes his eyes and imagines waves lapping softly against the side of *Joker*. Suddenly, Shunichi is overwhelmed by a longing to drop anchor in a quiet cove, where cooling summer breezes carry the tang of salt air. The unreachable notion of solitude at sea has crept into his living room, lingering in the golden light.

Shunichi is Shyobu and Jiroichi Isoki's middle son, the firstborn in Canada and the only surviving son. His older brother, Ichio, died when he was a child in the whaling village in Wakayama where he was born. Some years after Shunichi was born in Chemainus in 1915, his nine-month-old brother died in his birthplace too.

His sister Yoshiko is his only Canadian sibling still living in Canada. Both of his other Canadian-born sisters emigrated to Japan before the war. Of his three sisters born in Japan, only one is still alive.

With his wife's help, Shunichi keeps his complicated family history up to date in a *senzo dai dai*. Crafted from a type of Japanese cedar called *sugi*, the antique polished box contains drawers with tiny memorial tablets that document generations of ancestors. To understand the complexity of his generation requires insight into the pressures his parents faced. To flee poverty was one thing; to leave one's offspring behind was another. But like many *issei*, his parents intended on uniting the children of two worlds in Japan. The fact that the *senzo dai dai* is in Shunichi's care in Canada is striking evidence that circumstance dictated otherwise.

Jiroichi Isoki and his brother Tanezo are youngsters when the worst whaling disaster in their village's 700-year whaling history occurs. On the shores of the Wakayama village of Taiji in 1878, one of the hereditary leaders gives the order to harpoon a female right whale with a calf. Although he knows it defies a strict code of conduct in the ritualized hunt, Taiji Kakuemon argues with his counterpart that the poverty-stricken village needs a whale. At the sound of conch shells blowing from beach lookouts, the whalers pump their sculling oars toward the mother whale. A net is thrown and she is harpooned. It is late and growing dark when the dying whale drags the whalers into a stormy sea. A few days later, Taiji counts its dead at about 120. With most of its fleet destroyed and the best whalers gone, the town slumps into a depression and the ancient tradition of small net whaling fleets seems doomed.

Around the turn of the century, Jiroichi and Tanezo join those trying to sustain that way of life. But by 1910, whaling for humpback, grey, bryde, sperm and right whales enters a new technological phase, complete with large modern vessels and fire-powered harpoons. Unable to compete, Jiroichi and Tanezo abandon their whaling fleet and join the emigration wave across the Pacific, hoping to make a fortune and return.

After settling in Chemainus, the brothers buy a fish boat and begin charting the best spots for cod. The harvest is abundant, but the price for their catch is poor. Forced to accept that earning a fortune is not going to be a short-lived goal, Jiroichi sends for his wife. Shyobu leaves her daughters and joins him in 1914. A year later, Shunichi is born in their humble home across from the Chemainus lumber yard.

Shunichi's first memory is of sea. Bursts of sunlight hopscotch across the water and bounce off the sheer cliff that towers above him. He is fishing for "shiners" that flash through the translucent jade current. It is the summer the Isokis are living aboard *Joker*, fishing the reefs around Crofton and Maple Bay. Wrapped in a blanket and propped up on deck, Shunichi views the world with the unbridled clarity of a four-year-old.

In contrast to the scenic life at sea, most of his early years are spent in one of the shacks along Oak Street that his family rents from Giichi Nakashima. There is nothing notable about their home, but Shunichi loves the trek up to Nakashima's "ranch" past the railway station. The main attraction is an old horse that Giichi hitches to a sleigh when it snows. Even though icy gusts numb his cheeks, Shunichi laughs as the horse trots over the rolling hills. In the summertime, the aroma of ripening apples and peaches lingers on the property into dusk.

The neighbourhood does not change much when Gihei Kawahara becomes their landlord after the sawmill burns down in 1923, although a few tense months pass before the mill owners announce they will rebuild. Mr. Nakashima's chrysanthemum garden is an unfortunate casualty when Gihei builds a bunkhouse to accommodate the influx of working bachelors, but little else changes.

The day the Kawaharas move in, Shunichi notices a heavy-set boy his age shuffling aimlessly about. He walks up and introduces himself.

"My name's Takayoshi," the boy replies.

"Is that your father over there?" Shunichi asks.

Takayoshi glances across his shoulder. "Yes, that's Papa."

"I guess he's our new landlord, then."

Takayoshi nods. "What's there to do around here?"

"Let me see," Shunichi says. "Want to play cowboys and Indians?"

Takayoshi's eyes widen. "Sure!"

"C'mon, follow me."

Shunichi shows him how to make a sling-shot type of rubber gun with wood and old tire tubing, and they head for the rock bluffs behind the neighbourhood. As the weeks go by, Takayoshi learns all kinds of new tricks. The boys attach wire hoops to discarded iron wheels and roll them along the dirt street, hooting and hollering as they race their pretend cars and motorcycles recklessly through Kawahara camp. They fish for rock cod off the government wharf and sell their catch to their Chinese neighbours: the Chang brothers, Tong Puck and Hong Hing. With ten cents tucked neatly in their pockets, they scurry up to the community hall by the railway station to watch silent movies of cowboys and Indians on Saturday afternoons.

As Shunichi and Takayoshi grow strong, Hong Hing hires them to lug firewood off the beach. One wet Saturday morning in March, the boys heave water-logged driftwood up the steep, short hill to Hong Hing's house.

"God, this is heavy," Takayoshi grunts, trying to shift the weight onto his hip.

"Yeah. He better pay us that twenty-five cents he promised."

"He will. Look at him down there, watching us sweat," Takayoshi remarks as he drops the wood by Hong Hing's chopping block.

"He's a good foreman, eh?" Shunichi replies, giggling. "Hey, did you know his real name is Fong Yen Lew. He's from Canton. That's what his brother told me."

"How does he get Hong Hing from that?"

"Who knows. Race you back to the beach. He won't pay us until we've hauled at least three more loads."

When they are done, the old man invites them inside for a meal. Takayoshi's eyes light up when he sees Chinese cookies, some made from peanuts, others filled with a sweet white paste, but it's Shunichi who discovers the pork buns: mouth-watering and rich after a morning's wet work.

At school, the boys mingle and play team sports. In the spring, between rugby and baseball, they swing lumpy bags of marbles to and from school.

"You going to play that Danish boy at recess?" Takayoshi asks.

"I don't know. Why?"

"Well, I heard him bragging yesterday about how he can beat anybody. You ought to beat him for a change. You're good enough."

"Aw, c'mon. I've played him lots before. He beats me every time," Shunichi says, kicking a stone at his feet.

"I bet you can beat him," Takayoshi replies, turning onto the schoolyard.

Sure enough, during recess Shunichi is in the ring at the centre of the largest crowd. He plays several rounds with the Danish boy and knocks every one of his rival's marbles outside the ring.

When recess is over, Takayoshi clears a path to his friend.

"Knew you could do it," he shouts, slapping Shunichi on the back and grinning.

Shunichi beams and marches back to class, swollen with victory. The second the lunch bell rings, he is out the door. Takayoshi scuffles past some classmates, knowing his chances of beating Shunichi to the comics today are nil. He glimpses his friend up ahead, splashing through a swamp, cutting across backyards and soaring down the alley to Esplanade. Takayoshi is almost a breathless block away when Shunichi crashes through the pool room door and grabs the *Vancouver Sun* comic strip that a Japanese bachelor leaves for them. Takayoshi is puffing so hard when he arrives that Shunichi bursts out laughing.

"You rat," Takayoshi says, hobbling toward him.

"Slow poke," Shunichi teases. "Hey, did you see me beat him, Tak?"

Takayoshi grins and tumbles to the floor where they read the comics together.

As patrol leaders in the 2nd Chemainus boy scout troop, Takayoshi and Shunichi spend countless Saturdays practicing Morse code. They run copper wires under the roof connecting Shunichi's home to Takayoshi's bedroom above the store. With wires attached to flashlight batteries and bulbs on boards at each end, they press out one word at a time. Then to make sure the communique is getting through, they employ their sisters to verify each word. Taking their part as seriously as the boys, the girls sprint up and down the boardwalk piecing each critical message together.

Pretend emergencies aside, the boys take the ethics of scouting to heart. Almost a year after the troop forms in 1930, sixteen-year-old Shunichi tests his bravery. Swimming with friends off the government wharf one afternoon in May, he notices ten-year-old Yoshi Higashi flailing in deep water.

"Hold on, Yoshi," he yells. "I'll save you."

Shunichi swims as hard as he can to reach the boy. Between gulps of saltwater, Yoshi manages to spit out the word "cramps."

"It's okay. I'm here now," Shunichi says, propping the boy under his arm as he treads water. Then, struggling toward rocky shallows, he discovers the rescue is not so simple. Waves wash over their heads as he fights against the undertow. When he finally makes it to shore, Shunichi is shaking and vows to learn better rescuing techniques. By the time a national scouting executive awards him a medal of merit at the community hall months later, he has.

Before joining the scout troop, Shunichi spent most of his spare time helping his father. Sometimes they'd go fishing or to Southey Point, where there is a long shoal of shells. After shovelling broken clam and oyster shells into sacks, they hauled them back to *Joker* in a rowboat. In town, a Chinese chicken farmer gave them pennies for their labour.

It was hard work for young Shunichi, but he enjoyed exploring the waters with his father. Sometimes when they were motoring along, he thought about what he'd like to do when he finished school. A bright student, he had been promoted two grades. As he neared the end of grade eight, the principal urged him to go to high school. But Shunichi knew his carefree days were numbered. His parents simply couldn't afford to send him to high school when he could be earning a living. A few months after his fourteenth birthday in May 1929, Shunichi begins fishing full-time with his father.

He doesn't care much for fishing at first, especially when it means missing the baseball season. But he is attentive and learns where to go for the best catches of ling cod during his first summer out. They often motor to Active Pass to catch herring for bait before seeking out the rocky shoals where cod swim.

Shunichi learns an important lesson on one of their trips to Active Pass. Waiting to fish for herring at flood tide, Jiroichi and Shunichi tie *Joker* to several kelp-heads near Helen Point on Mayne Island.

"Let's have lunch while we wait for the tide, Papa."

Jiroichi nods.

Shunichi goes below for last night's leftover rice and *matsue take* mushrooms. Sitting against the gunwales with the sun on their faces, they eat their lunch. A short while later, Shunichi leans over the gunwale and studies the water.

"I think we've drifted onto a reef."

Jiroichi checks over the stern and throws up his hands. *Joker* is stuck. "It's too late now. We'll have to wait for the tide," he says, frowning.

Shunichi eyes the channel. "Sure hope one of the *Princess* ferries isn't steaming this way right now."

Jiroichi checks both ends of the pass. They are thinking the same thing: a swell from one of those ships would probably knock them over.

Fortunately, the tide changes within the hour. They are motoring toward the raging whirlpools of Georgeson Bay to fish for bait long before a ferry cruises through the pass.

Except when the fishing season closes in January and February, Shunichi rises with his parents at dawn, eats breakfast, and sets out with the tide, weather permitting. After getting their bait, father and son might fish for a week before going home. They are lonely stretches for young Shunichi, who longs for friends his age while sharing meals at anchor with other *issei* fishermen.

During the fall herring runs, Jiroichi takes Shunichi south to Pender Island where a friend from Wakayama runs a herring saltery at Beddis Rock. They stand at the conveyor belt that rolls the catch up to huge vats, picking out the larger herring to sell as kippers. It is tedious, smelly work, but they make a reasonable profit in the short-lived season.

En route, they pass seine boats setting their nets in vast schools of herring. Fascinated, Shunichi watches a two-man crew row out to the twisting, flashing silver mass. Without winches, the men haul a 400-ton catch into their scow for hours on end while bald eagles circle above. Shunichi stops associating life at sea with monotony.

As time goes by, he also begins to enjoy their quiet summer evenings at anchor. Schools of minnows ripple across the glassy harbour, while salmon splash through the surface. A flaming orange sun sinks below a shimmering ridge of cedar. Orcas sound down the channel, fine spray spewing out their blowholes, their dorsal fins cutting across the horizon like samurai spears.

Shunichi prays for such a night the first time he sleeps alone on the boat, anchored in a small bay off Tent Island in Stuart Channel. He has learned all he is going to learn about fishing from Jiroichi, who was targetted when the government tightened restrictions on Japanese fishermen. A few short months after saving Yoshi from drowning, sixteen-year-old Shunichi is on his own at sea. Now fifty-six, Jiroichi finds menial work at the mill, cutting firewood out of scrap lumber.

Shunichi fishes the waters around Chemainus his first day out alone, trying his luck off the reefs in Stuart Channel. He still uses the names men like his father gave to various islands and reefs, but he knows the English names from his marine chart. Among the *issei*, Tent Island is known as *Hyotanshima* for its gourd-like shape. Because of its length, Willy Island is called *Nagashima*, meaning "long island." Likewise, the Catholic school on Kuper Island led them to name a nearby reef *Gakkonomae*, meaning "in front of the school."

Shunichi revisits these fishing spots in his mind while his moderate catch lolls about in the watertight bulkhead. Aware the fish buyer will be at Porlier Pass tomorrow, he decides not to go home. He wants to increase his catch by getting an early start in the morning.

He motors into a small bay off Tent Island and sets the anchor. After putting a pot of rice on his cookstove in the galley, Shunichi sits in the cockpit and plans the day ahead. He decides to fish nearby, then round the south end of Kuper Island and head north along Trincomali Channel to the tip of Galiano. By the time the rice is cooked, the ocean and sky are indigo. Chemainus twinkles in the distance. Shunichi goes below, lights a coal oil lamp and eats his supper.

He sprinkles dry seaweed over his steaming bowl and thinks of the Sunday excursion last winter when he and his family scraped sandy seaweed off the rocks on Galiano. He wonders what they are eating tonight. Perhaps they have some dried mushrooms and pickles to go with their rice and fish.

Shunichi cleans up his dishes and goes to bed. Though tired, he can't sleep. Wishing the gentle lapping of waves against the wooden hull would lull him to sleep, he tosses and turns, fighting a mounting sense of fear. Alone and vulnerable, he imagines Indians on the rampage. They are not the jovial Native longshoremen at the Chemainus dock, or the sad children at the residential school perched on a hill to the north of his anchorage. They are warriors from the silent movies of his youth, brandishing tomahawks and screaming blood-curdling war cries as they lunge at him from the bow of their great voyager canoe.

It is a long night. Shunichi is relieved when dawn finally creeps into his cabin. Once up and going, he laughs at himself. The sun warms his back as he steers *Joker* out of the bay. He is never afraid on his boat again.

By noon, another fifty pounds of ling cod are floating in Shunichi's holding tank. He puts his East Hope engine in gear and points *Joker* north into Trincomali Channel. Musing about his wretched night, he smiles when the lighthouse at Porlier Pass comes into view.

The fish buyers from Vancouver are busy. Shunichi manouevres his boat among the others and begins dressing the cod while he waits. It being summer, he stands to gain about eight cents a pound for his catch. The price drops to less than two cents a pound in the spring, when the market is glutted before salmon season opens up.

Of the many buyers at the pass, Shunichi usually sells his catch to Chomatsu Koyanagi. Initially, he brought bread to sell to the fishermen, but then he started giving it away in order to keep his clients. Shunichi sees an opening and pulls up alongside Chomatsu's boat.

"Greetings, Koyanagi-san. Got room for more fish?" Shunichi asks, grinning.

"For your catch, always. What have you got?"

Shunichi hauls the cod from his tank and heaves it onto the deck.

"It's a fair catch," Chomatsu says, rolling a toothpick between his teeth and squinting into the sun. He lifts the cod onto his scales and hands Shunichi a duplicate bill, crediting him seventy-five pounds. Chomatsu will calculate the value and pay Shunichi on his next trip, minus whatever dry goods he might order.

"So long," Shunichi says, waving as he pulls away. He heads towards Mrs. Gear's marine gas station in Lighthouse Bay. A kind Welsh woman with a son about Shunichi's age, she lost her husband during the First World War. Now she smiles and embraces everyone as if they are kin and earns the title "Mama" from all the Japanese fishermen.

Shunichi anchors *Joker* in the harbour, rows to shore and scrambles up the bluff to the large, neat cottage. Although plenty of fishermen rely on the gas station for fuel, most are *issei* who speak little English. Isolated from community life, the Gears are especially delighted whenever Shunichi arrives at their door.

Humming under her breath, Mrs. Gear ties her apron around her ample girth and cooks up her guest's favourite meal: a chunky pot of clam chowder. After dinner, they catch up on island news and play rummy at the kitchen table. A large woodstove crackling at their backs, Teddy Gear and Shunichi talk about their dreams and ambitions. Some hours pass, and Mrs. Gear serves up large pieces of rich chocolate cake. After saying good night, Shunichi rows back to *Joker* under a star-studded sky. His oars stir the phosphorescence in gleaming black waters as he slides toward the shadow of his boat.

Tonight, he sleeps like a baby.

Leaving adolescence behind, Shunichi grows into a handsome young man and a proficient fisherman. His range extends north of Chemainus from Ruxton Island south to Osborn Bay off Crofton, along reefs in Stuart and Trincomali Channels. The shape of the ocean floor becomes part of his inner landscape as he works the rocky reefs with his line.

It is not a particularly lucrative business, but the family manages as well as any. Bartering fish for vegetables and fruit provides a more balanced diet, a common practice that extends beyond the Japanese community. In the waters around Yellow Point, farmers row out to meet fishermen who come close to shore, where they exchange fish for fruit at sea.

But Mr. Iwasaki's strawberry farm north of Vesuvius on Saltspring Island is Shunichi's favourite bartering stop. His farm spreads over a particularly sunny stretch of waterfront, where his strawberries ripen early in the season. Whenever Shunichi thinks of summer, he envisions Mr. Iwasaki's strawberries and unsullied afternoons aboard *Joker*. Cupping a bowl in his hands as he idles along the channel, he sucks the sweet red juice from the plump fruit as warm breezes rush past.

Home from fishing before Christmas in 1934, nineteen-year-old Shunichi steps outside one afternoon. Strolling up Esplanade and rounding the corner, he listens to the unusual quiet, as if a vacuum has sucked life out of the street. He glances to the west and notices dark clouds cresting over Mount Brenton. Suddenly, the wind descends, roaring down from the mountains like a tornado.

Stepping back into a doorway for shelter, Shunichi watches the storm wreak havoc around him. Wood from the lumber yard is flying in all directions, as is anything lying about. The roof of the thousand-foot storage and loading shed lifts with a crack and slams onto the bank. The storefront window at Taniwas' smashes and shards of glass join the flying debris. Shunichi peers out to sea, hoping *Joker* is safely moored. Several ocean freighters anchored in the harbour start their engines and head into the wind to avoid being blown onto nearby reefs.

Praying that *Joker* is secure, Shunichi pulls his cap down with a tug and turns to go home. He takes one step and almost bumps into Takayoshi.

"God almighty, this is some storm," Takayoshi yells.

"What on earth are you doing?" Shunichi asks, eyeing the garbage can lid in his friend's hand.

"I'm using this as a shield while I work my way through camp. I've got to warn people to douse the fire in their stoves, or we'll have a worse disaster on our hands."

Takayoshi carries on before he can respond. Shunichi debates whether to go after him and offer to help, but decides he'd better go home and check his own stove. His parents and Yoshiko are huddling near the front window when he dashes inside.

"Shunichi, where were you? What is happening out there?" Yoshiko asks.

"Tornado, maybe a hurricane, I don't know. Look, we've got to put the fire out in the stove *now*."

Yoshiko stares at her brother as he runs to the kitchen and grabs a bucket of water. When the smoke clears, Shunichi listens to the stovepipe rattling and sighs with relief.

The next morning the community assesses the damage. Everyone is out sweeping up debris or repairing windows, twisted frames and roofs. Miraculously, no one is hurt.

The following year, the Isokis move to Sidney so Shunichi can try out new fishing grounds around southern Vancouver Island. Initially, Shige Yoshida comes along as his partner, hustling Shunichi's catch wherever he can find a buyer. But there is less business than they hoped, so Shige returns to Chemainus leaving Shunichi to sell his own catch.

He works hard over the next three years, fishing and building up a modest clientele. But in 1938, customers start turning away. Press coverage of Japan's military prowess in Asia is fueling long-simmering tensions. On his rounds one Saturday morning, Shunichi meets racism face-to-face.

A regular customer opens the door and shakes her head. "I have nothing against you personally," she begins. "It's just that I have to keep peace with my neighbours, and they don't like me buying fish from Japanese. I'm sorry."

Shunichi stands on the porch and stares blankly at the closed door.

At home that evening, he is depressed, not sure how to break the news. "Mama," he begins.

Shyobu looks up from her knitting. "Yes?"

"I'm not sure if. . . . Oh, never mind." He wants to shelter her from the guilt, the shame.

Shyobu puts down the socks. "It's time to return to Chemainus, isn't it?"

"Yes. I can't sell my fish here anymore. From Chemainus, I can always go to the buyers at Porlier Pass."

"Well, we must move back anyways. We have to prepare for your sister's wedding."

"Yoshiko is getting married? When? To who?"

"Next February. To Takayoshi."

With Yoshiko secure in marriage and Shunichi a grown man, Jiroichi and Shyobu book their passage to Japan in 1939. Among other considerations, they want to see their daughters in Wakayama, although one died in childbirth years ago. Their youngest is getting married, so weddings mark their departure from Canada and return to Japan like bookends. Now in their sixties, they opt to live out their days in their homeland. Caught between cultures, they say farewell to Shunichi and Yoshiko with the same stoic face that marked their days as immigrants.

With his parents gone and his only remaining sister living at the Kawaharas', Shunichi rents a room and spends more time aboard *Joker*. He has always looked forward to the cruise up Stuart Channel, where the Bare Point lighthouse comes into view. From the days when he fished with his father until recently, the red-and-white tower signals his homecoming—a time for shared family meals and a fun Japanese card game called *Gaji* after dinner. Outings to pick mushrooms in the forest or jaunts to Galiano to gather seaweed have come to an end. Although his sister and friends are in Chemainus, Shunichi feels more lonely in town than at sea. Fishermen friends anchor regularly alongside at night. Kanichi

Nakatsu and Genichi Nakahara, also from Chemainus, often share supper with Shunichi in bays sheltered from gusting winds.

A little over a year after his parents leave, a new market opens up. Dudley Cole, a Victoria man working for an American firm, is buying dog fish livers, which are boiled down for oil used by arms' manufacturers. Early in 1941, Shunichi hires Minoru Nagasawa as his deckhand. They rig *Joker* for gillnetting dog fish, fishing that year from Seymour Narrows near Campbell River to the Race Rocks lighthouse in Juan de Fuca Strait south of Victoria. Genichi and Kanichi do the same, the two Chemainus boats often trailing each other and tying up together at night.

Although more lucrative, the work is harder than fishing for ling cod. Rather than bringing in his catch with one single line, Shunichi has to set and haul nets by hand. And because clubbing a dogfish to death is virtually impossible, Shunichi plugs the holes in his bulkhead and throws the fish in there to die. Minoru's help and companionship is one big consolation, particularly during the long rainy winter months.

One miserable afternoon, Shunichi decides to call it a day. A storm is brewing, the grey ocean swells rising and the wind picking up in the strait off Qualicum Beach. He calls to Minoru to haul in the nets so they can head for shelter. Minoru looks skyward and nods. After clearing the nets, Shunichi putters toward a harbour. Halfway there, he comes up alongside a small power boat in trouble.

A woman is rocking a little girl in her arms. The child wails into the gusting wind, her weary mother distraught. Their engine has stalled, and the ashen-faced father is trying to keep the boat from drifting further into the Strait of Georgia. With only a small anchor and a length of rode that falls short of the sandy bottom some twenty fathoms below, he hasn't a hope.

Shunichi and Minoru eye each other anxiously. "Where are you going?" Minoru asks.

"Powell River," the man replies. "We have no supplies on board to ride out the storm."

Shunichi surveys the chop, figuring they can make it across before the full force of the gale hits. Throwing out a tow line, he goes below and puts his eight-horsepower one-cylinder East Hope engine in gear. Shunichi tightens his Cowichan sweater around his neck and begins the long, rough tow across Strait of Georgia. About halfway, waves crash against the southern shores of Lasqueti and Texada Islands on their port side. Bucking through the chop, Shunichi and Minoru pray for the tow line to hold.

Just before dark, *Joker* chugs into Powell River harbour. Minoru is securing the boats to the dock when the family scrambles ashore and disappears. Feeling quite ravenous, Shunichi begins preparing a simple supper.

The rice is still cooking when the man reappears with a half pound of bacon. "I can't give you much, so take this," he says.

"You don't have to give me this, you know," Shunichi replies. But he has already gone. Back in the galley, Shunichi waves the bacon in front of Minoru. "I would have preferred a handshake and a thank you. But I guess thanking a Japanese is beneath him."

Lying in his bunk later, Shunichi closes his eyes and listens to the wind. The little girl's face looms before him, and he sighs. Resentment towards her father subsides as he pictures the child tucked in her bed, safe from the storm. He pulls the covers up to his neck and slides into a deep, dreamless sleep.

As it turns out, the year of dog fishing is his last. Moored at the docks in Sidney harbour on the morning of December 7, 1941,

Shunichi, Minoru, Genichi and Kanichi are awakened by a friend warning them to leave quickly. News of Pearl Harbor is spreading fast, and nearby James Island has a stockpile of dynamite. People might think them capable of sabotage and send a posse out after them.

It is like waking up to a nightmare that will last for years.

Shunichi and his fishermen friends motor up to Chemainus that morning. The next day, a Scottish fish inspector orders them to deliver their boats to Nanaimo. Shunichi, Kanichi, and Jinpachi Yamashita, an *issei* fisherman, solemnly slip away from the docks one by one. Out in the channel, the sea is choppy but not dangerously rough. It is a typical early December day, overcast, damp and cold.

Fighting excessive currents as he passes through Dodd Narrows, Shunichi remembers one of his Japanese language school teachers. He can still hear Mrs. Yonemura telling the class, "You must become good Canadians. Go ahead and mix with the white children and join the boy scout troop." Both she and Mr. Yonemura, a UBC graduate who worked on the boom in Okada camp, were more modern in their thinking than most of their peers. But her message, which once seemed all important, now rings hollow.

The next morning the men join a fleet of boats heading for the mouth of the Fraser River. Shunichi crosses the Strait of Georgia among the others without incident, but the trip is a blur. Later, he vaguely recalls tying *Joker* to the Fraser River dock—his last glimpse of her bobbing alongside Kanichi's boat, stranded in a sea of vessels.

Before going home, Shunichi and Kanichi travel to the immigration building, hoping to see Otoji Okinobu. Perhaps he will explain why the RCMP picked him up the day after Pearl Harbor. But guards prevent them from getting any closer than the parking lot outside the building. Someone inside sees them and brings Otoji to a window. Shunichi and Kanichi wave and he waves back. They never see or hear of him again.

With nothing more to do, Shunichi and Kanichi catch the next ship back to Nanaimo and ride a bus to Chemainus in silence.

Meanwhile, Dudley Cole is busy making phone calls from Victoria. Rather than lose one of his most hardworking and trusted fishermen, Dudley pleads with various authorities to allow Shunichi to continue fishing for him. He suggests a sailor equipped with a radio phone could go aboard *Joker* as added security. When his efforts fail, Dudley contacts Shunichi and offers to sell his thirty-two-foot fish boat. A few weeks later, Shunichi gets a cheque for $600—much less than the boat that he rebuilt in 1938 is worth, but much more than he would get from the government. Worse still, she might just sink into the muddy sludge in the river delta. Such is the fate of Jinpachi's boat, squeezed between bigger boats that crush her hull.

Back in Chemainus, Shunichi makes plans to visit his fiancee in Cumberland. The day before Christmas, he boards a bus and travels north to the small mining settlement on the eastern edge of the Comox Valley, where Hanaye Nakauchi lives with her family.

Gihei Kawahara and a friend of Hana's father arranged the engagement earlier that fall. The young couple hope to marry next year, but they have not yet set a date. Rumours of evacuation now threaten to thwart their plans altogether.

Shunichi's chest feels tight as he rides the bus and mulls over recent events. He cannot shake the image of Mr. Okinobu waving, tiny, from his window. He closes his eyes and listens to the bus engine rumble as they twist their way up island. He searches for *Joker* in his mind, but hordes of fish boats obscure her from view. She merges with the large menacing mass of the unknown.

When Shunichi reaches the Japanese section in Cumberland, the Nakauchis give him a warm welcome and the dismal cloud fades. He settles comfortably into their home, enjoying the closeness of a family at Christmas. It is not a big celebration, but it is meaningful. Hana and he know full well it might be their first and last together on home turf, but her parents inspire a certain courage. Clearly prepared to face any difficulty, they rely on their pioneering spirit to see them through. Concern clouds their eyes, but not despair.

The tight-knit Cumberland Japanese community adheres to the old ways. Their language school is arguably the best on the coast. Hana is well educated for her generation—a grade twelve graduate and perfectly bilingual. She has also been taught morals at the Japanese language school. The textbook for the *shushin* class reinforces lessons that began at home: perseverance, obedience, honesty, hard work, patience, kindness to animals, and respect for elders. Of all these qualities, extraordinary perseverance will sustain her through extraordinary times.

Without his boat, Shunichi spends his last days in Kawahara camp, bracing himself for the next government order and wondering what will become of them all. The Kawaharas give him room and board in exchange for work around the neighbourhood. When rumours about the evacuation turn to hard fact, Shunichi helps board up windows and move storage crates into the community hall. Yoshiko is nearing the end of her third pregnancy, so the family goes to Vancouver when Gihei departs for road camp, leaving Shunichi to look after the property and prepare to close everything down.

Emptiness echoes in the house. Mrs. Kawahara and her

sister-in-law continue cooking for the bachelors, but Shunichi
bumps into a shadowy presence as he walks the halls. In that
respect, the evacuation doesn't come too soon.

The lighthouse on Bare Point, which once signalled his homecoming, disappears as the SS *Princess Adelaide* rounds Tent
Island and steams up Trincomali Channel. Standing on the
ship's deck, Shunichi wonders when that welcoming beacon
will come into view again. It recedes behind the forests on
Kuper Island as the past slips from his grip with the force of an
ebb tide at full moon.

As the steamship cruises toward Porlier Pass, he relives his
years as a fisherman, pointing out the spots where he fished
and anchored to friends on deck. Chugging through the pass,
he closes his eyes and inhales deeply: the scent of Mrs. Gear's
clam chowder lingers. All of it sails behind him as the ship
steams into the open waters of the Strait of Georgia, where
snow-capped cobalt mountains on the mainland stretch in the
distance. The spring sun is warm and the breezes, light. He is
travelling toward *Joker* at the Fraser River dock, the whole
sorry mess of boats suddenly unforgettably distinct.

Hana and Shunichi marry a month later in May 1942 at a
Buddhist church in Vancouver. It is a simple ceremony, followed by a meal with close friends and family in a Chinatown
restaurant. But it is hardly a time for celebration. On a three-
day pass from Hastings Parks, Shunichi and Hana begin their
married life together aimlessly walking Vancouver's streets.
They have no money to enjoy some of the city's attractions,
and there's no escaping the stench and chaos that awaits them
in separate dormitories at the end of their so-called honeymoon.

Knowing they could have waited to marry under more fa-
vourable circumstances, the couple decided marriage offered

the only hope of staying together. Otherwise Shunichi would surely be shipped east to join the road camp crews. He goes to Lemon Creek instead, where a work crew is busy assembling the shacks that will be home for the next three to four years. Kaname Izumi accompanies him to the interior where they live in leaky tents for the summer, their hammers pounding down the valley for weeks. When Hana finally joins him that fall, they are ready to make the most of a bad situation.

Life falls into a routine without a future. Confined to the camp but allowed to work in the bush nearby, Shunichi piles lumber for a small logging operation while Hana volunteers to teach school. Since the provincial government reneged on its obligation to provide education for camp children, the B.C. Security Commission steps in to fund grades one to eight. Staffed mainly by high-school graduates like Hana, the primary schools offer the children an adequate education. Finally, missionaries are given permission to teach kindergarten and high school classes after church groups apply pressure on the government.

Pregnant with her first child within a year, Hana leaves teaching. In February 1945, she brings a son home from the Slocan hospital to the tiny shack in Lemon Creek that they share with her parents and siblings. Had they been American citizens, they might have been on their way home, albeit not necessarily to a friendly one. The U.S. Supreme Court is about to rule that restricting the movement of loyal Americans is unconstitutional when authorities announce Japanese Americans can go home in January 1945. But for Shunichi and Hana, home will never be the ones they left behind. Home is an elusive concept from the past and imagined for the future, a concept that they struggle to pull into the present.

In the spring of 1945, Mackenzie King's Liberal government presents internees with two choices: go east of the Rockies or "repatriate" to Japan. The political pressure comes from the White Canada Association and certain British Columbia MPs, whose self-appointed campaign is: "Not a Japanese from the Rockies to the Sea."

Faced with the uncertainty of starting over in the east, Shunichi and Hana sign up to go to Japan. The choice is made somewhat less difficult by the fact that Shunichi wants to see his parents again. Although he has never been to Japan, he feels he will be going "home" to his mother and father.

In August 1946, the Isokis pack their belongings and carry eighteen-month-old Stanley aboard a steamship at a Vancouver dock. The two-week crossing has its moments. Crammed into the ship's hold with other deportees, they nearly suffocate from heat as they steam through tropical waters. When it becomes unbearable, Shunichi asks a sailor to open a door. Cool air rushes in, but a passing officer reprimands the sailor. "Make those people suffer," he commands, slamming the door. Shunichi complains to the ship's captain, who replies, "I can't do anything for you. It's out of my jurisdiction."

When he sets foot on Japanese soil, Shunichi finally shakes the racism. In that sense, he does arrive home. But the trade-off rocks his sensibilities. The steamship anchors in waters south of Tokyo Bay while passengers are ferried ashore to Kurihama. Approaching the dock, Shunichi and Hana watch people scrambling like rats after cigarettes being cast ashore. Hana shifts Stanley's weight and returns her husband's glance. They recognize their mistake, too late.

Images on the train are equally shocking. People in rags flood the stations, welcoming strangers and friends home from the war. Perhaps they think the Isokis are returning from Manchuria or the South Seas, but none guess they are Canadians. Shunichi and Hana accept the homecoming welcome with mixed feelings: disoriented, to be sure, but touched by the compassion of those who regard them as fellow survivors. The atrocities committed in the Japanese prisoner-of-war camps are like the injustices perpetrated in Canada in one regard: a minority with influence and power practised a patriotism gone berserk, beyond the knowledge of ordinary, albeit often brain-washed, civilians.

Shunichi works for the American occupation forces over the next four years, first in Atsugi manning a telephone switch-board, then in the foreign mail section in Osaka, translating and summarizing prisoner-of-war letters from Manchuria for the benefit of American officers.

While in Osaka, he lives in a dormitory for foreign nation-als and battles loneliness on his stints away from his family. At the end of a long day, Shunichi enters the dormitory one after-noon and discovers there is a package for him. Troubled from fighting the dull ache of depression all day, he flushes when he sees the Canadian stamps and then the return address: Kaname Izumi, Hamilton, Ontario. Shunichi strides toward his bed and opens the box. Gingerly, he pulls out neatly folded socks, underwear, and a few shirts. Candies, cookies, and other goodies intended for Hana and Stanley are nestled in between. Such treats are impossible to find here. He rummages through the tissue and finds a note in Kaname's elegant handwriting:

"Shunichi, I have a good job, and we are doing fairly well. If you need anything, don't hesitate to write and ask for what-ever it is. Chiyo sends her love. We hope you're all well. Write soon, Kaname."

Falling onto his bed, Shunichi peers at cracks of sunlight cutting through bamboo blinds above his feet. He knows Kaname is probably fighting tough times too, but he sighs with relief. Happy memories flash across his mind, and his depression lifts: he has ambled out of the dark into sunshine, warmed by the thought that his boyhood friend remembered him.

As American army personnel, Shunichi and his family are well fed. But he cannot escape the starvation around him. Its face looms in the gaunt eyes of young children watching him nibble his lunch, and in mothers bent over sorry vegetables wherever they can scratch out a patch of soil. Its face haunts Hana too. She gives bits of food to destitute beggars who traipse onto his parent's small farm on the mountainside, which she tends for long backbreaking hours with her in-laws. It feeds a starvation of a different sort in them, a psychological hunger for home.

In 1950, Shunichi's sister Kikuno suggests he take his family back to Canada where they will be happy. His parents are home, but he cannot seem to find it with them. Jiroichi and Shyobu mingle among the wider community, free in ways they never knew in Canada. Faced with one of life's uncompromising realities, Shunichi decides to take his wife and five-year-old son to the only country where he can hope to find that peace.

Having said farewell to their children on both sides of the Pacific, his parents don't see them off at the train. The final parting with their only son revives old pains and promises new grief, so they say goodbye in their living room. For his part, Shunichi trails their memory across the Pacific Ocean and the North American continent, stretching the link into oblivion.

When they arrive in Fort William, Ontario, it is forty-below zero and Hana's turn to grieve. Her father died while they were en route.

Shunichi does manual labour of one sort or another while continuing to work toward a goal he has tucked under his belt since Lemon Creek. By coal oil lamplight in the internment camp shack, he completed his grade nine and ten math by correspondence. While working for the American army in

Japan, he polished off high school bookkeeping at night school.

After they settle with Hana's family in Fort William, Shunichi builds a cubbyhole next to the coal bin in the basement. For three years he comes home from his day job and retreats to his "study" to work on night school assignments. Following a job transfer to Toronto in 1956, Shunichi graduates as a registered industrial accountant. His first bookkeeping job enables him to work his way into accounting positions that secure his future until retirement.

It is a long way from the anchorages of his youth, where the winds and tides off British Columbia's coast once cradled him in sleep.

EPILOGUE

THE REUNION

O N AUGUST 9, 1991, several former Chemainus residents launch the reunion near the alley that had once been the main thoroughfare through Kawahara camp. Takayoshi Kawahara hangs his video camera around his neck and strolls along the dirt lane, pointing out where the *ofuro*, or Japanese bath, had been, the kitchen where his mother and wife cooked meals for the bachelors, and the bunkhouse that sat squat in what is now a vacant parking lot. The notary public's office on the corner had been his father's store and pool hall, which loomed much larger when he was young. Up the street on Esplanade, the duplex where his wife lived is one of few recognizable dwellings, a green and white cottage with a side porch, expansive lawn and pale pink rose bushes out front. Unbeknownst to all, it too will be gone in a few years, replaced by a square apartment building without history or character.

Takayoshi saunters back down the alley to Croft Street. The boardwalk that once connected neighbours together has, of course, disappeared—along with the homes, the blacksmith

shop made into judo hall, the woodsheds, outhouses, and stal-
wart apple tree that had been home base for hide-and-seek
games. Gone too was the plot where the community grew its
vegetables and the garage where his father kept his 1937
Chrysler Royal taxi. Takayoshi stares at the house in its place.
This is where everyone congregated to decorate the prize-win-
ning float for the 1939 parade.

He looks across the street and recognizes the flat roof on the
corner building. It was the store, pool hall and living quarters
that Risaburo Taniwa built for his son. Takayoshi recalls that
its proximity to his father's store undermined their family
business somewhat.

Turning back to face the east side of the street, he trundles
up to what was once the community hall. He remembers dragging himself up the front stairs to attend daily Japanese language lessons, wishing he could go play instead. That entrance
is gone, replaced by a side entrance. Standing back, he visual-
izes how the old school sat just so, the lay of the land un-
changed where fruit trees scattered their sweet harvest onto
the yard.

The street is a hubbub. Takayoshi's sister, Chiyoko, and her
husband are visiting from Honolulu where they now live. She
is as animated as the child who raced along the boardwalk
with Yoshiko to confirm the words he and Shunichi punched
out in Morse code back in their boy scout days. Hunched over
the hood of a car, she studies old school pictures brought out by
George Price, a nearby resident. Shunichi, Hana, and Yoshiko
chat in the middle of the street, remarking how things have
changed. Kaname Izumi strolls toward the corner with his
wife, pointing up Oak Street. The lumber yard today is a
fraction of its former self, when there was nothing but lumber
all the way to the highway. Tosh Kamino pauses alongside one
of her childhood friends, who swirls the gravel with her foot in
a lot where her house once stood. Shige and Sumiko Yoshida's

oldest daughter, Mitsi, arrives just as coal-grey clouds skirt overhead. A child of nine when they were evacuated, she cuts a striking figure now. About to celebrate her fifty-eighth birthday, she looks no more than forty, her eyes shining like iridescent black ponds.

The wind picks up and rolls down Croft Street. Those still milling about huddle under the shelter of the former Taniwa store entrance, continuing their reminiscences as the clouds split open. Across the street, Stanley Taniwa, the artist son of Matsue and her late husband, Norey, struggles to pull a piece of plastic sheeting over scaffolding to protect his mural. The unveiling is tomorrow, and he still has a few last-minute touches to do.

Stanley was six months old when Matsue carried him aboard the SS *Princess Adelaide* in April 1942. In the spring of 1990, he returned to Chemainus on a pilgrimage of sorts, hoping to piece his past together. His father, whom he idolized as a boy, had deserted the family in Fort William when he was eleven. Two years later, Norey died of cancer in a Vancouver hospital. His father's death thousands of miles away triggered a volatile and angry rebellion that would last decades. At forty-nine, he is beginning to make some sense of it all.

A tall, handsome man, he pulls his long, black hair into a ponytail, accentuating the broad features characteristic of Cree men he has known. Often mistaken for a Native, Stanley is no stranger to discrimination. Struggling against oppression is not peculiar to his parent's generation. For Stanley, it is lumped in with poverty and the loss of his father, a proud man made hollow by the indignities of the war experience.

Stanley believes it was more than coincidence that led him to Chemainus when the town needed an artist to paint a mural commemorating the Japanese community. After hearing about it from someone on the street, he went to the murals' society office where a kind woman brought out a file full of pictures. Among them was a photograph of the *Nippon* team, his father in uniform flanked by baseball buddies from his youth. Stanley wept. The heart of the puzzle clicked into place: the leap in his life's journey brought so much tumultuous, painful zig-zagging into focus with sudden, unexpected mercy.

In June 1991, Stanley left his home and studio in Clanwilliam, Manitoba and set out across the prairie in his old Volvo. When he arrived in Chemainus in early July, he set to work on the mural of *The Lone Scout*, across the street from the home where his mother nursed him as a newborn.

The murals' society hired him to depict the story of scoutmaster Shige Yoshida, and incorporate a picture of the Japanese community standing in front of the hall it built to celebrate Canada's Diamond Jubilee in 1927. One house away from that same community hall, where his father had entertained crowds in dazzling *Kabuki* performances, Stanley lines up his paints and brushes, sets out the photos for reference, and begins painting his people's history onto the side of a fish and chip restaurant.

Although Shige is the focus of the mural, Stanley paints his own family among those congregated in front of the old community hall. He paints himself as a little boy next to his father as a young boy in Japan, standing side by side in front of the white picket fence. He paints his father in his *Nippon* baseball uniform, sandwiched between Stanley's uncles, Iwao and Hitoshi. He paints his mother as a young woman and an old woman, surrounded by her children, holding a small bouquet of flowers. Tiny intricate portraits, they form the backdrop to the scoutmaster who symbolizes the resolute strength and spirit of his people. But Stanley is also bringing his family home, and with it, his personal struggle with bitterness and grief. He circles the community portrait with blossoming cherry branches, signifying rebirth and new life.

Just up the street from *The Lone Scout*, Joyce Kamikura is busy creating one of the most colourful murals in Chemainus, *The Winning Float*. Born in Steveston and interned in Slocan with her family as a child, she does not share Stanley's passion for bringing his family home. Her passion is purely artistic, gained in part from post-war years living in Japan where she escaped the discrimination of her peers in Canada. A vibrant and spontaneous woman, Joyce adapts a black-and-white photograph Mutt Otsu took in 1939. Five young girls dressed in fancy kimonos stand in a line before the Japanese float that won first prize in the parade celebrating the fiftieth anniversary of the Chemainus sawmill. Under Joyce's brush, the girls transform into elegant young women, their kimonos sweeping gracefully across the outside wall of a laundromat.

The next morning, sunlight streams through a grove of cedar and fir trees in the Chemainus cemetery. Ravens fly high overhead, their raucous cries penetrating the cool, still air. Reverend Harry Costerton has just spoken, and there is healing in the silence that follows his opening words. Words spoken forcefully, they cannot be misconstrued or disregarded, words as simple as the desecration of graves was shameful.

"What was done was wrong," he begins. "The wholesale removal of grave markers from this space should not have occurred—but it did. We join each other in having sorrow for that.

"The situation might have been corrected at the time by asking the families to come back here for the purpose of having them restore the markers according to their memory of where they should be.

"This opportunity was not taken, and because of the passing of time—and of people—and the absence of a written detailed record of the graves in this section, the location of each grave is now very difficult—it seems impossible—to determine.

"What sometimes is done with *really* old, old cemeteries, once centuries have gone by, is that the old grave markers that are still serviceable are assembled in an orderly manner—not on the graves but together in one smaller area—and the remainder of the property is developed for use as a park or a church yard, remembering that it has served as a cemetery.

"In what we have done here we are, unfortunately, ahead of the time, forced by necessity. We have assembled serviceable markers; we have added appropriate "common" markers. And this space, once used for graves, has become a little bit like a park.

"It is too bad that we are ahead of our time. But we are. I hope we can live with that."

The shrill, guttural caw of the ravens echoes overhead, but no one looks skyward. Shunichi Isoki and his sister Yoshiko are praying for their baby brother, Yoneji, who died of pneumonia before his first birthday; Kaname Izumi and his sister Sunao are absorbed in memories distant as well, the early death of their mother, Towa, and baby Nobuyuki whose life was extinguished almost as soon as it began; Hitoshi Okada stands tall next to his wife, Shizuka, remembering the hollow house his mother, Miki, left behind when she died of influenza, and the day his brother Takeshi did not come home from the waters off Bare Point; Mutt Otsu watches limbs of the cedar trees undulating in the breeze, transfixed by the memory of his stepfather, Tairyu Fujimoto; Shige and Sumiko Yoshida touch the memory of little Shigeru, taken from them so very long ago.

One by one, they, and others with family buried here, step forward to lay abundant flower wreaths at the foot of the memorial. When they are done, the marble platform is blanketed in gladiolas, chrysanthemums, and roses.

Shunichi faces the gathering. A lustrous black Buddhist altar at his side, he addresses the politicians and Chemainus residents huddled among the Japanese Canadian crowd from all regions of the country.

"In April 1942, we left our loved ones here, believing they at least wouldn't have to go through the anxieties of war. It made me very angry when I heard about the desecration of the Japanese Canadian graves in Chemainus. I knew that there were some individuals who did not like us, but I did not dream that anyone would bulldoze our graves. It is anathema to think that anyone could hate another race so much that they would spitefully destroy gravestones on a sacred resting place. It was indeed shocking news. I lost faith in the British "fair play" about which I had been taught in school.

"The unveiling and dedication of the monument is very significant for me. I have a baby brother who is buried here, and I am assured that now he can, indeed, rest in peace. I cannot forget the atrocity perpetrated upon our sacred grounds, but I can forgive. Let us pray that this is the beginning of the peace and harmony for which we are all striving."

Bishop Toshi Murakami comes forward in his long, flowing black robe to lead the *O-bon* service, the annual Buddhist ceremony lighting the way for spirits of the deceased to visit home and loved ones.

"The incense burning here symbolizes purity of intentions, the flowers are the glory of Buddha, and the sunlight shining upon us is the light of compassion and wisdom," he announces. And the ravens fly over again, their calls muted by the song of dedication ringing through the air.

Overcast skies threaten rain when Chemainus unveils *The Lone Scout* and *The Winning Float* that afternoon. The crowd on the street is as thick as the Chemainus River salmon run Shunichi remembers from his boyhood. It also reminds him of

the jostling at the sumo wrestling tournament Gihei Kawahara hosted here to celebrate his birthday in 1932.

Old baseball and school friends stumble into one another,
laughing, shaking hands, and reminiscing about ball games
won and lost. Names are dropped, sometimes jogging memories of those who have passed on: the war, cancer, strokes,
heart attacks. . . . Hitoshi Okada and George Ridgway speak
face to face, letting slip the memory of their last encounter
through the wire fence at Hastings Park. The man who used
to issue the sawmill paycheques hails Shige on the corner.
Others circulate, asking for Kaname and Shunichi—not by
the English names they used in school. Women in the crowd
seek classmates with whom they played jacks and skipping
rope.

When the speeches begin, Shige and Sumiko Yoshida are
among those sitting under a canopy, facing an archway of red
and white balloons bobbing upwards in the sky. The local
RCMP sergeant and a corporal are nearby sentries, their red
serge uniforms an ironic reminder of changing times. Shige
sits with hands folded lightly on his knee, his neck tilted as if to
catch some intangible breeze. Somewhere out on the sea, it is
stirring a cat's paw, delicate like the curve of his lips.

After various speakers have paid him tribute, he shuffles
over to the podium and chuckles: he has to climb onto a box in
order to reach the microphone. "I want to thank all of you," he
booms. Dressed in his original 1930s scoutmaster uniform, he
is frail but proud. "I feel so happy. When I left in 1942, I was
very sad. But I think it has come to a point where I can go
home with happiness."

Shige steps down from his box to a round of applause. Former scout leaders in navy blazers encircle their diminutive
hero as he pledges to keep alive the spirit of the scout movement. "On my honour, I promise that I will do my best to do
my duty to God and my country and to live in the deeper spirit

of the scout law," he vows. Then the Cowichan Valley Baden-Powell Guild makes him an honourary member.

As Shige returns to his seat, the spotlight falls on Matsue Taniwa briefly. Short, bald George Price calls her name from the podium, glancing down at his wife, Jessie, for encouragement. She nods her thin head and smiles. In the late 1940s, the couple bought a bakery where the Taniwas had their store. During some renovations in the 1960s, George discovered a portrait of Norey in the walls.

Surprised and slightly nervous, Matsue climbs onto the podium and unpins the yellow rose from the envelope. She opens it carefully, her elegant hands wavering in mid-air. The picture of her late husband was taken during his school days in Japan. Dressed smartly in a white judo suit, Norey gazes forcefully at her.

"Thank you," she says, smiling as George Price pins the rose on her lapel. She surveys the crowd briefly before stepping down. Matsue catches Stanley's eye, confirming her suspicion that he knew. But she misses Jessie Price's uplifted face, her grey eyes translucent like a lake at dawn.

The afternoon ends with a song. A young man from Calgary, Allen Desnoyers, accompanies himself on guitar and sings his composition, *Chemainus Harbour, April 21, 1942.*

I lived in Okada camp . . . until the war
Papa was a boom man like many men before
I grew up speaking English in 1942
The year the ship came to the bay to carry us away

I don't know where Pearl Harbor is, I do not want to know
I know it made my momma cry to hear it on the radio
I liked the horseshoe harbor where I'd while away the day
Until it let the ship come in to carry us away

I am a Canadian, I may look Japanese
But I was born in '32 in Chimunesu
It may seem like a drooping shack, it may be weathered
   as a bone
But this is still my Father's house and I don't want to leave
   my home. . . .

Hitoshi Okada sits among his peers, lost in thought. He glances at Kaname Izumi and Mutt Otsu, friends from his boyhood in Okada camp. All older than ten when the ship carried them away, they are not the boy in the song. They know the child intimately nonetheless.

He plays on the beach still, in front of his father's house.

GLOSSARY

baa-chan	grandmother
butsudana	small Buddhist shrine
dojo	an exercise hall, often used for martial arts
fujinkai	women's association
fukeiki	economic depression; hard times
gaji	card game
gambari-ya	diehards or holdouts
hahanokai	mothers' association
hakujin	Caucasians
issei	first-generation immigrants
jijikai	a self-governing body that looks after community affairs
kami	Shinto-Buddhist nature spirit; deity; god
kesho-mawashi	floor-length apron worn during ring-entering ceremony of a *sumo* tournament
koto	classical Japanese stringed instrument
manju	sweet bean cake
matsutake	pine mushroom
nee-san	older sister
nii-san	older brother
nikkei	of Japanese descent, living outside of Japan
nisei	second-generation immigrants (children of *issei*)
O-bon	annual Buddhist ritual to commemorate the dead
odori	type of Japanese dance
ofuro	bath; public bath
okaeshi	a return gift for a present received
senzo dai dai	a box containing record of family lineage
shikataga-nai	expression meaning "It can't be helped"
shushin	morals; ethics
sugi	type of Japanese cedar tree
taikun	tycoon

INDEX